Chinese Policy toward Indonesia, 1949–1967

By the same author

Chinese Foreign Policy and the Cultural Revolution, 1970

Chinese Policy toward Indonesia, 1949–1967

DAVID MOZINGO

Cornell University Press | ITHACA AND LONDON

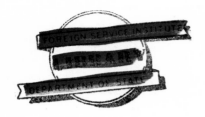

Copyright © 1976 by Cornell University

First published 1976 by Cornell University Press.
Published in the United Kingdom by Cornell University Press Ltd.,
2-4 Brook Street, London W1Y 1AA.

International Standard Book Number 0-8014-0921-7
Library of Congress Catalog Card Number 75-14719
Printed in the United States of America

In memory of my father

Acknowledgments

I am indebted to many persons for helpful suggestions, criticism, and encouragement received during the preparation of this work. Most of all I am grateful to H. Arthur Steiner and George McT. Kahin. The first introduced me to, and taught me how to study, China; the second helped me to understand the societies and history of Southeast Asia and, through the example of his own work, inspired this study. I would also like to give special thanks to Benedict R. O'G. Anderson, Herbert S. Dinerstein, Edward Friedman, Alexander George, Melvin Gurtov, Paul F. Langer, John W. Lewis, Ruth McVey, Guy Pauker, Myron Rush, and David A. Wilson. Many Indonesian and Chinese friends contributed much of the information on which this book is based. Because the issue of relations with China is still politically sensitive in Indonesia, no purpose would be served by mentioning their names. But without their help and confidence I would not have been able to finish this project.

The Ford Foundation gave generous financial support that made it possible for me to undertake language and political studies at Cornell University and to complete field research in Indonesia and Hong Kong. Subsequent grants from the China-Japan Program and the International Relations of East Asia Project, both of Cornell University, freed me from teaching obligations long enough to bring this work to completion.

DAVID MOZINGO

Ithaca, New York

Contents

Abbreviations

ANZUS   Australia–New Zealand–United States Defense Treaty
CCP   Chinese Communist party
CPR   Chinese People's Republic
CPSU   Communist Party of the Soviet Union
KMT (Kuomintang)   Chinese Nationalist party
NASAKOM (Nationalisme-Agama-Komunisme)   Acronym for fusion of nationalism, religion, and communism
NCNA   New China News Agency
NEFO   New Emerging Forces
PKI   Indonesian Communist party
PNI   Indonesian Nationalist party
PSI   Indonesian Socialist party
SEATO   Southeast Asia Treaty Organization

Chinese Policy toward Indonesia,
1949–1967

Introduction

On August 17, 1965, in a speech commemorating the twentieth anniversary of Indonesia's proclamation of independence, President Sukarno announced the existence of a diplomatic and political alignment between the Chinese People's Republic and the Republic of Indonesia. Although a *de facto* entente between the two powers had been steadily developing since late in 1963, Sukarno's speech included the first official acknowledgment that the purpose of the alignment was to break up the Federation of Malaysia, to outflank the Anglo-American position in Southeast Asia, and to organize an Afro-Asian coalition of "newly emerging forces" opposed to the Western powers.

Six weeks after the speech the Peking-Djarkarta axis suddenly began to disintegrate, following an abortive coup on October 1st by junior army officers, aided by the Indonesian Communist party (PKI), which aimed at liquidating the pro-Western Indonesian army high command. The coup attempt set off a massive anticommunist chain reaction that led, in rapid succession, to the bloody suppression of the PKI, the overthrow of the Sukarno government by a right-wing military junta, a complete diplomatic rupture with Peking, and the restoration of Indonesia's close ties with the Western powers. Almost overnight an alliance with Indonesia that appeared to be the most spectacular achievement of China's diplomatic strategy in a decade had resulted in a major foreign-policy disaster for China.

The short-lived Peking-Djakarta axis and the 1965 Indonesian coup are the two events that most dramatically demonstrate the unstable foundation of Chinese policy in Indonesia. In the seventeen years between the establishment of diplomatic relations in 1950 and their suspension in 1967, Chinese policy in Indonesia underwent a complete transformation but eventually came full circle. It began with an attitude of revolutionary militancy and hostility toward the newly independent Indonesian republic; shifted to a posture of peaceful coexistence and friendship in the mid-1950's; reached its zenith of success in the period of the Peking-Djakarta axis; and returned to its original revolutionary attitudes in 1967, following an anticommunist counterrevolution in Indonesia and the radicalization of China's foreign policy during the Great Proletarian Cultural Revolution. The stages in the evolution of Chinese policy in Indonesia during this period corresponded, in general, to the phases in the development of her policies toward the entire Afro-Asian world after 1949. An analysis of the Sino-Indonesian relationship may, therefore, make more apparent the larger patterns of Peking's policies in the Third World generally and toward her noncommunist Asian neighbors particularly. The history of Chinese diplomacy indicates clearly that Peking's relations with all these nations, including Indonesia, have been persistently ambivalent.

The test of an effective foreign policy is not, of course, that it manifests no ambivalence. Few foreign policies would be able to pass this test. Nor should the effectiveness of a policy be measured by its stability, consistency, or success in producing harmonious relations with other states, for acquiring these attributes may not be its main or even its desired goal. The only reasonable criterion of effectiveness is whether, on balance, a policy achieves those objectives desired by its makers. According to this standard, Chinese policy in Indonesia was clearly a failure, whether one concludes that its basic goal was to maximize Chinese and communist influence or, as the present writer believes, to strengthen those elements in Indonesia that wanted to make their country independent of the major capitalist powers and the Soviet Union. There were spasms of momentary success, to be sure, but in the end the entire policy met with crushing defeat.

The central question this study explores is why China's policy in Indonesia failed. Theoretically, the general or any specific bilateral policy of a state may fail for one or a combination of reasons: (1) the goals of a state may not be commensurate with the resources available or committed to achieve them; (2) the policy makers' assessment of the external situation may be unrealistic; (3) important new factors may emerge or events occur that may invalidate a previously successful policy; and (4) faulty execution may, of course, cause the failure of the most carefully fashioned Machiavellian schemes. From the mid-1950's until the 1965 coup, China's policy in Indonesia appeared to skillfully navigate among these shoals and to be on the verge of a major triumph that might have far-reaching geopolitical consequences. The occurrence that altered the emerging Chinese gain was the Indonesian coup, an unexpected and disastrous event that Peking could not have prevented. It might be argued that, in a sense, Chinese policy in Indonesia was not actually defeated but simply proved vulnerable to the kind of internal upheaval abroad that periodically undermines the foreign policies of all the great powers.

More fundamentally, however, the policies of the Chinese leaders themselves were the factors most responsible for the failure in Indonesia. It was a matter of choice, not accident, that they decided not to pursue modest objectives and not to employ a cautious strategy, which would have been better calculated to avoid potential disaster than the goals and tactics they chose. China's leaders opted for an ambitious policy, a power alignment with the highly unpredictable and unstable Sukarno government. They were evidently willing to incur high risks despite the well-known influence of pro-Western generals in his regime, widespread Indonesian suspicion of Peking because of its ties with the Indonesian communists, and China's lack of the power resources to bend this alliance to her will or, if threatened from outside, to defend it. In view of its own earlier experience with bourgeois nationalist elements during the Chinese civil war and the wavering record of Third World governments led by these classes after 1949, the Chinese leadership ought to have foreseen that a close relationship with Sukarno's Indonesia was fraught with danger.

But perceived opportunity, not justifiable suspicions, governed Chinese policy, especially from 1961 on, when the prospect of an alliance with Indonesia became a significant component of Peking's global anti-imperialist strategy. In the main, that strategy was forced on China, because she perceived, with good reason, that the United States and the Soviet Union were bent on encircling her, and she was determined to oppose them. This well-grounded fear, however, hardly made a highly risky alliance with the Sukarno regime and its PKI supporters seem a necessary or even an attainable means of organizing an anti-imperialist counterstrategy. Indeed, the venture in Indonesia was in marked contrast to the general style of Chinese foreign policy during the preceding seventeen years, a policy which had been characterized by great caution and deftness. Was the conduct of the policy in Indonesia merely an exception to the general norm? Or was it the product of more pervasive pressures operating on Chinese foreign policy as a whole, which eventually had a cumulative effect in relation to Indonesia? This study finds that the evidence sustains the second interpretation.

From what perspective can the forces and events leading to the collapse of Chinese policy in Indonesia best be understood? Basically, the Sino-Indonesian relationship was the outgrowth of two kinds of pressures: those exerted by the nature and course of the Cold War and those stemming from the domestic evolution of the Chinese and Indonesian polities. The Cold War was significant because the rivalry among its principal actors dominated and defined the international environment in which the relationship between the two powers evolved. Particularly in the early years, the foreign policies of China and Indonesia, as well as their respective leaders' images of each other, to a great extent reflected the fact that the former was oriented toward the Soviet camp while the latter leaned heavily toward the United States. And primarily because these Cold War alignments did not satisfy the national aspirations of either power, China and Indonesia moved progressively closer after 1961, despite their seemingly incompatible social values and state systems. The Cold War also may be said to explain the eventual outcome of the relationship, since Indonesia abandoned the alliance with China in order to reattach herself economically and politically to the capitalist world, while China rejected Indonesia as a suitable partner in the anti-imperialist camp.

While Cold War pressures played a major role in effecting changes in Chinese policy, the decisive factors in the Sino-Indonesian relationship were internal ones. The controlling importance of events inside Indonesia and China on the association between the two powers is the central theme that emerges from a historical study of their interaction, especially at its zenith in 1965. What shattered the alliance was the attempted coup, the culmination of internal conflicts among the Indonesian elite that finally burst through the feeble edifice Sukarno had tried to erect to contain them. Similarly, the Cultural Revolution brought the schisms among the Chinese elite to a head a year later, in 1966. Because the Cultural Revolution wreaked havoc on China's foreign policy for sometime thereafter, the Peking-Djakarta entente would probably have been terminated as a result of the domestic Chinese upheavals if those in Indonesia had not occurred first.

Though the internal factors were dominant, an examination

of Chinese diplomacy reveals that throughout the 1949 to 1967 period the Chinese government's conception of what was necessary for carrying on its struggle with America (and later Russia) ultimately determined its policy in Indonesia. Each major shift in Peking's attitude toward Djakarta—in 1951, 1954, 1958, 1961, 1963, and 1967—closely corresponds to each phase through which her global policies passed. On a number of occasions these shifts in global policy ran parallel to, and therefore complemented, specific bilateral trends that were developing in relations between the two powers. In other instances the conflicting imperatives of her global and her Indonesian interests pulled China in opposite directions. But in no case can it be shown that problems or opportunities arising from the latter concerns were sufficient to nullify, or even to modify, significantly the former.

Yet, remarkably, both the major successes and failures of Chinese diplomacy during nearly two decades resulted, not from the effectiveness with which Peking's general foreign-policy line applied to Indonesia, but from the extent to which political currents in that country ran with or against China's internationally oriented policies. All of China's significant diplomatic triumphs—including the 1955 Dual Nationality Treaty and the winning over of Sukarno and the PKI—were the products, first and foremost, of favorable political changes in Djakarta. Peking's diplomacy adroitly responded to, but did not create, these preconditions. Similarly, China's main setbacks in Indonesia—such as the increase in American and Soviet influence and the repeated mistreatment of Chinese nationals—had almost no connection with China's foreign policy. Invariably they were entirely the consequence of internal forces in Indonesia which had an impact on foreign-policy issues.

The inability to harmonize competing imperatives during its relationship with Indonesia seems to point up certain weaknesses in the theoretical framework the Chinese leadership uses to analyze international politics and in the basic foreign-policy strategies it employs. Like the acts of other foreign-policy-making elites, the international actions of the Chinese leaders grow out of a dialectical process: an analysis of actual situations they are confronted with or wish to change and the more subjective images they have about what is happening or what can be done. There is nothing especially subtle or communist about this process. All foreign-policy makers try to reconcile their ideas with reality. The Chinese leaders may differ from the others, but only in degree, in the extent to which their conceptions of how to understand and to act in response to perceived reality have, during an extensive period of codification and practice, attained the status of doctrine. The ability to identify the main form and content of "contradictions" (whether in a national or international setting) is, from the Chinese communist perspective, the fundamental task of policy analysis. Correct identification, they believe, will reveal the basic strategic problems to be solved, the main adversaries to be opposed, the potential friends to be conciliated, and the general policy line to be pursued during a particular phase or era. Failure to grasp the nature of the "contradictions" must result in erroneous policies and may even invite defeat. If we were to apply the Chinese leadership's test to the Chinese experience in Indonesia, we would be forced to conclude that the leaders had fundamentally misperceived the whole situation.

With respect to strategy, the CPR (Chinese People's Republic) is a conventional international actor in the sense that it uses elements of national power—force, diplomacy, and political and economic leverage—to achieve the external aims of the state. Its methods of employing these tools have been distinguished from those of capitalist states (and, to a degree, also of other socialist states) by the Chinese preference for strategies which embody the united-front concept. This Marxist-Leninist device, which is by no means the special property of the Chinese—though they may be said to have most fully developed and relied on it—has a long history and an important place in Chinese revolutionary practice. Boiled down to essentials, united-front politics is a method of coalition-building that the Chinese communists have used to strengthen their support at home and abroad. Its relationship to the theory of contradictions, and hence to the decisive factors in the development and implementation of policy goals, is direct and absolute. Simply stated, the identification and analysis of the main contradiction determine what kind of united-front or coalition policy China follows. In other words, whereas the theory of contradictions is used to establish general policy goals, the united front is the vehicle by means of which broad policies are implemented.

Chinese diplomatic strategy in Indonesia involved complicated, sometimes interlocking attempts at coalition-building—international (with anti-imperialist forces), bilateral (between China and Indonesia), and fraternal (between the CCP and the PKI). An analysis of the evolution of Chinese united-front policies, therefore, provides a basis for interpreting the most important developments in the Sino-Indonesian relationship. This approach has the additional advantage of adopting, to the extent possible for the outside observer, the frame of reference of Chinese policy makers. It may also help to avoid a flagrant and persistent misconception apparent in many Western writings: that the Chinese think and act in response to the motives that foreign anticommunist analysts attribute to them instead of the motives that they themselves say inspire their policies.

Employing the categories the Chinese use to analyze and implement policies may result in an interpretation that seems to present what China does and why she does it in overly mechanistic or dogmatic terms. It may be useful, therefore, to remind readers that although the conceptual vocabulary of Marxism-Leninism-Maoism has a rigid quality (some might say it is "systematic"), in actual practice the Chinese have interpreted its terms quite flexibly, in order to allow their decision makers the maximum choice of policies. Far from being the prisoners of an allegedly rigid ideology, in the conduct of foreign policy the Chinese leaders have basic analytical and diplomatic tools as adaptable and "modern"—and also with the same limitations—as their counterparts in other countries have. In an attempt to find the reasons why Chinese policy in Indonesia failed, surely the frame of mind and the instrumentalities behind that policy are prime subjects for investigation, as would be the case in a similar analysis of the foreign affairs of another state. The objective of the present study, therefore, is to assess the strengths and weaknesses of the theory and strategy of Chinese foreign policy and to determine, insofar as is possible, what part these elements, in comparison with other factors, played in bringing about the final outcome.

When the unfavorable geopolitical realities are taken into consideration, the fact that China's leaders thought they could compete with America and Russia for influence in Indonesia appears all the more remarkable. Indonesia's inclusion in the sphere of Anglo-American air and naval dominance prevented China from bringing any meaningful pressure to bear either on her adversaries or on behalf of her supporters in that country. The United States and the Soviet Union, particularly the former, could exert much greater leverage. Moreover, the balance of political forces inside Indonesia consistently favored the anticommunist, anti-Chinese elements. And finally, the complete independence of the Indonesian Communist party, especially as its size and influence grew, frustrated more than it helped Chinese diplomatic strategy.

Very largely because of these handicaps, China had great difficulty in designing united-front policies capable of reconciling persistent conflicts between her international and her bilateral aims in Indonesia. Increasingly the policy toward Indonesia became subordinated to the preponderant importance of China's struggle with America and Russia. The significance of the global rivalry with the two superpowers began to emerge in the late 1950's, and had begun to play the paramount role in Chinese diplomacy by 1963, when the Sino-Soviet dispute became irreconcilable. By that time Sukarno's radical nationalist foreign policy had thrust Indonesia forward as a leading exponent of Afro-Asian struggle against the Western presence in the colonial world; and the PKI, having become by far the largest effective political force in Indonesia, was engaged in a desperate competition with the army to establish, before he passed from the scene, its succession to Sukarno. Indonesia, therefore, provided an acid test of the Chinese leaders' major argument in their polemics against Moscow: that the ideological and power aims of the socialist camp could be simultaneously pursued by means of a united-front strategy linking communist revolutions and anti-imperialist nationalism in the colonial world. When Peking's alliance with Sukarno and the PKI was destroyed by the Indonesian coup this argument was largely invalidated. China's apparent attempt to compete with the great powers as the center of a Third World coalition also collapsed. Another consequence of the defeat was that her own credibility as a champion of anti-imperialists and revolutionaries was severely tarnished, possibly for a long time to come.

Thus it must be concluded that the experience in Indonesia played a part in Peking's decision, after 1967, to continue her verbal and economic support of anti-imperialist movements in the Afro-Asian world but to avoid direct external entanglements. This reorientation of policy, which survived the Cultural Revolution and characterizes Chinese diplomacy in the present era of expanding international contacts and the détente with the United States, owes much of its impetus to what Peking learned from the failures of her attempt to pursue great-power policies in the 1960's. The venture in Indonesia occupied a cardinal position in those policies, and its failures suggest some of the reasons for the reorientation of Chinese foreign policy after the Cultural Revolution.

1

The Indonesian Setting

The interaction of geopolitical, socioeconomic, and historical factors determined the essential nature of the Indonesian state that confronted China in 1950. A discussion of the most salient characteristics of Indonesian society and the relations between Indonesia and mainland China before 1950 is necessary to provide the background for an understanding of subsequent phases of their relationship.

Geopolitical and Sociocultural Aspects

Indonesia is the world's largest archipelago, a sprawling chain of islands linking the Asian and Australian continents. For nearly two thousand years this oil- and mineral-rich country has served as a major crossroad of trade, cultures, and ideas. Its natural resources and strategic position invited European domination as early as the seventeenth century. In the twentieth century alone Indonesia has experienced a Japanese invasion and occupation (1942–1945), a colonial war of independence against the Dutch (1945–1949), and since 1950 the more covert forms of aggrandizement spawned by Cold War power rivalries.

Indonesia's 125,000,000 people inhabit more than two thousand islands occupying a total land-water area approximately the size of the United States.[1] As such, it is the third most populous

[1] For basic geographical and social data on Indonesia see Karl J. Pelzer, "Physical and Human Resource Patterns," in Ruth T. McVey, ed., *Indonesia* (New Haven, Conn.: Human Relations Area Files Press, 1963), pp. 1–23.

Asian nation, ranking behind China and India, and is historically linked to other Third World countries in the race to overcome poverty and backwardness. Indonesia's size and underdevelopment are quite important for an understanding of its place in world politics, for the major Cold War adversaries—Russia, China, and the United States—all contend that the form the modernization process takes in the emerging countries of Asia, Africa, and Latin America—that is, whether it is inspired by doctrines originating in the capitalist or the communist systems— will decisively affect the future balance of power in the world. Each of these great powers has, therefore, been quite reluctant to permit Indonesia to determine independently the form her own modernization and political development will take, since they all see that process affecting their own aspirations and interests. As a result, the open and clandestine political warfare Russia, China, and the United States have waged in Indonesia beginning in 1950 has seriously impaired her capacity to develop free of unwanted foreign interference, and it has undermined the authority of every government in Djakarta since independence was won in 1949. Dissidents of the Left or Right have always known they had powerful friends abroad ready to support subversive causes.

The guerrilla and rebel movements that have erupted during Indonesia's turbulent postindependence era have usually been able to find many natural sanctuaries in the vast mountains and rain forests of Sumatra, Borneo, and Celebes. In general, however, Indonesia's geography is unfavorable to the development and continuance of insurgent warfare. With the notable exception of a mountainous region in West Java, where the Darul Islam rebels were able to hold out for more than a decade after 1949, in Indonesia the terrain best suited for the harboring of rebellious guerrillas is not contiguous to the major areas of population concentration, which insurgents would have to win and keep to be successful.

Population density is highest on Java and Bali, and on both

islands there is widespread rural poverty,[2] one of the conditions most readily exploited by revolutionary movements in the underdeveloped countries. But neither island has a large remote hinterland capable of safeguarding insurgent forces from the stronger military power of the government in Djakarta. In the outer islands the geographic situation is basically reversed. Ideal guerrilla terrain abounds, but the peasant community, in comparison with Java's, is both small and economically better off. At various times since 1949 rebel movements outside Java have been able, temporarily, to defy Djakarta, but they have never been able to gain control of a large enough population base to be able to conquer or hold any of the outer islands, much less pose a serious challenge to Djakarta's control of all Indonesia. Hence the familiar demographic configuration which, on mainland Southeast Asia, has worked to the advantage of revolutionaries—hill and jungle redoubts adjacent to peasant concentrations in the valleys and deltas of major river systems—is not characteristic of Indonesia. The lack of strategically useful terrain contributed heavily to the final defeats suffered by the Darul Islam and by participants in the Sumatran and Sulawesi revolt of 1958. This same geopolitical reality also frustrated the efforts of the PKI to generate a peasant rebellion in East and Central Java in the wake of the 1966 overthrow of the Sukarno regime by the Indonesian army. Chinese communist theories about "surrounding the cities from the countryside" would, therefore, at any time confront formidable obstacles if they were adapted to Indonesian conditions.

The pattern of economic relationships in Indonesia is also not generally conducive to revolution in the countryside. Most of the population is made up of small, independent subsistence farmers, but massive rural poverty is largely confined to areas of Central and East Java and Bali. Even there, despite intense

[2] *Ibid.*, pp. 13–20.

population pressures and a rise in absentee landlordism after 1950, social and political tensions seem never to have reached the level characteristic of prerevolutionary China or Vietnam. The Indonesian landlord class is not large, cruel, or very wealthy in comparison with the tenant and landless groups, or with landlord elements in other lands. Moreover, in many of the impoverished districts on Java a tradition of communalistic land ownership and use in the villages served, during most of the 1950's and 1960's, to blunt the potential appeal of class war in the countryside.[3] Rural socioeconomic radicalism upsurged in the early 1960's, but the subsequent annihilation of the PKI ended this brief threat and has forced the Indonesian peasantry to continue its conservative, passive traditions. In the outer islands, which have favorable land-population ratios, rural poverty has yet to become an explosive political factor.

Poverty, as a potential source of discontent, is also present in the cities and towns. As in other underdeveloped countries, Indonesia's urban centers have had to absorb heavy migrations of unemployed or discontented villagers seeking—but rarely finding—a better life in the cities. Partly because of the growth of a large, impoverished urban population, the Indonesian communists were forced to concentrate their organizational and political effort in the cities, although the party's doctrine stressed the peasantry as the basic element of the Indonesian revolution.[4] This situation was disadvantageous to the communists strategically, because the heavy concentrations of military, police, and commercial activity were mainly in urban, not rural, communities. And because, after 1949, the real levers of power were

[3] For an excellent treatment of the Indonesian social structure and its role in the country's economic history see W. F. Wertheim, *Indonesian Society in Transition: A Study of Social Change* (The Hague: W. van Hoeve, 1959).

[4] See D. N. Aidit, *Indonesian Society and the Indonesian Revolution* (Djakarta: Jajasan "Pembaruan," 1958), p. 69.

always in the hands of anticommunists, who were strong in the cities, they always occupied the commanding political-military position during any internal upheaval.

Because Indonesia is a preindustrial country it does not have a powerful capitalist class or a trade-union movement, at least in the Western sense.[5] The absence of a strong labor movement limited the extent to which Indonesian communism could expect to pursue successfully a genuine "proletarian" strategy. On the other hand, lacking an equivalent of Western-type "captains of industry," Indonesia's entrepreneurial class is not basically capitalist but mercantilist. Actually, owing to the fact that army officers, since 1957, have operated nearly all the enterprises confiscated by the government that carry on a large part of the nation's industry, "bureaucratic capitalism" is a more appropriate term. The country has a long tradition of energetic trading classes; the most vigorous ethnic components are primarily the Bataks and Minangkabau of Sumatra, the Makassarese of South Celebes, and, most important, the resident three million foreign- and local-born Chinese.[6] On the other hand, the dominant ethnic group, the Javanese, who constitute over 40 percent of the population, have not produced a strong class of merchants and traders. The occupation that has most attracted enterprising Javanese is government service;

[5] For a general summary of the Indonesian trade-union movement see Everett D. Hawkins, "Labor in Transition," in McVey, *Indonesia*, pp. 257–269; and Iskandar Tedjasukmana, *The Political Character of the Indonesian Trade Union Movement* (Ithaca: Cornell Modern Indonesia Project, 1959).

[6] On the economic role of the Chinese in Indonesia the best studies are W. J. Cater, *The Economic Position of the Chinese in the Netherlands Indies* (Chicago: University of Chicago Press, 1936); H. F. Mac-Nair, *The Chinese Abroad* (Shanghai: Commercial Press, 1925); J. S. Furnivall, *Netherlands India: A Study of Plural Economy* (Cambridge: Cambridge University Press, 1939); and Victor Purcell, *The Chinese in Southeast Asia* (London: Oxford University Press, 1951).

they are predominate in military and bureaucratic roles, especially at the national level.

These differentiations within the Indonesian community have resulted in several important forms of economically generated political friction. The greater entrepreneurial prowess and wealth of the outer islanders have fostered demands for increased regional autonomy—demands which have conflicted with persistent Javanese efforts to centralize power in Djakarta.[7] Yet it is not the numerically dominant Javanese but the commercially vigorous outer-island natives and the Chinese who constitute most of the Indonesian middle class. This class, however, has not been allowed to play the principal role in national politics, as is the case in most other underdeveloped countries, because it is composed of ethnic and racial minorities which, in national politics, have had to yield to Javanese numerical supremacy.

The dominant position of the Chinese minority in the local economy is greatly resented by both the bureaucratically oriented Javanese—who, nevertheless, traditionally extort large sums from the Chinese in exchange for protection, licenses, and so forth—and the outer-island traders. As a result, one of the few political sentiments that unite the indigenous elite classes is a deep antipathy toward the Chinese community. Indonesians have tended to project this hostility onto any Chinese government—whether in Singapore, Taipei, or Peking—in the belief, not entirely unfounded, that this minority gives its true loyalty to one Chinese state or another, but certainly not to Indonesia.

Since the winning of Indonesian independence numerous government regulations have been designed to curb Chinese control of the local economy. These measures have, indeed, greatly reduced the wealth and efficiency of the Chinese mer-

[7] This problem is discussed in J. D. Legge, *Central Authority and Regional Autonomy in Indonesia: A Study in Local Administration* (Ithaca: Cornell University Press, 1961).

chants but have not generated substantial Indonesian entrepreneurial talent and energy to replace the role of the Chinese. From time to time state-operated enterprises or cooperatives have been attempted as economic alternatives to the Chinese traders; to date such experiments have not proved very effective. Nevertheless, discriminatory measures against the Chinese, whatever the degree of their legality and despite their harmful consequences for the economy, have been politically quite popular.

In spite of characteristics that make for cohesion, Indonesia's cultural and ethnic composition presents serious obstacles to national integration. Most of the approximately 250 spoken languages belong to the Malayo-Polynesian family, and the national language, Bahasa Indonesia, is very widely used. About 90 percent of the population practices or professes Islam. A long history of interisland commercial and cultural contacts has also resulted in many commonly shared values and customs.[8] Nevertheless, there are over 300 separate ethnic groups and much strong identification with a particular region or culture. The inevitable tendency of a Java-dominated Djakarta government to exercise hegemony over the Indonesian agglomeration has, on the whole, had the effect of impeding the development of a larger, integrated nationalism. It would, however, be misleading to overemphasize the centrifugal tendencies and frictions arising from Indonesia's diverse cultural makeup. Historically, the country has adopted a receptive, though selective, attitude toward successive waves of cultural, religious, and ideological influences. Indonesia has borrowed extensively from her contacts with the Hindu, Islamic, and Western traditions,

[8] Among the most important works on Indonesian culture, its roots and adaptations, are B. J. O. Schrieke, *Indonesian Sociological Studies* (2 vols.; The Hague: W. van Hoeve, 1957); Clifford Geertz, *The Religion of Java* (Glencoe, Ill.: Free Press, 1960); and Wertheim, *Indonesian Society in Transition.*

weaving what was compatible or simply useful into the existing cultural fabric without losing her own identity.

Political and Ideological Influences

The capacity to absorb and "Indonesianize" diverse foreign influences has been less effective at the political level. Indonesia has received her basic political ideas from very different sources: an indigenous authoritarian tradition; Western social-democratic and Marxist philosophies introduced by the Dutch; and Islamic beliefs. These largely conflicting ideas have not yet been successfully synthesized. The official state ideology, Pantjasila (the Five Principles), first proclaimed in 1945, and Sukarno's ill-fated "guided democracy," espoused after 1959, were reflections of the country's continuing search for a harmonious integration of the major political creeds that have taken root in the course of its history.

Although Islam is the dominant religious belief, it has not exerted a correspondingly strong influence on Indonesia's political history,[9] partly because Indonesia received primarily "modernist" Islamic teachings, less militant than the versions usually found in the Middle East. Being already a moderate form of Islam, it was susceptible to the absorptive process of Indonesianization. But Islam also has never registered its full potential political impact because soon after independence was won the Moslems split into two rival party organizations (Masjumi and Nahdatul Ulama), roughly equal in strength, an event which greatly weakened the force of Islam in national politics.[10] More-

[9] An analysis of the strengths and weaknesses of Islamic political parties, as compared to other forces in the country in the 1949 to 1955 period, is in Soedjatmoko, "The Role of Political Parties in Indonesia," in Phillip W. Thayer, ed., *Nationalism and Progress in Free Asia* (Baltimore: Johns Hopkins Press, 1956), pp. 128–140.

[10] This process is discussed in Herbert Feith, *The Decline of Constitutional Democracy in Indonesia* (Ithaca: Cornell University Press, 1962).

over, the fact that Moslems led the Darul Islam and Sumatran rebellions while seeking aid from foreign powers also served to discredit the Islamic political class as genuine nationalist spokesmen.

Historically, the appeals of Marxism have also been weakened by the split between the national communists (represented by Tan Malaka and, later, the Murba party) and the internationally affiliated PKI.[11] The PKI's identification with Russia and China could never be entirely removed and, consequently, has always acted to undermine its quest for nationalist credentials. On the other hand, communism's emphasis on class struggle little suited the society's traditional values of harmony and compromise. In the decade from 1954 to 1964 the PKI successfully exploited rising social-economic tensions between the more prosperous, strongly Moslem *santri* class and the poorer, non-Moslem *abangans*. The subsequent bloody suppression of the PKI and its supporters, however, reaffirmed the power and the willingness of the dominant segments of Indonesian society to resist radical social change. Standing between the Islamic and communist groups, a variety of secular nationalist parties bore the brunt of the effort to provide the nation with a set of political ideas that combined Western-derived notions of representative democracy and social-economic justice with traditional Indonesian conceptions of leadership and decision-making.[12] The largest of these, the PNI (Indonesian Nationalist Party), founded by Sukarno, though it was persistently hobbled by

[11] On the origins and problems of communism in Indonesia see Ruth T. McVey, *The Rise of Indonesian Communism* (Ithaca: Cornell University Press, 1965).

[12] The struggle between the nationalist and communist factions in Indonesia from the early 1900's to 1950 is fully analyzed in George McT. Kahin's classic study *Nationalism and Revolution in Indonesia* (Ithaca: Cornell University Press, 1952), and from 1950 to 1957 in Feith, *The Decline of Constitutional Democracy in Indonesia*.

factional splits, usually offered the main alternative to those who rejected the rigidities of Islam and communism.

Under conditions of such ideological divergence it is not surprising that postindependence Indonesia was unable to reach a viable consensus on the basic questions of national political life: the form of the state and the institutions through which legitimate authority was to be exercised. The country's strongest political tradition, before and during the Dutch period, was elitist and authoritarian. The men who led the independence struggle, partly from personal conviction and also because they hoped to win the support of the Western democracies, attempted to transplant parliamentary government to Indonesian soil.[13] This effort was not destined to survive for long the society's very strong authoritarian impulses. All the major contenders for power—Sukarno, the army, and the leaders of the communist, Islamic, and nationalist parties—soon proved unwilling to carry on their rivalry solely in accordance with the republic's formal institutions and laws. Instead, all the rivals worked outside the system, tried to subvert it, and thus deprived the constitutional experiment of the basic condition necessary for its success.

Historical Background

Despite all the setbacks Indonesia has suffered since 1949, her leaders have succeeded in creating an Indonesian state with boundaries encompassing roughly the area once dominated by the maritime powers of Shrivijaya and Madjapahit, the great Indonesian empires of the ninth and fourteenth centuries.[14]

[13] See Feith's treatment in *The Decline of Constitutional Democracy in Indonesia.*

[14] Sources consulted for the historical background include D. G. E. Hall, ed., *A History of Southeast Asia* (London: Macmillan, 1955); Bernard H. M. Vlekke, *Nusantara: A History of the East Indian Archipelago* (2d ed., The Hague: W. van Hoeve, 1960); and J. C. Van Leur, *Indonesian Trade and Society: Essays in Asian Social and Economic History* (The Hague: W. van Hoeve, 1955).

Like contemporary Indonesia, these empires were loose political entities whose control over outlying territories was always tenuous, though at one time or another ancient Indonesia seems to have extended as far as parts of what today are the Philippines, Cambodia, and Malaysia.

As maritime trading powers, ancient Indonesian kingdoms had rather extensive contact with China from about the sixth century A.D., and gradually a small flow of Chinese traders settled in the islands. But the sending of Indonesian diplomatic missions and emissaries to China was, as far as is known, quite irregular until the Dutch colonial period.[15] In no sense was the Indonesian archipelago ever under Chinese domination. During periods of the Ming and Ch'ing dynasties, however, the Chinese tended to regard Java, at least theoretically, as part of their tributary system.

The Mongol (Yuan dynasty) invasions of Southeast Asia in the late thirteenth century led to a brief conflict with Madjapahit which is of some significance because it is an early example of the rivalry that might have been expected to develop between China and Indonesia when both countries were strong and expansionist. Following Madjapahit's mistreatment of Kublai Khan's envoys, who had come to demand submission to the new emperor of China, in 1292 the Mongols sent a punitive military expedition to Java. The expedition met with failure, however, and was soon forced to retire. No subsequent attempt was ever made by China to subjugate the islands.[16] When the Ming dynasty sent its famous naval expeditions to Indonesia, India, and beyond in the early fifteenth century, the imperial fleet stopped to mete out punishment, this time to the Chinese-ruled settlement at Palembang in Sumatra.[17] With the Javanese king-

---

[15] This conclusion is based on the official Chinese dynastic records discussed in W. P. Grnoeneveldt, *Historical Notes on Indonesia and Malaya* (Djakarta: Bhratara, 1960).

[16] *Ibid.*, pp. 20–34.

[17] *Ibid.*, pp. 34–45.

dom, on the other hand, the Ming envoys cultivated friendly diplomatic and commercial ties, apparently seeking to bring the Javanese more completely into the Chinese tributary system.

If the pattern of relations which began to emerge during Ming times had continued, harmonious intercourse rather than conflict between the two countries might have grown and developed. As it turned out, however, in later years China and Indonesia were destined to be driven apart by forces neither country was responsible for generating. Imperial China's decline under the impact of the West, the rise of Islam, and the Dutch conquest of Indonesia were the three major developments which, cumulatively, resulted in serious frictions between the two societies. These historically based frictions have lasted and have aggravated the Sino-Indonesian relationship until the present day.

The early Chinese settlers in Indonesia were few and largely confined to the commercial cities along the coast, where a lively trade between the Indies and China had developed.[18] By the fourteenth century the different cultural practices and ethical beliefs of the Chinese had not caused any serious antagonism between them and the native population. Harmonious co-existence was possible until that time because the value system of the indigenous people was quite tolerant and, moreover, because the Chinese had little close contact with Indonesian society outside the coastal cities. But with the spread of Islam throughout the islands in the fifteenth century the formerly tranquil relations between Indonesians and Chinese began to deteriorate. Islam introduced not only a religious creed sharply antagonistic to Chinese beliefs and customs, but also a rival Moslem merchant class anxious to displace the Chinese traders. Potential dissension between the native population and the

[18] The single best overall English-language account of the Chinese in Indonesia is Purcell, pp. 11–54, 441–568.

Chinese settlers was still in an embryonic stage when the Dutch began the conquest of Indonesia in the seventeenth century, at which point the situation changed completely.

The Dutch discovered that the Chinese could perform several key economic roles in the colony: as middlemen collecting agricultural produce for export; as retail merchants; and as licensed operators of salt, opium, and other revenue-producing monopolies. Because it helped implement the Dutch plan of exploitation, Chinese economic dominance in the villages and towns was encouraged. As a result, Chinese traders quickly displaced the already less vigorous native merchants. By the nineteenth century the Dutch had begun to encourage large-scale Chinese migration from the mainland as a source of cheap labor to work in the colony's mines and plantations. Many of the Chinese who originally came to Indonesia as indigent laborers eventually toiled and saved enough to start in business for themselves, usually as small traders. Not infrequently, Chinese who began as humble merchants in the villages and towns became wealthy and economically powerful in the Netherlands Indies.

The short-run economic advantages of indirectly using the Chinese to exploit the colony were of considerable importance in the maintenance of Dutch rule. Through their support of a Chinese-dominated middleman system the Dutch effectively prevented the development of a strong native entrepreneurial class that might become politically troublesome. In turn, the pervasive economic dominance of the Chinese in the towns and villages helped to deflect some of the natives' rising discontent from the alien Europeans to the alien Asians in their midst.

The Chinese obtained little of enduring value from their role as middlemen. At one time or another they did enjoy both preferential legal status and pronounced economic advantages in comparison with the Indonesians. More important in its effect on the long-term interests of the Chinese was the fact that the Dutch consistently discouraged assimilation with the native population. By failing to do this the Dutch greatly diminished the prospects for social peace in the future. Ultimately, it became Dutch policy to prevent the Chinese from owning land in the villages (though some form of renting or leasing was usually possible), to foster separate Chinese schools, guilds, and so forth, and to treat the Chinese as a special category of Netherlands subjects distinct from both the European and the native populations. Many Chinese, especially second-generation, local-born *peranakans* did, however, intermarry with, and adopt the customs of, the Indonesians. But among the foreign-born, *totok* Chinese, who were more numerous and more conscious of their cultural identity, Dutch policies encouraged the growth and strengthening of a separatist Chinese community.

The long-term consequences of Dutch colonial policy proved to be exceedingly detrimental to relations between the resident Chinese and the indigenous population. A strong native entrepreneurial class could not develop, and the weak one that did harbored deep resentment against its Chinese competitors. These feelings were shared by many Indonesian farmers and laborers as well, since the Chinese largely controlled the credit system and the marketing of goods in the villages and towns. Furthermore, the generally separatist attitudes of the Chinese, which not infrequently resulted in their looking down on the native population, helped to stamp them, in the view of most Indonesians, as alien exploiters who had a vested interest in the perpetuation of Dutch rule.

By the twentieth century the socioeconomic situation had made inevitable the isolation of the Chinese from the mainstream of the Indonesian movement for national independence. Indeed, the initial stimulus to this movement was the increasing Chinese commercial predominance over the already hardpressed native merchant class, from which emerged the first large nationalist organization, Sarekat Islam, formed in 1912 as a cooperative trade association for protection against the Chinese.[19] A few Chinese who understood the implications of Indonesian nationalism for future relations between the two races joined the independence movement. But a much greater number of Chinese in Indonesia were more excited by another political phenomenon of the early twentieth-century—the rise of nationalism in mainland China.

Traditionally, imperial China had recognized all Chinese descendants through the male line as its subjects, regardless of where they were born or whether they had acquired the citizenship of a foreign country. In practice, however, subjects who chose to live in a "barbarian" land were regarded as outcasts, undeserving of the emperor's protection or his concern for their welfare. Therefore, although many hoped to return eventually to their motherland, most overseas Chinese felt they had little reason to be politically loyal to, or even particularly oriented toward, the mainland. This attitude began to change in the last two decades (1891-1911) of the Manchu dynasty. In a reversal of traditional attitudes, Peking suddenly began to take a serious interest in the overseas Chinese—passing laws confirming their Chinese citizenship, soliciting remittances from them, dispatching various commercial and educational delegations to overseas Chinese communities, and so forth. At length, in order to develop closer ties with these communities, Peking began negotiating with the Western powers for the establishment of Chinese consulates in their colonies.[20] Largely as a

[19] The impact of the Chinese economic stranglehold on the development of the Indonesian nationalist movement is analyzed by Kahin, pp. 37–63.

[20] For the major events in this process see Donald E. Willmott, *The National Status of the Chinese in Indonesia, 1900–1958* (Ithaca: Cornell Modern Indonesia Project, 1961), pp. 2–11, 15–19; Lea E. Williams, *Overseas Chinese Nationalism: The Genesis of the Pan-Chinese Movement in Indonesia, 1900–1916* (Glencoe, Ill.: Free Press, 1960); and Purcell, pp. 511–525.

result of the growth of such contacts, many Chinese in Indonesia, unassimilated with either the native or the European population, soon developed a strong attachment to the Chinese mainland they did not formerly have.

Dutch efforts to control and check the spread of mainland-Chinese influence were successful legally but not politically. Peking was allowed to open consulates in Indonesia in 1910, but on the condition that Dutch law, rather than Chinese, would determine the status of the local Chinese.[21] In this way, an attempt was made to force Peking to abandon its citizenship claims on those Chinese residents the Dutch considered the Netherlands' subjects. In practice, this effort had little effect, since Peking's consulates proceeded to register, and solicit funds from, local- and mainland-born Chinese alike, despite repeated Dutch protests and restrictions. Moreover, there was really no way the Dutch could prevent the developing Chinese revolution on the mainland from exerting a politicizing effect on concerned Chinese in Indonesia. This was becoming quite evident as early as 1927, when the rupture of the first KMT (Nationalist Party of China) -CCP alliance triggered a similar split among the politically active segments of the Indonesian Chinese community. Later, during the Sino-Japanese War, (1937-1945) most Chinese groups in Indonesia put aside their internal differences to organize various anti-Japanese bond drives and boycotts in support of the Nationalist Chinese government.[22] On the eve of World War II it had become clear that Dutch colonial power might be able to slow down but could not entirely arrest the attraction to the nationalistic symbols stirring the mainland felt by the politically conscious elements in the Indonesian Chinese community.

Because the Chinese minority had given visible evidence of support for Chiang Kai-shek's government it was inevitably

[21] Purcell, pp. 514–515.
[22] *Ibid.,* p. 544.

exposed to harsh treatment at the hands of the Japanese during the latter's conquest of Indonesia between 1942 and 1945. In destroying Dutch rule the Japanese did more than abolish the colonial system under which the Chinese had acquired wealth and preferential status. During the occupation the Japanese facilitated the growth of Indonesian nationalist organizations, with the aim of creating native puppet support for Japan's "Greater East Asian Co-Prosperity Sphere." This objective the Indonesian nationalist leaders were prepared to serve, as a temporary tactic, because it enabled them to build the kind of mass movement the Dutch had thoroughly suppressed and because they hoped to win independence eventually, even if it could only be achieved by means of a period of tutelage by, and dependence on, Japan.[23] The Japanese did not attempt to break the Chinese stranglehold on the economy. But by allowing the nationalist elements to build a rudimentary political-military organization, they did provide the Indonesians with the means for taking effective action against the Chinese traders if the native population ever freed itself from foreign rule.

In view of the long-pent-up resentments against them, the local Chinese suffered less during Indonesia's 1945 to 1949 independence struggle than might have been expected.[24] To some extent this was because a number of Chinese fought along-side the Indonesians against the Dutch, while others held prominent positions in the republican government formed during the independence struggle. Primarily, however, it was owing to the fact that the principal nationalist leaders, such as Sukarno, Mohammad Hatta, and Sjahrir, were not racist or anti-Chinese. They were politically alert to the dangers which might stem from repressive actions likely to create a thoroughly alienated

[23] On the Japanese occupation period see Harry Benda, *The Crescent and the Rising Sun: Indonesian Islam under the Japanese Occupation* (The Hague: W. van Hoeve, 1958); and Kahin, pp. 101–132.

[24] For this period see Purcell, pp. 551–568, and Willmott, pp. 19–24.

Chinese minority to contend with after independence was won. International considerations also must have influenced the Indonesian leaders' attitudes toward their Chinese problem. To encourage anti-Chinese actions would have undermined the republic's diplomatic efforts to win the support of the major foreign powers at the United Nations. One of these was Nationalist China, a veto-exercising member of the Security Council and a staunch advocate of Indonesian independence from the beginning of the struggle against the Dutch.

The fact that the Indonesian nationalist leaders were political moderates thus helped to keep the revolutionary struggle from simultaneously becoming an internal racial conflict. Nevertheless, when the Dutch attempted to restore colonial rule in 1945, the resulting war for independence created conditions for periodic anti-Chinese violence by the native population. Conflict between the Chinese and Indonesian communities was especially sharp in some of the Dutch-occupied and contested territories. Generally, the Chinese attempted to remain neutral during the independence struggle, offering no resistance to the Dutch but giving little or no active support to the revolutionaries. The Chinese position proved to be untenable. To the Indonesians, the Chinese seemed to be continuing "business as usual," profiteering from the war and *de facto* alignment with the Dutch.

Following several localized but bloody anti-Chinese massacres— the worst occurred in 1946 at Tangerang in West Java and took more than six hundred lives—the Chinese formed local "self-protection forces" (*pao-an tui*), sometimes with Dutch assistance and weapons.[25] A natural response under the circumstances, the existence of these paramilitary units nevertheless freed some Dutch troops to attack the republic and once again had the effect of identifying the Chinese as enemies of the Indonesian nationalist movement. To make matters worse, as

[25] Purcell, pp. 554–566.

in the Japanese-occupation period, the economic dominance of the Chinese was not broken during the war against the Dutch; in fact it was strengthened. Many Indonesian independence fighters came home from the war to find that the major beneficiary of their hard-won victory was the much resented local Chinese minority.

Tension arising from the Chinese-minority issue was only one of the divisive factors built into the new state of Indonesia. Nationalist, Islamic, and Marxist political groups had toiled together in the opening phases of the independence struggle. In 1948, however, the PKI suddenly bolted from its alliance with the noncommunist parties and attempted to seize the leadership of the independence movement. Although it was then in a weak military position vis-à-vis the Dutch, the republican government under Sukarno-Hatta thoroughly crushed the PKI challenge.[26] This action won Indonesia the decisive support of the United States in pressuring the Dutch to grant independence, but it also stamped her leaders as anticommunists and "imperialist lackeys" in the view of foreign communist states and parties.

The terms under which Indonesia was granted independence, in December 1949, largely confirmed the communists' analysis of the new state's neocolonialist status. Her leaders were obliged to settle for a Dutch-rigged federal republic—although they desired a unitary state; to shoulder a huge war debt owed to the Dutch; to protect all Dutch and other foreign economic assets; to become junior partners in the Netherlands-Indonesian Union formed in 1949; and to accept Dutch retention of sovereignty over the West Irian territory, subject to a vague formula for future negotiations. The disposition of West Irian clearly symbolized the fragility and incompleteness of Indonesian independence. Such provisions virtually ensured that Indonesia

[26] The background and development of the split are carefully analyzed in Kahin, pp. 256–303.

would be weak, disunited, and dependent on the Dutch and their Western capitalist allies.[27]

The wisdom of accepting a much compromised independence and the question of when and how the situation could be rectified were issues that divided the leaders of the new Indonesian state from the outset. That their country was within the economic and geopolitical orbit of the Western powers was a fact the political elite fully recognized.[28] But they were divided on whether Indonesia's national goals and interests should be pursued by accepting this reality or by challenging it.

President Sukarno became the main, but by no means the only, exponent of the radical nationalist belief that modern Indonesia was to be the successor to the ancient glories of Madjapahit and Shrivijaya, a destiny which could be fulfilled only by breaking out of the Western orbit.[29] At the very least, this view required an Indonesian foreign policy of neutralism in the Cold War. That the policy might also have strong anti-Western overtones was clear from the fact that Sukarno, like most of the educated elite, had been heavily influenced by the

[27] Ibid., pp. 421–445.

[28] The clearest admission of this fact is in former Prime Minister Mohammad Hatta's "Indonesia's Foreign Policy," Foreign Affairs, 31 (April 1953), 441–452. The same view was also expressed, with somewhat greater reluctance, by another prime minister, Sutan Sjahrir, in Perdjoeangan Kita (Our Struggle [Jogjakarta, 1946]).

[29] For the expansionist, anti-Western view of Indonesia's place in the world see Muhammad Yamin's address of May 31, 1945, to the Investigating Committee for the Preparation of Indonesian Independence, in Yamin's Nasah Persiapan Undang-Undgang Dasar 1945 (The Drafting of the 1945 Constitution) (Djakarta: Jajasan Prapantja, 1959), I, 126–135. In this speech Yamin developed the "Greater Indonesia" doctrine which underlay Sukarno's foreign policies after 1961. Yamin argued that the territorial basis of the Indonesian state should include West Irian, Portugese Timor, British North Borneo, and the Malayan states. While Hatta took issue with these imperialist notions at this conference, Sukarno's speech at the meeting supported Yamin's thesis.

Leninist theory of imperialism, which argued that capitalist states would attempt to dominate and exploit Afro-Asian countries. The behavior of the Western powers toward Indonesia, before and after 1949, did much to strengthen this theory's credibility. Aside from Sukarno, however, other Indonesian leaders, especially those representing economic and military interest groups, had more modest ambitions for their country. They too accepted the desirability of neutralism in the Cold War but believed such a policy could be asserted even though Indonesia remained within the Western orbit, where it would be possible to take advantage of capitalist aid and the strategic protection Anglo-American power afforded her vis-à-vis any potential external communist danger. This conception of Indonesia's place in the world was ascendant in the immediate post-1949 period; and consequently, Djakarta's foreign-policy aims were neither ambitious nor assertively pursued.

Although conflict between proponents of an Islamic and of a secular nationalist Indonesian state existed from the outset and was never wholly resolved, the ruling elite was able to develop a measure of consensus on certain basic questions concerning the country's internal order. They were prepared to give parliamentary institutions a trial—some because compromise was expedient, others because of principle and conviction. A modified form of the capitalist system was accepted, even though this meant prolonged Dutch-Chinese control of the economy and though most of the governing elite nominally espoused one variant or another of welfare or Marxist socialism as necessary for the creation of a "just and prosperous" society. How such a society was to be created by an elite singularly lacking in economic and administrative expertise and representing, in essence, the Western-educated offsprings of a colonial aristocracy was an early problem. One political fact of life was clear. In crushing the 1948 PKI bid for power, Indonesia's post-independence-era elite served notice of the fate that awaited those who might attempt violent or radical change of the existing social order.

It may be useful to summarize briefly the main characteristics of the Indonesian polity that confronted the Chinese leaders late in 1949 and to suggest the main issues that were likely to shape the pattern of future Sino-Indonesian relations:

1. Because Indonesia had been subject to predominantly Hindu, Islamic, and Western influences, she was outside the traditional Chinese sphere of influence. The sense of a special mission and of a kinship with countries such as Korea and Vietnam that has affected ancient and modern Chinese policies was not, therefore, likely to be significant in motivating Peking's post-1949 aims and interests in Indonesia. Probably, therefore, China's policies would be shaped primarily by compelling recent events in China, such as the resurgence of antiforeign nationalism and the existence of a revolutionary ethos in an elite which had just come to power in the first indigenously created Marxist state in Asia. Indonesia, on the other hand, emerged as the successor to a Western colonial entity—albeit after a struggle—and her leaders were pledged, not to radicalism or basic reform, but to dependence on the leading capitalist democracies and the adoption of some of their institutions. Because the motivations of the two countries were fundamentally different, there was a strong likelihood that the resulting opposed nationalistic interests would clash sharply and soon, if the opportunity arose.

2. The most immediate source of friction between Peking and Djakarta was almost certain to be the status of the Indonesian Chinese minority and any relationship the communist mainland might try to establish with it. Although this minority had proved highly responsive to influence exerted by China in the past, in 1949 Peking's capacity to manipulate the Indonesian

Chinese was, in fact, sharply limited. By playing on such themes as nationalism or the nostalgia of the overseas Chinese for the mainland, Peking could expect to win the support of some Indonesian Chinese. But an essentially petty-bourgeois trading class, after all, could not be expected to embrace the basic economic and political tenets of communism unless the Indonesians made life intolerable for the resilient Chinese. Moreover, if the communist government of China followed in the path of the previous Manchu, republican, and nationalist governments—whipping up enthusiasm and support for mainland causes—the Indonesian Chinese would almost certainly be exposed to violence, possibly to massacres, as had happened in the past. The end result could only be an impairment of the diplomatic position of China and an improvement of that of her enemies, who might be expected to profit from any racially inspired Sino-Indonesian conflict.

3. As an underdeveloped island-state more than two thousand miles to the south, without military power and overwhelmingly occupied with its internal problems, Indonesia itself posed no direct security threat to Peking. The apparent weakness did not, however, conceal from the Chinese communist the larger geopolitical reality: Indonesia was a creature of neocolonialism, in effect an appendage of the powerful and warlike imperialist system. Because the influence of the Western powers was dominant in Djakarta, the Chinese leaders automatically assumed that Indonesia would be used to further imperialist aims directed, not only against the Chinese People's Republic, but also against the true interests of the Indonesian people and other Asian-African people struggling for national liberation. The elimination of Western influence or at least of imperialist control over Indonesia was, therefore, a central objective of any policy the Chinese leaders might adopt.

4. Because of Indonesia's political, economic, and ideological

cleavages, her foreign and domestic affairs were likely to be highly unstable. Such a situation was certain to invite intervention by powers interested in preserving Indonesia's dependence on the capitalist states, as well as by such powers as the CPR, which were interested in promoting anti-Western revolutions. The instability of Djakarta's relations with the West, a consequence of the Indonesian elite's dissatisfaction with their country's mortgaged, semi-independent status, would afford communist powers an opportunity to fish in troubled waters. On the other hand, the possibility that foreign communists might successfully exploit anti-Western nationalism in order to ignite a radical revolution seemed most unpromising in the light of the 1948 suppression of the PKI. And any Chinese government seeking to promote a class war in Indonesia had to reckon with the certainty that its own kinsmen, the overseas Chinese, would immediately become its first victims.

The restraints on any forward or interventionist Chinese policy toward Indonesia after 1949 were, from the outset, exceedingly formidable. Peking was faced with a very large, distant, complex, and volatile neighbor—not a placid Laos, Cambodia, or Thailand, and not a small Vietnam or Korea that could easily be made to feel the weight of Chinese power. Yet the new leadership in Peking did not arrive at an assessment that China's interests were limited or that its capacity to influence future development in Indonesia was marginal. Why Peking assumed that an assertive, active policy in Indonesia was possible is the subject of the next chapter.

2

Chinese Foreign Policy:
Theory and Strategy

How much of the sociopolitical history of Indonesia before 1949 was familiar to the men who fashioned the foreign policy of the CPR is impossible to ascertain. Even if the Chinese leaders knew the history fairly well—which seems unlikely, since they had only a limited acquaintance with the outside world before taking power—their interpretation of conditions in that country would almost certainly not accord with many of the views outlined in the previous chapter. On the other hand, because of their perspective as Marxist-Leninist revolutionaries and the record of what their subsequent diplomacy tried to achieve, it seems reasonable to conclude that they were generally optimistic about the long-term future course of relations between China and Indonesia.

The basic views that have motivated China's international behavior and her perception of the realities of the world she lives in but has also tried to change are interrelated. These two aspects, ideas and realities, cannot be separated for analytical purposes, because the principles behind a state's actions are rarely formulated in a political vacuum, and a nation's conduct cannot be interpreted accurately as simply a series of *ad hoc* moves, a sort of chain of intellectually unconnected responses to events or conditions thrust up by the environment. Because ideas and reality must be considered together as a composite whole, rather than separately as independent influences, attempts to explain the foreign policy of China or of any other state as mainly a function of ideology, power, or national interest invariably result in theses which raise more questions than they solve.

To some observers China's foreign policy seems to derive largely from a more or less explicit communist theoretical outline. Others tend to see the role of various Marxist, Leninist, Stalinist, and Maoist ideas as less important in determining the actual practice of the Chinese than the international situation they have had to cope with, which has required that communist doctrines be adjusted. Adherents of both persuasions cite numerous passages from communist classics to buttress their points of view, an exercise that to my mind proves practically nothing. There are, however, two essential points on which those who have closely studied the Chinese communist movement should be able to agree. First, the principles underlying its foreign as well as its domestic policies have developed and changed in response to specific historical experiences. Second—as should be equally obvious—despite the evolutionary process that has modified these principles, Chinese communism has retained a central core of ideas and theories that continue to define how Chinese communists see and react to reality.

An explanation of how communist ideas and concrete political reality have together shaped Chinese policy in Indonesia must begin with the international situation of the late 1940's. By that time, the main features of the international system that was to affect Asia for the next two decades had already emerged. In China, an essentially rural-based communist movement was in the process of winning basic victory in, and leadership of, a vast social revolution which also had strong anti-imperialist overtones. Elsewhere in Asia, other anticolonial movements also led to a breaking away from direct European rule, but it was by no means certain that they had finally or completely put an end to imperialism. The most important reality that affected the international relations of postwar Asia was the emergence of the

United States as the dominant power in the Pacific. Though Washington generally supported decolonialization where it had reason to believe that the successor states would be dependent on, and therefore would cooperate with, the Western capitalist democracies, it consistently opposed other, equally nationalistic liberation movements that were led by communists or nationalists thought to be radically anti-Western and therefore potentially friendly to the Soviet Union. From her military bases stretching from Korea and Japan through Okinawa to the Philippines, the United States, because of the region's postwar economic dependence on her, exercised unprecedented power and influence. Postwar American actions in Asia made it clear, moreover, that she did not intend to relinquish the dominance she had acquired as a result of defeating Japan. Rather than accept the propositions that some retrenchment was unavoidable and that the affairs of Asia would have to be determined mainly by the indigenous countries of the area, American leaders chose to use their dominant power to create a status quo supportive of what they deemed to be the larger economic and military interests of the Western alliance that had been formed in opposition to the Soviet Union and its allies.

The defeat of its Nationalist Chinese ally in 1949 had the effect of suspending, temporarily, adherence to the previous pattern of direct American intervention in mainland Chinese affairs. But it did not deter her from interfering in the internal affairs of other Asian countries. Despite her recent experience in China, in early 1949, before the CRP was established the following October, Washington undertook a commitment to back up French colonialism in Indochina. This move followed from the far-reaching decision the United States had made earlier that year to prevent the perceived threat of a chain of communist revolutions in Asia as a consequence of the "loss" of mainland China. In Indonesia, American policy was similar to that in Indochina—economic and indirect military support of the Dutch reconquest of the former colony—and it was reversed in 1949, only after the nationalist insurgents had thoroughly suppressed the communist faction of the independence movement and, as a result, convinced Washington that the Sukarno-Hatta leadership would not lead the country out of the Western orbit.

Similar considerations were reflected during the emergence of the states of India, Pakistan, and Burma from British rule. There, too, the fact that the main currents of nationalism were both decidedly anticommunist and opposed to radical social reforms made the granting of political independence a price the West could well afford to pay in light of its larger economic and military interest in backing conservative regimes throughout the area. What this process meant was that a mapping of certain Cold War boundaries and America's commitment to a general containment strategy in East Asia had begun before the Chinese revolution was completed, that is to say before Peking had become a major factor in the politics of the region.

The new leaders in Peking did not have to be conditioned by Marxist ideas to conclude that countries like Indonesia— weak, fragmented, and still tied economically to their former colonial masters—were not genuinely autonomous nation-states. Marxism-Leininism did, however, explain that the neocolonial countries were the product of a special international system— imperialism—and that the contradictions in this system determined both the nature of the socioeconomic conflict within these states and the basis of their foreign and domestic policies. To understand how the perceived reality and the theory of imperialism influenced Peking's foreign policy after 1949 it is necessary to examine China's conception of the workings of the international system.

Theory of International Relations

The Chinese communist view of international relations proceeds from the basic conception laid out in Lenin's theory of imperialism.[1] According to this theory, the present era will witness the final collapse of the world imperialist system. This system, which is the culmination of monopoly capitalism, is regarded as the root cause of poverty, war, and the oppression of one state or people by another. These destructive consequences are considered to be inherent in the nature of the imperialist system, for the industrialized capitalist countries must become increasingly expansionist and aggressive, must seek control of the colonial nations and the lesser capitalist states in order to secure the markets and resources necessary to stave off their own eventual internal economic collapse and revolution.

Like other Marxists, the Chinese leaders hold that the final overthrow of the imperialist system is inevitable, because its destruction has been predetermined by the dialectical laws governing the development of economic forces. However, the complete destruction of imperialism ultimately requires violence, because the classes responsible for the system will not step down from their historical places peacefully. On the contrary, communist theory posits that as the crisis within and between imperialist states deepens, the imperialist leaders will be compelled to launch foreign wars, to grab new colonies, and to dominate the economies of other nations in an attempt to perpetuate their moribund system. Socialist states are also believed to be threatened by the decaying capitalist order, for they not only represent the new world order that will replace imperialism but are major obstacles in the path of the more aggressive capitalist states.

In this theory of international politics the colonial and semicolonial countries of the Third World are of prime importance in two respects. First, because they are principal sources of

[1] V. I. Lenin, "Imperialism, the Highest Stage of Capitalism," in *Selected Works* (Moscow: Foreign Languages Publishing House, 1952), I, 433–568.

scarce raw materials, cheap labor, and markets for surplus products, the imperialists must hold and exploit these nations in order to survive. Second, they are imperilism's Achilles heel, because they are perceived as sources of a rising tide of national liberation movements. The Chinese communists therefore believe that since imperialism is the common enemy, the socialist states and the national liberation movements should, in the historical sense, be natural allies. In other words, communism and nationalism should support each other's struggles, because it is the nature of imperialism to commit aggression against people outside its orbit; hence the people of various nations should join together in the fight against their common enemy. Finally, because the enemy is inherently incapable of voluntarily abandoning its aggressive behavior, no lasting peace, only temporary accommodation, is possible with imperialist states.

As the leading capitalist power, during most of the Cold War, U.S. imperialism was depicted as the "main enemy" of the socialist and Third World nations, the chief—but by no means the only—opponent whose global policies must be defeated before the complete liberation of colonial areas and the genuine independence of nation-states could be secured. Adherence to the Leninist theory of imperialism thus imbues the Chinese leaders with a strong belief that their posture vis-à-vis American imperialism and what they currently label Soviet "social imperialism" is one of self-defense. But the most fundamental point to emphasize is that, owing to China's prolonged domination and mistreatment by the West, the theory of imperialism has acquired a strong truth, not only in the minds of Peking's leaders, but probably also of the vast majority of their countrymen. Mao Tse-tung and the Chinese Communist party did not invent an imperialist enemy; the Chinese nation has accumulated ample experience demonstrating this fact during the past hundred years. What the Chinese communists did provide was a quiet credible interpretation of how and why imperialism behaves the way it does. Their theory obviously does not conform to the conception leaders in the capitalist states have of their policies. But in view of the past record it should surprise no one that present-day Chinese leaders are prone to assume that the actions of capitalist nations, in their dealings with China, are motivated by ulterior and exploitative aims. The leaders make the same assumption with respect to the policies of such states toward other socialist and underdeveloped countries.[2]

The specific source of Peking's enmity toward the United States is the latter's long-standing record of intervention in China's internal affairs. This intervention, which began before the end of the Chinese civil war but still continues, was a decisive factor in the creation of a *de facto* Nationalist Chinese state on Taiwan and hence in the incompleteness of the Chinese revolution. While American obstruction of the CPR's sovereignty is the mainspring of Chinese anti-Americanism, other sources of tension besides the Taiwan issue have generated and continue to generate opposition to Washington's policies. For the United States has been consistently perceived as the leading member of a capitalist system which requires tension, war, and the domination of other countries in order to survive. These requirements, the Chinese believe, give rise to a global pattern of conflict in which America and China are usually arraigned on opposite sides. While it is conceivable that a different American attitude toward the Chinese civil war in the 1940's might have altered the Chinese leaders' perceptions of American aims in China, the fact is that Washington gave them no serious cause for reappraisal until the early 1970's. Moreover, for their

[2] For example, see Hu Sheng, *Imperialism and Chinese Politics* (Peking: Foreign Languages Press, 1955); Shao Tieh-chen, *Revolutionary Dialectics and How to Appraise Imperialism* (Peking: Foreign Languages Press, 1963); and *Imperialism and All Reactionaries Are Paper Tigers* (Peking: Foreign Languages Press, 1958).

more general conviction that the United States was the leader of the world imperialist system to have changed, radical changes in the global policies America has pursued since the late 1940's would have been required, and such changes seem virtually inconceivable. In the absence of either precondition it is hardly surprising that Peking's point of departure in international affairs was the fundamental assumption of a continuing antagonism between herself and the United States. In fact this view was established well before the communist victory in China, the emergence of the Taiwan dispute, or the onset of the East-West rivalry. The image of a hostile America has waxed and waned with the course of the Cold War, but even during the current period of détente it remains a basic, if less stridently discussed, element of the Chinese world outlook.

According to Mao Tse-tung's analysis of the international situation in 1946, the United States had replaced Nazi Germany and Japan as the leading imperialist predator. He believed America was attempting to gain control over most of the world, including the Far East, in order eventually to attack the Soviet Union and the socialist system. Mao concluded that before this attack could be launched the American imperialists would have to subjugate "a vast zone which includes many capitalist, colonial and semi-colonial countries in Europe, Asia and Africa." If a new war was to be prevented, he said, the people in this zone would have to unite with those in the socialist movement and struggle; otherwise war was unavoidable.[3]

The expectation of a new imperialist-instigated war, the strategic importance of an intermediate zone of countries between the United States and the socialist states, and the necessity for a global struggle against imperialism were thus put forward as fundamental political tenets of the Chinese com-

[3] Mao Tse-tung, "Talk with the American Correspondent Anna Louise Strong," in *Selected Readings from the Works of Mao Tse-tung* (Peking: Foreign Languages Press, 1967), pp. 283–284.

munists well before the two powers became active rivals in Asia. So strong are the roots of this anti-imperialist ethic that it is reflected in virtually every aspect of Peking's foreign policy, coloring her attitudes and her relations with all countries, and is unlikely to disappear altogether. Accordingly, any favorable changes in American policy toward China—such as those that preceded and followed the Nixon visit—must be interpreted in Peking as resulting from a weakened American position in the capitalist system, not from a sudden "change of heart" in Washington. Chinese communist theory thus takes into account the possibility that the aggressive policies of imperialist nations like the United States can change. But the change is due to the emergence of deep crises within the imperialist world. In this sense, nothing in Chinese theory automatically designates a particular capitalist power as the permanent enemy of China; from her perspective that role is a function of historical forces that are in a constant state of flux. By the same token, however, the Chinese theories of imperialism cause her leaders to be skeptical about the possibility of long-lasting good relations with a country like America in the absence of profound changes in its economic and political base.

Next in importance to the theory of imperialism, and closely related to it, is the Chinese conception of the revolutionary process in the colonial countries. The basic formulation of the concept is also Leninist. In his theory of the "New Democracy," however, Mao Tse-tung introduced important modifications of Lenin with respect to (1) how revolutionary movements would unfold in colonial and semicolonial countries; (2) the role of these movements in the struggle against imperialism; and (3) the relationship of colonial liberation struggles to the socialist movement.[4] On these issues, Mao's theoretical innovations

[4] *On New Democracy* (Peking: Foreign Languages Press, 1954), pp. 18–27.

amounted to an argument that stressed the overriding importance of colonial revolutions in bringing about radical changes in the global balance of power between socialism and imperialism. The full implication of his ideas, originally developed in the context of China's resistance against the Japanese invader, only became apparent twenty years later when, in opposition to Soviet foreign policy, Peking tried to persuade the socialist camp that the main arena of the struggle with imperialism was the Third World, not Europe.

Basic Leninism conceived of the revolution in colonial, pre-capitalistic countries as developing in two sequential phases: a bourgeois-democratic stage in which the national bourgeoisie, bent on establishing the supremacy of native capitalism, would lead the struggle for independence against imperialism and feudalism in the country; and a transition-to-socialism stage in which the proletariat (i.e., the local communist party) would establish a worker-peasant dictatorship and proceed to complete the socialist revolution. Ever since Lenin's time bourgeois-democratic revolutions struggling against imperialism have been regarded by communists as useful allies, but primarily in a tactical sense: the disruption of imperialism's "weak link"—the colonies—can greatly advance the struggle against the Western industrial powers. However, until these revolutions had entered the second, or transition, stage they were not considered, in Leninist theory, an integral part of the world proletarian-socialist revolution.[5]

Mao's 1940 New Democracy formulation altered Leninist theory in two ways. First, Mao argued that in semicolonial countries waging a liberation struggle against imperialism (as

[5] Lenin's basic thesis on the united front was adopted at the Second Comintern Congress in 1920. See Jane Degras, ed., *The Communist International, 1919–1943* (London: Oxford University Press, 1956–1965), I, 143–144.

was the case in China) the bourgeois-democratic revolution would not be led by the bourgeoisie alone but by the "joint revolutionary-democratic dictatorship of several revolutionary classes." In other words, the Communist party and its supporters could begin the process of challenging the leading role of the bourgeoisie well before, instead of after, the completion of the national revolution. Mao's conception of the multiclass revolutionary alliance was further refined and carried forward in his 1949 work, *On People's Democratic Dictatorship*.[6] Here he proclaimed that a dictatorship of all the revolutionary classes, led by the CCP, would also characterize the transition-to-socialism stage—a concept which in effect replaced Lenin's idea of hegemony by the proletariat alone after the seizure of power. Thus the New Democracy departed significantly from Leninist theory by indicating that Lenin's two-stage revolution could be transformed or compressed, during a substantial period of time, into essentially one stage. In terms of how to forge an effective revolutionary strategy the basic idea was that before the bourgeois-democratic revolution was actually completed, it might be possible for the communists to become the leaders of a multiclass alliance in certain colonial and semicolonial countries in which the national struggle against foreign domination clearly superseded, in importance, the internal struggle between the proletariat and the bourgeoisie.

The second revision of Leninism that grew out of Mao's 1940 theory was his contention that New Democracy-type revolutions in colonial and semicolonial countries were actually integral parts of the "proletarian-socialist world revolution," despite the fact they had not yet entered the transition stage. Mao argued that anticolonial movements such as China's New Democracy were already sufficiently proletarian in character,

[6] Mao Tse-tung, *On People's Democratic Dictatorship* (Peking: Foreign Languages Press, 1950), pp. 1–26.

because they represented "the new type of revolution," a revolution "led by the proletariat [that] aims at establishing a new democratic society and a state under the joint dictatorship of all revolutionary classes" and thus "serves to clear a path even wider for the development of socialism."[7] In effect, Mao was arguing that anti-imperialist revolutions implicitly became part of a general movement toward socialism rather than toward captitalism once proletarian elements were in a position to assert a challenge for the leadership of a national multiclass alliance.

Neither of the innovations was presented, at the time or later, as applicable only to the Chinese revolution because of its special character. On the contrary, the New Democracy formula was stated in general terms; it was relevant, presumably, to colonial revolutions in which conditions were similar to China's.

The projection of Mao's ideas onto external colonial settings revealed several basic assumptions underlying his analysis of the dynamics at work in the international system. It seems clear, for example, that the New Democracy theory presupposed a high degree of congruence between the anticolonial and the socialist movements in waging anti-imperialist struggles—a presupposition that was not in the thinking of Lenin or his successors. Similarly, New Democracy's prominent optimism about the prospects for a "new type of revolution" which would enable the proletariat to establish its leadership during the bourgeois-democratic stage was in marked contrast to the more pessimistic conclusions Moscow was forced to reach after 1918 concerning what communist parties in the colonies could be expected to achieve in the first stage of the revolution.[8]

[7] *Ibid.*, pp. 11–12.

[8] Moscow's disenchantment with the prospects for revolution in the colonies has a long history. It is rooted in the setbacks suffered by the Comintern in the 1920's, when various efforts to support and subvert national independence movements resulted in crushing defeats for Moscow and the Asian communist parties, without producing any compen-

The assumption that seems to have had the most pervasive impact on Peking's analysis of Third World politics in the post-1949 period is the strong implication in New Democracy that anti-imperialist revolutions in the developing countries are integral parts of the world proletarian-socialist revolution. This conception appears to assign to anti-imperialist revolutions a far more important role and status in the international communist movement than Lenin, Stalin, or Khrushchev ever conceded in defining the Kremlin's attitude toward anti-imperialist nationalism in the Third World. The impact this basic Maoist reinterpretation of Leninist doctrine was to have on Soviet-Chinese accord in foreign policy began to be felt only in the late 1950's, when Peking started to argue that the socialist camp should concentrate its strategy in the Afro-Asian countries. But the rationale for the theory that the colonial struggle was such a significant constituent of the world socialist revolution that it should determine that revolution's direction and emphasis actually had its roots in Mao's concept of New Democracy, announced nearly twenty years earlier.

Peking's general attitude toward international relations has also been shaped by Mao's theory of contradictions, first advanced in 1937.[9] This innovation also derived from an earlier Marxist classic theory, the theory of dialectical materialism. The key significance of this Maoist theory is that the Chinese communists use it in analyzing major internal and external policy issues.

---

satory weakening of the imperialist system. Similar consequences attended the post-1948 Kremlin effort to disrupt the Western alliance by encouraging another round of communist revolts in Southeast Asia. Ironically, the two Asian communist movements which did succeed, in China and in Vietnam, did not have Soviet encouragement until victory seemed assured.

[9] Mao Tse-tung, *On Contradictions* (Peking: Foreign Languages Press, 1965), I, 311–347.

Basically, "contradictions" theory develops the idea that all human and natural phenomena are in a process of constant change; the motive force is the uninterrupted emergence of contradictions, which are inherent in everything. The operative part of this theory holds that although every process has a number of contradictions, only one of them is the "principal contradiction" (*chu-yao mao-tun*) at any given time. This principal contradiction plays "the leading and decisive role while the rest occupy a secondary or subordinate position." The important link between this theory and the actualities of Chinese communist policy-making was established long ago when Mao said: "Therefore, in studying any complex process . . . we must devote every effort to finding its principal contradiction. Once this principal is grasped, all problems can be readily resolved."[10] That the Chinese leaders, in fact, have consistently and conscientiously analyzed the domestic and international problems of their revolution in the framework of contradictions theory has been pointed out in several scholarly studies.[11]

The range and importance of foreign-policy decisions that may be affected by employing contradictions theory are substantial because the Chinese use it to guide them in finding answers to such questions as: What is the central problem to be solved? What hostile force or forces are to be regarded as the "main enemy"? With what force or forces can we unite in order to defeat the enemy? What strategy and tactics should be adopted? In non-Chinese parlance, operationalizing contradictions theory means making an application, at the strategic decision-making

---

[10] *Ibid.*, pp. 331–332.

[11] For example, see Franz Schurmann, *Ideology and Organization in Communist China* (Berkeley: University of California Press, 1966), pp. 101–104; John Wilson Lewis, *Leadership in Communist China* (Ithaca: Cornell University Press, 1963), pp. 47–52; and Peter Van Ness, *Revolution and Chinese Foreign Policy* (Berkeley: University of California Press, 1970), pp. 24–29.

level, of class-analysis techniques in order to diagnose the implications of various policy choices facing the leadership and thus to choose the optimal one. Because determining the principal contradiction is regarded as crucial, the Chinese elite consider that determination to be the acid test of their abilities as statesmen and strategists.

Since few theories command respect unless their explanatory power has proved to be significant, it is important to understand the historical context in which Mao's ideas about contradictions emerged. He first advanced the theory in 1937, at the time of the Japanese invasion of China, the event that marked the decisive turning point in the fortunes of the CCP and, indeed, the whole course of the Chinese revolution. Mao used the theory to demonstrate the strategic necessity of subordinating the internal class contradictions between the proletariat and the bourgeoisie in China to the external but principal contradiction between the Chinese nation and Japanese imperialism. On the basis of this analysis the CCP entered into a tactical anti-imperialist united front with the Kuomintang—a union that subsequently enabled the communists to mobilize the military forces and the mass political support necessary to win the final victory. The fact that Mao's decisions proved to be correct at this crucial juncture and at later points no doubt strengthened the credibility of policy analyses based on the contradictions theory. In essence, China's leaders believe that a correct application of the theory reveals not only the main strategic problem to be solved, but also the tactics that should be employed. The foreign relations of China are especially affected by the leadership's application of the theory, because the identification of the principal contradiction determines who the main international adversary is and therefore which united-front policy to adopt in opposing him.

While the alliance with the Soviet Union was intact Peking did not publicly invoke the contradictions theory to argue the case for the primacy of confronting imperialism in the colonial world. Instead, several fundamental contradictions were usually identified but not openly discussed in any particular order of importance.[12] Although the prime significance of the struggle between imperialism and the oppressed nations and peoples had been emphasized in Chinese writings since the early 1950's, it was not explicitly singled out as the most crucial conflict until 1963,[13] and it was not designated the principal contradiction until 1965.[14] By that time the relations between state and party had so deteriorated that the Sino-Soviet ideological dispute was more a reflection than a cause of their differences. It seems quite probable, nevertheless, that China's leaders, or at least Mao and those closest to him, all along regarded the colonial world, the setting of the struggle against imperialism, as the decisive strategic battleground—an appraisal that also reflected primarily the fact that Peking's most vital interests were centered in this arena—even though their assessment was not openly proclaimed until the break with Moscow. It would appear, therefore, that the great importance attached to the struggle over the Third World was closely connected to the kind of strategic thought

[12] Although the precise wording and number varied in Peking's usage, generally there were said to be four "fundamental contradictions": between the imperialist and the socialist camps; between the bourgeoisie and the proletariat in capitalist countries; between the oppressed nations and imperialism; and between the imperialist countries. These were spelled out definitively in the letter of the Chinese Communist Party Central Committee of June 14, 1963; in *The Polemic on the General Line of the International Communist Movement* (Peking: Foreign Languages Press, 1965), pp. 6–7.

[13] See "A Proposal Concerning the General Line of the International Communist Movement," of the Central Committee of the Communist party of the Soviet Union, in *The Polemic,* pp. 3–54; and Shao Tieh-chen, *Revolutionary Dialetics,* p. 20.

[14] Former Politbureau member P'eng Chen made the Chinese analysis a matter of public record on May 25, 1965 in a speech in Indonesia, in *Hung-ch'i* (Red Flag), 6 (June 1965), 4.

which produced Mao's 1946 concept of the intermediate zone, the 1949 advocacy of Maoist-type colonial revolutions, the post-1954 Chinese emphasis on Afro-Asian anti-imperialist unity, and the 1965 proclamation of the "people's war" doctrine.

Underlying each concept which found expression in a major phase of Chinese foreign policy was the implicit assumption that the fundamental contradictions between imperialism and the colonial and semicolonial world had to be confronted, either to defend the basic national interests of socialist states or to honor the ideological commitment to support anti-Western revolutions. In subordinating the internal class struggle to the external contradiction between the Chinese nation and Japanese imperialism during the thirties and forties, the Chinese had used a method they apparently believed other Third World communist parties and revolutionary movements could also successfully employ, under similar conditions, to break away from Western domination. In projecting this strategy to the international scene of the late 1950's and 1960's, Peking essentially meant that the communist powers should be prepared to subordinate the struggle between the developed socialist and imperialist states to the allegedly more decisive conflicts stemming from the contradictions between imperialism and the oppressed nations and peoples. In other words, the Chinese argued, the outcome of the struggles of Third World countries to liberate themselves from the American-led imperialist system was the decisive factor in the long-term contest between socialism and capitalism.

Thus the common thread that runs through the major theoretical underpinnings of Chinese foreign policy is the significance of the conflict between imperialism and the countries of Asia, Africa, and Latin America in shaping the evolution of the international system. According to the Chinese view, the nature of this conflict not only predetermines the aggressive behavior of the imperialist powers but also creates interests common to both socialist and Third World countries. China's foreign-policy theory also helps her leaders to identify what they believe are the imperialists' fatal political weaknesses, in particular their opposition to genuine national independence. From their interpretation of the worldwide conflict the Chinese communists have developed, in essence, a theory of international relations which provides both a framework of perceptions and a set of general policy guidelines.

Chinese Foreign-Policy Strategy

Given the international power realities of the fifties and sixties, it seems, in retrospect, strangely out of character for the leaders of China to conclude that an active, assertive policy in Indonesia was possible, for such a policy seemingly required the capabilities of a great power. Peking could do very little, on her own, to weaken the Western economic and military position, to improve the fortunes of the Indonesian communists, to determine Soviet policy toward Indonesia—much less toward Southeast Asia—or even to protect her own nationals in a foreign land. On the other hand, the leading capitalist powers could exert powerful leverage as consumers of Indonesia's exports, suppliers of technical aid and credit, and, crucially, trainers of her military officers. Actually, the Americans and the Dutch did not have to rely heavily on their overwhelming naval and air forces to influence decisively the turn of events inside Indonesia; they already had powerful interest groups inside the country ready to help them. Moreover, such power as the socialist camp could muster, even as it grew in proportion to that of the West, remained substantially under Soviet control. Therefore, an independent Chinese strategy in Indonesia depended almost entirely on China's conducting a diplomatic campaign superior to that of the stronger Western powers. Peking would have to respond adroitly to opportunities created by the course of the rivalry among the powers and the relations between them and the unstable Indonesian government.

Yet the evidence to be presented in this study shows that the Chinese leaders consistently strove to attain the kinds of foreign-policy influence that are sought by great powers. Part of this drive undoubtedly stemmed, as it does in other nations, from exaggerated ambitions. Another factor, no doubt, was a belief that aggressive pressures were being exerted by her enemies, especially the United States, and, after 1956, the Soviet Union. But these elements, though they may possibly have been the underlying motivations for policies, do not account for the Chinese leaders' apparently extraordinary confidence in their ability to compete with, and ultimately prevail over, objectively stronger opponents. To understand this crucial dimension of Chinese policy it is necessary to turn to an analysis of the body of strategy and tactics the leaders had developed over a long period of time, which they believed had repeatedly enabled them to triumph over physically more powerful adversaries. At the heart of the Chinese leadership's strategic philosophy is a deep-seated rejection of conventional power relationships which, in the West, are regarded as decisive in determining the outcome of political-military conflicts. A formidable period of revolutionary experience appears to have proved to the satisfaction of the Chinese that their enemies, though outwardly strong, in reality have fatal weaknesses that can be exploited in the course of a protracted struggle which pits superior understanding of historical forces and political organization against purely military and economic power.[15]

From this basic perception flow such standard Chinese communist sayings as "The enemy is a paper tiger"; "Man is more important than weapons"; and "Despise the enemy strategically;

[15] The best statement of the Chinese depreciation of the enemies' power—including their nuclear weapons—is Mao's "Talk with the American Correspondent Anna Louise Strong."

take full account of him tactically." These slogans are not, as some observers have supposed, simply psychological boosters to compensate for the CPR's relative military and industrial inferiority. They are genuine reflections of an abiding confidence in the importance of social change, which the leadership believes fundamentally determines the outcome of political war. Because the CPR has been a comparatively weak power, in virtually every international conflict affecting the CPR since 1949 her leaders have assumed that the adversaries initially had the advantage. The Chinese believe, however, that the adversaries' contradictions must eventually, as the contest evolves, undermine their temporary physical superiority. Indeed, Chinese strategy most excels in the exploitation of the opponents' vulnerable points and their mistakes over a long period of time. This strategy is evident in the classic successes the Chinese have achieved over the Japanese, the Kuomintang, and, most recently, the Americans, who after twenty years were politically defeated and forced to abandon their anti-China containment policy. The Chinese communists did not physically overcome any of these opponents—not even Chiang Kai-shek's armies, which for the most part melted away as a result of massive desertions starting in late 1948. But China's staying power, based on a correct assessment of the strategic situation and on superior mass organization, effectively counteracted these enemies' material superiority, which proved, eventually, an inadequate substitute for policies that lacked a solid political base.

The core element of the strategy is Mao Tse-tung's famous three-part revolutionary model: party, army, and united front.[16] By party he means a disciplined communist leadership, skilled in the theory and practice of Marxism-Leninism and closely linked with the masses. The second component, the army, must be led by the Communist party and must eventually develop

[16] Mao presented a succinct formulation of the model in *On People's Democratic Dictatorship*, p. 23.

enough independent military power to secure a population base and military sanctuaries and to wage armed warfare in the countryside. Finally, the united front must be a broad national alliance of all those forces opposing imperialism and feudalism, and it must be a revolutionary united front whose purpose is to seize state power.

In the Chinese strategy, these three components are inter-related to form a single entity. Army and united front serve as the strategy's principal weapons. The former is necessary to guarantee eventual communist control over, or at a minimum independence within, the united front. By means of the united front the revolutionaries seek to divide and isolate their enemies while organizing potential allies into a broad national coalition. The party plays the role of the grand strategist wielding these weapons.

The successful employment of this model in the Chinese revolution established Mao Tse-tung as a formidable strategist in the management of political-military conflict. That the Chinese have consciously tried to apply the strategic lessons of their long revolution to the pursuit of foreign-policy objectives since 1949 has been pointed out in several scholarly studies[17] and has been loudly proclaimed by the Peking government on various occasions.[18] Again, it must be noted that the relevance of the model to Peking's foreign policy necessarily derives, not only from its historically proved worth, but also from the fact that the Chinese leaders, in common with all Marxist-Leninists, see no fundamental distinction or separation between internal

[17] For example, see Tang Tsou and Morton H. Halperin, "Mao Tse-tung's Revolutionary Strategy and Peking's International Behavior," *American Political Science Review,* 59 (March 1965), 80–99.

[18] The best-known proclamations are Liu Shao-ch'i's opening speech at the Asian-Australasian Trade Union Conference on November 16, 1949, broadcast by the New China News Agency (NCNA) (Peking), November 23, 1949; and Lin Piao's "Long Live the Victory of People's Wars," *Peking Review,* 8 (Sept. 3, 1965), 9–30.

and external spheres of politics. From this point of view it follows that, since the class struggle permeates everything, political-military conflict situations at the subnational, national, and international levels can be diagnosed and acted upon by applying certain general rules—that is, the precepts of various time-tested Chinese strategies. Though the Chinese leaders' conception of how the philosophy and principles of their revolutionary strategy can be applied to problems of national statecraft does not, obviously, account for every initiative Peking takes or response she makes in international affairs, a knowledge of the conception is the main key to an understanding of her foreign policy.

Great though the lessons and usefulness of these strategies have been, several factors point to the conclusion that the Chinese leadership has not been altogether successful in transposing the domestic revolutionary model to foreign affairs. The logical international equivalent of the CCP component should have been the socialist camp and, by implication, Soviet rather than Chinese leadership of the communist movement. While the Sino-Soviet alliance was intact the Chinese accepted Russian leadership. Once the two powers came into open conflict, however, there really could not be an international equivalent of the unified, disciplined party the Maoist model requires. In the early 1960's, China tried to fill the gap by presenting the antirevisionist communist states and the parties that were oriented toward Peking as substitutes for the Sino-Soviet alliance. But this dialectical sleight of hand supplied the party component of the model only in a theoretical sense. Peking's anti-Soviet coalition had neither discipline or unity. That its members shared a common adherence to Chinese interpretations of Marxism-Leninism was, to say the least, very doubtful. Similarly, the combined military forces of the socialist camp—the equivalent of the Chinese Red Army in the model—could not fill the army's place after the Sino-Soviet rupture. Presumably, the anti-imperialist groups engaged in revolutionary struggles around the globe were regarded as effective substitutes. But these elements, troublesome though they might be to the imperialists, were never capable of performing the power role the Red Army had played in the Chinese domestic struggle. Even where such anti-imperialist forces were led by communists—usually they were not—none were controlled by Peking and hence could not be relied on to act in accordance with Chinese strategic preferences, let alone Chinese state interests. The successful national liberation movements, as in the case of Indochina, Algeria, and Cuba, were confined to local geographic regions and did not, by virtue of their victories, transform the international balance of power in a way analogous to the effect of the Red Army's triumphs over the Nationalist armies in the Chinese revolution. The absence of real international equivalents for the party and army components actually meant that the only element of the Maoist revolutionary model that could be employed in the service of China's foreign-policy strategy was the united front. An analysis of the Chinese ideas about this component will help to make apparent the general strengths and weaknesses of the united front and the role it performs in foreign policy.

Peking's conception of the united front is based on Leninist doctrine, which indicates that for all communist elites since the Russian revolution the necessity of forming or joining united fronts develops in response to a specific historical circumstance: the weak or threatened position of the revolutionary party prior to the time it is strong enough to seize power in a country. An extension of this premise to international politics makes evident the need of the socialist camp to form and join united fronts because of the great danger of imperialist attack—a threat that will continue until the imperialist system collapses.

The possibility of forming united fronts arises from the characteristic Marxist-Leninist analysis of power relationships among the main participants in a political conflict situation. At one end of the spectrum are the progressive forces, of which the most ideologically advanced is the proletariat. But the proletariat's leadership of the progressive elements may, in fact, be more apparent than real. At the other end of the spectrum are the reactionary elements—that is, the feudal and capitalist classes led by the imperialists and their anti-communist allies. Between the two poles are the middle-of-the-road groups, which, because they are composed of the vast majority of the people, are of primary importance to the contending Left and Right forces. In the competition for supremacy, the strength of the anticommunists is perceived as deriving mainly from their military power. On the other hand, the fundamental weakness of the reactionaries is political, since, according to Marxism-Leninism, the vast majority of the world's people want to throw off the capitalist yoke and engage in revolutions. Hence, virtually all communist parties embrace the doctrine that, in situations where the objective balance of forces is against the proletariat, the revolutionaries must attempt to organize a united front. If possible, the front should include the great majority of the people, which comprises the familiar four progressive classes: peasantry, workers, petty bourgeoisie, and national bourgeoisie. As Mao Tse-tung succinctly put it, the essential purpose of the united front is "to develop the progressive forces, to win over the middle-of-the-road forces and to isolate the diehards" (i.e., the imperialists and the reactionaries).[19]

Depending on the specific situation facing communist revolutionaries, the united front takes different forms and expresses different tactical objectives. Historically, two classic models of the united front have appeared: the united front from "below," wherein the communists attempt to lead a worker-peasant alliance to overthrow a capitalist or feudalist regime; and the united front from "above," wherein the communists attempt to collaborate with certain bourgeois governments and political parties which,

[19] *Selected Works* (London: Lawrence and Wishart, 1954), III, 194.

together with the communists, face the imminent threat of fascism (i.e., a particularly virulent form of imperialism). Either type of front can be employed to cope with internal as well as external conflicts. Historically, the "below" model has usually reflected a somewhat narrow revolutionary class base and a bid for power; the "above" model has ordinarily emerged when the communists, forced to take a defensive position, needed a broad front that included many nonproletarian elements. In general, every tactical situation justifies the formation of one or the other type of united front—hence its ubiquitous role in the history of communist parties.

Mao Tse-tung introduced yet another variation of Leninism when he succeeded in combining the united front from above and the united front from below.[20] Because China was a semi-colonial country in which the immediate national revolution against foreign domination took priority over the internal class struggle, Mao argued that it was possible to forge a coalition linking the proletarian-led worker-peasant alliance (the united front from below) with the patriotic segments of the bourgeoisie (the united front from above). Although this fusion of the CCP and the KMT was a military necessity for both sides, it greatly expanded the communists' political appeal as a nationalist movement fighting the foreign enemy and thus helped them to win over many noncommunists during the war against Japan. In this way the CCP was able to add to its main sources of strength, the peasants and workers. In Mao's formulation, however, the front from below must remain the basis of the alliance, since the peasants

[20] The significance of this variation and its implications for other Asian communist parties have been analyzed by John Kautsky, *Moscow and the Communist Party of India: A Study in the Post-War Evolution of International Communism Strategy.* (Cambridge, Mass.: M.I.T. Press, 1956), pp. 6–15. Mao Tse-tung showed why it was possible to integrate both types of fronts in a semicolonial country during the anti-imperialist struggle, in *On New Democracy.*

and workers make up the genuine and most dependable revolutionary forces. The front from above, on the other hand, Mao regarded as playing a subordinate or secondary role, owing to the fact that it represented the less reliable bourgeois classes that might waiver or betray the revolution at a future time. Theoretically, however, a combination of the two fronts was possible and desirable as long as the principal contradiction facing the revolutionaries required an overall anti-imperialist strategy.

Although the Chinese communists evidently regard the formation of united fronts as an important political objective, their effectiveness or safe use depends on two essential conditions. The front must be led by the proletariat rather than by its rival, the bourgeoisie; and the proletariat must retain independence of, and freedom of action within, the front.[21] These conditions are necessary to ensure that the front maintains a genuine revolutionary thrust. Otherwise there is the danger, as the Chinese see it, that the front might come under the hegemony of the bourgeoisie. This class, which is considered to have an anti-imperialist or antifeudal role to play in certain periods, is at best a waivering ally, prone at some point to betray the front and attack the revolutionaries. As all communist parties would agree, the bourgeoisie presents this threat because its class drive is to establish domestic capitalism and the revolutionaries will ultimately stand in the way, no matter whether the two camps see eye to eye, temporarily, on the anti-imperialist issue. The Chinese communists have especially good reason to be wary of alliances with bourgeois nationalists. Their first united front with the Kuomintang, which lasted from 1923 to 1927, ended with Chiang Kai-shek's bloody suppression of the communists. That bitter experience compelled the CCP thereafter to form united fronts only

[21] Mao Tse-tung, *The Question of Independence within the United Front* (Peking: Foreign Languages Press, 1960), pp. 1–6.

when it could be sure that the two crucial conditions—control and freedom of action—would be met. During the second CCP-KMT alliance (1936–1945), the communists had independent bases of political and military power which, in the circumstances of the Japanese occupation, could not be undermined by the Nationalists. Indeed the reverse occurred. By entering into the anti-Japanese united front, eventually millions of people came over to the communists' side.

An expectation of continuing competition with the bourgeoisie for control of the united front is, therefore, fundamental to the Chinese view of how this instrument can be used and what potential dangers it poses. Whether the struggle with the bourgeoisie takes predominantly an armed or a political form and whether the united front with that class lasts a long or a short time depends on different historical conditions.[22] Analyzing the future of the CCP-KMT alliance during the war against Japan, Mao correctly predicted that the united front would later "turn into an armed struggle when [the communists were] forced to split with the bourgeoisie."[23] After the final split, in 1946, the Chinese communists went on to seize power, having used the wartime collaboration with the KMT to expand greatly their military and political strength. After the victory in 1949 the CCP did not terminate the alliance with all its noncommunist allies. On the contrary, minus the KMT and a few other groups designated as reactionary, the united front of "all the revolutionary classes led by the proletariat" was not only retained as the political coalition that would exercise power in the period of "the people's democratic dictatorship," but the principle of the

[22] Li Wei-han, "The Struggle for Proletarian Leadership in the Period of the New-Democratic Revolution in China," *Peking Review,* 5 (March 2, 1962), 12.

[23] Mao Tse-tung, "Introductory Remarks to *The Communist*," *Selected Works,* III, 59–60.

united front achieved the status of a basic element of the 1954 CPR constitution.[24] The history of the Chinese revolutionaries shows that they have been wary, and justifiably so, of collaboration with noncommunist groups, especially when they have not controlled such relationships. But it also shows a disposition to regard united fronts, not simply as short-term devices, but as useful long-term solutions to various kinds of political-military problems.

The concept of the united front has been used by communist parties in other countries. It is not the special property of the CCP. To underscore what is distinctive in the Chinese adaptation, it may be useful to compare the Chinese and Soviet experiences. Historically, Moscow has employed united fronts on a number of occasions—both the "above" and the "below" models. From 1918 to 1920, for example, when the Bolsheviks incorrectly anticipated a revolutionary floodtide in the industrialized nations, they adopted a front-from-below policy aimed at mobilizing workers and peasants to seize power in Russia and other European states. When the European revolutions failed to materialize, the Kremlin shifted its attention to Asia. During the 1920's, Moscow tried to align itself with fledging bourgeois-led national liberation movements to China, India, and Indonesia in the hope of weakening Russia's main enemies, the Western colonial powers. This was the first appearance of the united front from "above" in Soviet foreign policy. The united front took a distinctly different "above" form, however, at various times between 1935 and 1945, when the Soviets devised the "Popular Front" concept and joined in a grand alliance with the governments of the capitalist democracies to defeat the Axis powers. Following the collapse of the wartime coalition, between 1947 and 1952,

[24] This is made explicit in the Preamble. See Liu Shao-ch'i, *Report on the Draft Constitution of the People's Republic of China* and the appended document, *Constitution of the People's Republic of China* (Peking: Foreign Languages Press, 1962), especially pp. 19–22 and 63.

Moscow's united-front line again reverted to the use of a "below" model, by backing communist-led uprisings in capitalist as well as colonial countries. By 1955 the Kremlin was again employing the "above" united-front model, which involved collaborating with certain Afro-Asian bourgeois nationalist regimes for the purpose of keeping them out of the American orbit. About this time Moscow commenced the more general policy of tacitly discouraging communist parties in the capitalist, newly independent, or colonial countries from engaging in revolutions that might undermine her primary aim of managing the Cold War within the framework of an American-Soviet bipolar power system.

Moscow's decreasing interest in united fronts since the mid-fifties is not difficult to understand. Russian communism was no longer a weak or isolated movement in great need of allies, but a nuclear superpower comparable in strength to the United States. Under these circumstances united fronts are rather unimportant in Moscow's foreign policy. Strategically, the Russian leaders are not dependent on winning over various anti-imperialist and nationalist forces in order to protect the Soviet state or even to advance the more distant, vague goal of world revolution. On the contrary, other communist and noncommunist states and nationalist movements seek Moscow's protection, patronage, and good will. As a result of this fundamental reversal in Russia's global position her leaders can afford to be relaxed about the bourgeois, capitalist, and feudalist elements with which the Kremlin chooses to cooperate from time to time. The Soviet experience thus seems to have led to the conclusion that united-front entanglements may be necessary in the early stages of development of communist power, but once this power is solidly established they can and should be dissolved, as they have been in socialist states that are responsive to Moscow's wishes.

Chinese experience led to a different conclusion. The course of China's revolution, both of the struggle for power and for socialist construction, indicated a strong possibility of transforming the united front into a permanent general strategy applicable to foreign and domestic affairs.[25] This high estimate of the worth of fronts is partly a result of its usefulness in retaining noncommunist support for domestic programs in China and in obtaining noncommunist allies abroad as defensive measures. In other words, the CPR, while Washington and Moscow were attempting to encircle and confine her, needed as many friends and supporters as she could muster, because the military-industrial base of her revolution was comparatively weak. In another sense, however, the importance the Chinese have attached to the united front reflects the strong populist undercurrent in Chinese communism, particularly in Maoist ideology, which assumes that the overwhelming mass of the Chinese people support communism. Internationally, the extension of this populist idea leads to the assumption that the people of various countries, and not solely on a class basis, oppose imperialism and can be won over to revolutionary programs. Accordingly, the development of political associations for the purpose of creating united fronts can lead to the conversion of noncommunist elements into permanent allies of China, both at home and abroad.

The transformation of the united front into a general strategy also appears to have been aided, indirectly, by Mao's earlier innovations in Marxism-Leninism. The "New Democracy" theory, it seems clear, contributed to the vitality of the united-front concept, because it envisioned a continuation of the multi-class alliance, not only until the socialist transition stage was reached, but also, implicitly, beyond that stage. Similarly, the contradictions theory, as it has been applied to problems of international power politics, has also tended to prolong the usefulness of the united front concept. For the whole line of reason-

[25] The most detailed analysis of this process is the excellent study by Lyman P. Van Slyke, *Enemies and Friends: The United Front in Chinese Communist History* (Stanford, Calif.: Stanford University Press, 1967), p. 278.

ing that developed from Chinese contradictions analysis after World War II (to the effect that the colonial and semicolonial countries were the decisive theatre of the struggle with imperialism) logically led to a foreign policy emphasizing long-term support of a variety of united-front strategies linking communism and nationalism in the Third World.

Because the Chinese use of the united front has been a function of national strategy, the analysis of the type or types of front policy being pursued at any given time has been, and continues to be, a very important diagnostic tool in trying to understand Peking's objectives in a variety of international contexts. The following chapters analyze China's policy in Indonesia primarily as it has affected or been affected by the shifting pattern of her united-front strategies, paying special attention to the relationships between their global and specifically Indonesian dimensions. This analysis seeks to explain three aspects of the relationship with Indonesia during the period 1949 to 1967: How did Peking's perception of the evolving international situation influence the general aims and forms of her policy toward Third World countries, especially in Asia? How did the several major shifts in China's global strategy affect her policy toward Indonesia? How effective was the united front, globally and in Indonesia, as an instrument of Chinese policy?

3

Revolution and Diplomacy: The Left United-Front Strategy

The Chinese communists formed their initial impressions of Indonesia in the context of the East-West Cold War. An analysis of the evolution of Peking-Djakarta relations should, therefore, begin with the impact this conflict had on their view of the international situation and, consequently, of the external forces they regarded as friends or enemies of China. The genesis of the Cold War, especially the question of Moscow's and Washington's relative responsibility for triggering it, is still a matter of scholarly debate and certainly cannot be dealt with here. The Chinese were not principals in the opening phase of this conflict, but because their attitude toward post–World War II nationalist movements was affected by the outbreak of the Cold War, it has a bearing on this study.

With the formation of the Cominform in September 1947 the international communist movement adopted a generally militant revolutionary attitude toward most capitalist, colonial, and newly independent countries. This stance was officially announced in Zhdanov's two-camp doctrine, which divided the entire world between the progressive and peace-loving forces headed by the Soviet Union on one hand, and, on the other, those led by the reactionaries, namely the United States imperialists and its "lackeys" in various parts of the world. All states, parties, and classes would have to choose to support either the camp of "peace and socialism" or the camp of "war and imperialism."[1] From the time of this authoritative pronouncement until the middle of the Korean War the communist parties (except Yugoslavia's) used the two-camp doctrine as a basic guide for external affairs; they cooperated with forces that were prepared to support revolutionary and anti-imperialist causes and engaged in various kinds of political or armed struggle against those elements that did not support Soviet foreign policy. Internationally, during this period, the Cominform's united-front program was defined in very narrow, revolutionary terms, and it admitted almost no possibility of cooperation with nations or groups that were not aligned with Moscow or local communist parties.

When the two-camp doctrine appeared, the Chinese communists had already made the final break with the Kuomintang. Armed conflict had begun and, by 1948, would lead to the destruction of the Chinese Nationalist armies and, soon thereafter, to communist victory on the mainland. Stalin's hard line toward the West thus fully accorded with the belief of the Chinese communists that a massive revolutionary floodtide was developing that would soon sweep over China and, eventually, result in the liberation of the rest of Asia from Western domination.[2] In a spirit of ideological solidarity and mutual interest the CCP in late 1947 welcomed the extension of the Cominform's

[1] A. Zhdanov, "The International Situation," *For a Lasting Peace for a People's Democracy* (Bucharest), 1 (Nov. 10, 1947), 2 (Cominform journal).

[2] Mao was certain that the Chinese revolution was soon going to inspire and strengthen the revolutionary struggle of oppressed peoples everywhere. See "The Present Situation and Our Tasks," in *Selected Works* (New York: International Publishers, 1956), V, 157–158. Another optimistic view of revolutionary potential at this time was in "Congratulations on the Opening of the Southeast Asia Youth Conference," NCNA report of North Shensi Radio broadcast, February 16, 1948.

revolutionary line to Asia.[3] By endorsing the Cominform position, the Chinese communists made it very clear, nearly two years before the CPR was established and with virtually no experience outside the Chinese context, that they regarded neighboring Asian countries as parts of the world's revolutionary storm center. Certainly, therefore, their conception of the anticolonial upheavals then shaking this region must have accorded with the existing Cold War divisions. The fact that in China and in other Asian countries the United States and its European allies sought to oppose or control national revolutions created, quite apart from ideological considerations, strong bonds of unity between the Chinese communists and Moscow.

During its first phase, the Indonesian independence movement corresponded to the Cominform's definition of a progressive, anti-imperialist force. Although the Indonesian communists had not attained leadership in the movement, until 1948 they were allied with noncommunist bourgeois parties in an anticolonial war against the Dutch, a united front of sorts that could be viewed as supporting the larger, global anti-imperialist struggle.[4] After January 1948, however, the position of the PKI began to change rapidly. In that month the Renville agreements for a cease-fire were signed, following a mediation effort by the United States to resolve the conflict through negotiations. The decision to accept these arrangements split the Indonesian nationalist movement and led to the resignation of the Sjarifuddin cabinet, which had signed the agreement on behalf of the republic. Instantly the Cominform attacked this settlement as a sell-out to the imperialists.[5] The Chinese communists joined in, calling the

[3] "The Present Situation and Our Tasks," p. 173.

[4] For a detailed analysis of the Soviet attitude, which was in effect the basic Cominform position toward the Indonesian revolution during the 1945–1949 period, see Ruth T. McVey, *The Soviet View of the Indonesian Revolution* (Ithaca: Cornell Modern Indonesia Project, 1957), pp. 66–90.

[5] McVey, *ibid.*, pp. 74–75.

Renville agreements "disgraceful," the result of "vacillation [by] upper elements within the country" and of the schemes of "American imperialists [who worked to] buy up Indonesian reactionaries to split the Indonesian national camp."[6]

At the beginning of August 1948 the old Indonesian communist leader Musso, who had been for many years an exiled refugee in the Soviet Union, returned to Indonesia and shortly thereafter took charge of the PKI.[7] The situation appeared to be quite favorable for the Indonesian communists at this time, for the Renville agreements separating the Dutch and Republican forces had recently broken down, sporadic fighting had occurred, and there was widespread disillusionment in nationalist circles because of the failure of the United States to support their cause. Musso proclaimed a "Djalan Baru" ("New Road") program to organize a more broadly based united-front alliance enabling the PKI to align with those segments that were actively fighting the Dutch and were not opposed to the PKI's efforts to mobilize popular support for itself.[8] The fact that Musso had openly called the "Djalan Baru" his "Gottwald Plan" for Indonesia spoke plainly enough of the PKI's intention of taking the government of the republic from Sukarno and Hatta—apparently by political means rather than by armed insurrection, as Gottwald's forces had done in Czechoslovakia a few months earlier. In the event that political struggle was not successful, however, Musso's plan included the possibility of armed struggle as soon as the PKI had developed sufficient strength. The most careful accounts of this

[6] NCNA report of North Shensi Radio broadcast, Feb. 16, 1948.

[7] My interpretation of events in Indonesia from 1945 to 1949 relies heavily on Kahin, *Nationalism and Revolution in Indonesia,* especially pp. 256–303.

[8] Musso, *Djalan Baru untuk Republik Indonesia* (The New Road for the Republic of Indonesia) (Djakarta: Jajasan "Pembaruan," 1953). This was the resolution adopted by the PKI Politbureau in August 1948 after Musso took over the leadership of the party.

period have concluded that Musso regarded an armed uprising as an emergency rather than a preferred strategy.[9]

Musso's adaptation of the Czech model proved to be ill-fated for several reasons. The republican leaders learned of the plans early, and the Indonesian communists were, in any case, not themselves strong or united enough to take power. The implementation of Musso's program required time, but events moved too rapidly. By mid-September, before Musso could fully organize the PKI, the Hatta government had begun to purge the republican army of procommunist officers and to disband unreliable military units. This move apparently prompted local communist political and military leaders in the Madiun-Surakarta area (Central Java) to counteract Musso's gradualist strategy by staging a coup and beginning an armed insurrection. On September 19, 1948, Sukarno, in a radio broadcast, presented the Indonesian people with a choice between himself and communism. Although Musso did not, in fact, call for the overthrow of Sukarno and Hatta until after this speech, Sukarno effectively accused the PKI of forcing a total confrontation. The end result was the bloody defeat of the insurgents' forces at Madiun and the virtual annihilation of the PKI as a political organization. Many senior communist leaders, including Musso, were killed.[10]

The nationalist victory at Madiun eliminated the possibility that the Indonesian revolution might take a radical direction. Because it put the moderate bourgeois nationalists securely in charge of the revolution, it decisively shortened Indonesia's struggle for independence. Before Madiun, the Dutch possessed military power too great for the republic to overcome, and they generally also enjoyed the indispensable advantage of American diplomatic support and military aid. After Madiun, Washington was no longer easily persuaded, as she had been earlier, that the Sukarno-Hatta leadership was a leftist group.

[9] Kahin, pp. 282–288.
[10] *Ibid.*, pp. 288–303.

A number of factors contributed to Washington's disenchantment with the Dutch attempt to hold on to Indonesia. The logic of the Cold War after 1948 tended to cause American policy to develop its own two-camp doctrine. Nationalists who had shown themselves to be anticommunists were welcomed as representatives of the "free world"; other neutralist or anti-Western leaders were, to say the least, often suspected of being the agents or dupes of Moscow. As a consequence of these simplistic notions, Indonesia's independence struggle suddenly acquired an importance, largely because of its recent anticommunist overtones, it did not have before. Soon after Madiun, the United States threatened to cut off Marshall Plan aid to the Netherlands unless she reached a settlement with her rebellious colony. By such methods Washington applied diplomatic pressures that resulted in the Round Table Conference Agreements of December 1949 that granted Indonesia independence within the Netherlands-Indonesian Union.

Although the events at Madiun won Indonesia the decisive support of the United States, they earned her the strong enmity of communist nations. By early 1949 authoritative Chinese communist publications were already leveling ideological broadsides against the Indonesian nationalist leaders. A particularly critical example of the Chinese attitude described the leaders of the Sukarno-Hatta government as "feudal aristocrats" and "fascist stooges of the Japanese occupation period" who opposed the "people," "weakened anti-imperialist strength," and had the same outlook as the "Nehrus, Jinnahs, Luang Phibun Songgrams, Quirinos, Syngman Rhees" and other "feeble-minded bourgeoisie of the East." The "shameless bourgeoisie of Indonesia" had placed themselves "in complete opposition to the people at home and abroad," had pursued "anti-Communist and anti-popular policies," and could "only lead the national struggle towards defeat and capitulation."[11]

[11] Sha Ping, "Lessons from Indonesia," *China Digest,* 5 (April 5,

Such an expression, in early 1949, of strong ideological hostility toward the Indonesian leaders did not preclude the possibility that once the CPR was established, Peking might be prepared to enter into diplomatic relations with the bourgeois government in Djakarta. As early as June 1949, Mao Tse-tung proclaimed that in its relations with foreign countries the CPR would oppose "exclusively the imperialist system and its plots against the Chinese people." Peking would be "willing to discuss" with "any foreign government" the possibility of developing diplomatic relations on the basis of "equality, mutual benefit and mutual respect for territorial integrity and sovereignty." Further conditions required foreign governments to "sever relations" with Nationalist China and to adopt a "genuine attitude" of friendship toward the CPR. On these terms, "friendly cooperation" would be possible with the "people" of all countries.[12]

At the same time Mao did not try to conceal the fact that the CPR's willingness to establish normal diplomatic relations with bourgeois states would not be purchased by abandoning its anti-imperialist stance. In his basic policy statement of June 30, 1949, Mao reaffirmed the Cominform's two-camp doctrine as the foundation of China's foreign policy, declaring that all nations and classes, "without exception," must "lean to one side," toward either "socialism" or "imperialism." There was no "third road," and neutrality was merely a "camouflage."[13] By taking this posi-

---

1949), 5–6. Harsh attacks on the Indonesian elite continued until early 1950. See *Chieh-fang Jih-pao* (Liberation Daily), December 11–12, 1949; and Soong Ching-ling, "The Difference between Soviet and American Foreign Policies," in *700 Millions for Peace and Democracy* (Peking: Foreign Languages Press, 1950), p. 25.

[12] Speech by Mao Tse-tung at the Preparatory Committee Meeting of the Chinese People's Political Consultative Conference, June 15, 1949; in *On People's Democratic Dictatorship*, pp. 33–34. He repeated this offer in a speech in Peking on October 1, in *Jen-min Jih-pao* (People's Daily), Oct. 2, 1949.

[13] *On People's Democratic Dictatorship*, p. 11.

tion the Chinese leader essentially implied that genuine friendship was possible only with members of the communist bloc, anti-imperialist nations, and other revolutionary forces. In the 1949 context, "lean to one side" almost certainly indicated hostility toward bourgeois nationalist-led governments like Indonesia, which had stopped opposing imperialism and hence could hardly be acceptable, politically, to Moscow or Peking. The principal objective in offering to establish diplomatic ties with states like Indonesia, therefore, seemed to be to make direct contact with potential revolutionary groups and supporters in these countries.

This was the background for Liu Shao-ch'i's famous November 16, 1949, speech advocating that certain types of colonial and semicolonial countries follow "the path taken by the Chinese people in defeating imperialism and its lackeys." Liu restated the Maoist revolutionary strategy in a four-point formula that may be summarized as follows: (1) There must be a broad, national united front of all those classes and elements opposing imperialism and domestic reactionaries. (2) The basis of this front must be a worker-peasant alliance led by the Communist party, not by the classes or parties of the bourgeoisie, which are inherently unreliable. (3) The Communist party must be of a special type: it must be thoroughly skilled in Marxist-Leninist theory, strategy, and tactics and closely linked to the masses. (4) "Wherever and whenever" possible, colonial peoples must organize a "liberation army" led by the Communist party to carry on an "armed struggle," the main form of struggle in many countries.[14]

The statement of the formula removed any doubt about whom the Chinese regarded as their friends and enemies in the newly independent states. But it also revealed that some revolutionary objectives had a much greater priority than others in China's foreign policy. By late 1949 the Chinese communists were well aware that in Indonesia and in every other newly independent

[14] Opening address to the Asian-Australasian Trade Union Conference, NCNA (Peking), Nov. 23, 1949.

Asian country except Vietnam, armed struggle after 1947 had led to the crushing defeat of communist parties and, consequently, to the political isolation of revolutionaries in a number of countries, including Indonesia. Awareness of this hard fact was reflected in other passages of Liu's speech that have not received the attention they deserve. In substance, they tend to qualify substantially the call for armed struggle with which this speech is usually identified. For Liu also proposed that in countries where premature uprisings had failed, the main task confronting the communists was to organize and to begin creating multiclass united fronts. On the whole, the theme that was set forth in "the path of the Chinese people" in late 1949 and early 1950 was not, as is usually suggested, a call for "armed struggle" along Chinese civil war lines, but rather a call for an indefinite period of communist organizational and ideological spadework in many countries until a time when, together with international and domestic factors, revolutionary prospects were more favorable.[15]

The Recognition Issue

The fact that the Chinese communists regarded Indonesia as a neocolonialist creation of the Americans and the Dutch did not deter the new leaders in Djakarta from deciding to seek diplomatic relations with Peking. This was a surprising development in one sense, since the decision aroused much controversy in many Indonesian groups, especially some of the political parties. In anticommunist Moslem circles there was a strong feeling that relations with all communist states should be avoided, as the

[15] *Ibid.* The bulk of this speech was not devoted to eulogizing the Chinese revolutionary model but rather to an analysis of the present international situation, especially the difficulties facing the communist parties in the colonial and semicolonial countries. Liu laid particular stress on the need for these parties to develop local worker-peasant alliances and a national multiclass united front. The Chinese model favors armed struggle—an idea Liu mentioned last in summarizing Mao's path—at some point in the revolution but not unless mass support and political organizations have been built to sustain it.

recent Madiun experience demonstrated to the satisfaction of many. Among others there was a justified suspicion that Peking's diplomatic presence in Indonesia would intensify the Indonesian Chinese community's sympathy for mainland Chinese nationalism, whatever form it took.[16]

The prevailing opinion in the government of the time, however, expressed by Prime Minister Hatta (himself staunchly anticommunist), was that Indonesia could not ignore the CPR, for to do so would discredit the country's proclaimed independent, neutral foreign policy.[17] The leaders' decision was not easy to make, because the American government, to which Djakarta looked for aid and diplomatic support in the early years after 1949, opposed, and invariably exerted a variety of pressures to prevent, any state's establishing relations with communist China. Hatta also feared that Nationalist China, a permanent member of the Security Council, might veto Indonesia's application for United Nations membership if she established diplomatic ties with Peking.[18] Djakarta decided to risk the displeasure of anticommunist states in order to assert an independent foreign policy. Her leaders hoped this expression of autonomy would be recognized in Moscow and Peking and that it would help to promote a limited normalization of relations with the communist powers.

Indonesian independence was proclaimed on December 27, 1949. Most of the international community promptly recognized the new state. Even the Soviet Union, whose past criticism of the "reactionary" Sukarno-Hatta leadership had been no less virulent than Peking's, announced its recognition of Indonesia within three weeks, on January 15, 1950.[19] China was in a position to do

[16] Interview with former Prime Minister Mohammad Hatta, June 8, 1961.

[17] *Ibid.*

[18] *Ibid.*

[19] Ministry of Information, *Report on Indonesia* (Djakarta, Feb. 10, 1950), p. 1.

the same, since, according to diplomatic practice, the fact that the CPR had been established previously, on October 1, 1949, conferred on her the prerogative of recognizing a junior state. It had been expected that China's recognition would follow Moscow's as a matter of course, but a positive signal was not forthcoming, even though Hatta cabled a formal request for recognition to Peking via the Dutch government on January 11, 1950.[20] For reasons this writer was unable to discover the Dutch did not forward his communication to Peking until February 27. Though that was more than a month after the Soviet response, Chou En-lai waited another month before cabling the CPR's recognition on March 28, 1950.[21] Although the transmission of Hatta's message via the Dutch, rather than directly to China, may have offended protocol-conscious Peking and thus prompted her to wait another month before replying to it, a more serious circumstance appears to have caused the delay: the ambiguous relationship between Indonesia and Nationalist China.

At the time of the transfer of sovereignty Nationalist China maintained seven consulates in Indonesia, which had been established during the period of Dutch colonial rule. The Nationalist Chinese had been staunch supporters of the Indonesian independence cause, and for this reason alone had some hope that the new government in Djakarta would decide to establish relations with Taipei. To this end Nationalist China immediately recognized Indonesia on December 27, 1949, and, leaving no stone unturned, dispatched a special mission under General

[20] "Ho-lan cheng-fu te chao-hui" (Communication of the Dutch Government), March 27, 1950; in *Chung-hua jen-min kung-ho-kuo tui wai kuan-hsi wen-chien chi* (Selected Documents on the Foreign Relations of the People's Republic of China). Vol. I: 1949–1950 (Peking: Shih-chieh chih-shih ch'u-pan-she, 1957), 31.

[21] "Chung-kuo cheng-fu chih yin-tu-ni-hsi-ya lien-pang kung-ho-kuo cheng-fu te chao-hui" (Communication of the Chinese Government to the Government of the Republic of the United States of Indonesia), March 28, 1950, in *ibid.*, I, 31–32.

Wu Teh-chuan to Djakarta, hoping to enter into negotiations about future relations between the two states.[22] In view of the fact that the Nationalist consulates were still in operation, another Taiwan mission was also on its way to Indonesia, and since Djakarta had thus far done nothing to terminate its *de facto* relations with Taipei, it is hardly surprising that Peking temporized. Under the circumstances her probable suspicion that Djakarta might be trying to achieve recognition from both Chinas was not entirely unjustified. Since any suggestion of two Chinas was wholly unacceptable to the Chinese leaders, they apparently decided to withhold recognition until the exact nature of the Taiwan-Indonesia relationship was clarified to their complete satisfaction.

Actually, Hatta's cable to Peking was in no sense a two-Chinas scheme, for he promptly informed General Wu of his government's intention to establish relations with communist China. At the same time he notified General Wu that Nationalist China's consulates in Indonesia would have to be closed within a few months.[23] Although the consulates were not closed until early April, news of the decision and of the KMT's diplomatic setback no doubt quickly reached Peking. Once the course Djakarta would follow was clear, Peking could play down the fact that the Chinese Nationalist consulates had not actually ceased operations before she formally extended recognition to Indonesia.

Chou En-lai's cable of March 28 to Hatta acknowledged the CPR's willingness to establish "regular diplomatic relations" with Djakarta "on the basis of equality, mutual benefit and mutual respect for territory and sovereignty." Hatta replied on April 13, stating that his government was "gratified" by the CPR's earnest desire to establish relations with Indonesia and that he agreed with Chou's statement of the principles on which relations should

[22] Aneta (Indonesian News Service) (Djakarta), Dec. 29, 1949.
[23] Interview with Hatta, June 8, 1961. The Nationalist Chinese consulate did close in early April. See *Sin Po* (Djakarta), April 5–11, 1950.

be based.[24] In May, Chou sent another cable, suggesting that diplomatic missions be exchanged at the ambassadorial level and proposing Wang Jen-shu as the first CPR ambassador.[25] Hatta agreed to these proposals in a reply sent to Peking in June. Because, however, Indonesia had not yet chosen an ambassador, he proposed to appoint a chargé d'affaires to serve ad interim in Peking.[26] Wang Jen-shu's appointment was announced in Peking on July 20; after arriving in Indonesia, he presented his credentials to President Sukarno on August 14 in Djakarta.[27] Almost six months later, on January 21, 1951, chargé d'affaires Isak Mahdi presented his credentials to Foreign Minister Chou En-lai in Peking.[28] Although four and a half years would pass before the Indonesian government actually appointed an ambassador to China, the original barriers to diplomatic relations between the two states had been removed.

Diplomatic Representation

The question of CPR consular representation in Indonesia had not been raised in the initial diplomatic communications between Peking and Djakarta. This was a matter of first priority to Peking, since an adequate consular establishment would be necessary to act on behalf of the Chinese citizens in Indonesia.[29] Consulates

[24] "Yin-tu-ni-hsi-ya lien-pang kung-ho-kuo cheng-fu te fu-chao" (Reply of the Government of the Republic of the United States of Indonesia), April 13, 1950; in *Chung-hua jen-min kung-ho-kuo tui wai kuan-hsi wen-chien chi*, I, 32.

[25] Interview with Hatta, June 8, 1961. I have not found the text of this note in the Chinese documentation.

[26] *Ibid.*

[27] See *Jen-min Jih-pao*, July 20, 1950, and *Sin Po*, August 15, 1950.

[28] *Current Background* (Hong Kong: United States Consulate General), No. 31 (Feb. 1, 1955), 4.

[29] The Common Program, adopted by the First Plenary Session of the Chinese People's Political Consultative Conference on September 29, 1949, as the CPR's basic constitutional document (it was replaced in

also would be useful in achieving the longer-range political goal of undermining the KMT's position in Indonesia.

Kuomintang influence in the Indonesian Chinese community had been paramount for twenty years, and the retreat of the Nationalist government to Taiwan in 1949 did not decisively weaken it. Because Taiwan's claim to represent China was now, more than ever, heavily dependent on the support she received from the thirteen million Chinese subjects abroad, over 95 percent of whom were domiciled in southeast Asia, the early severing of the ties was a major objective of Peking's foreign policy. As in other southeast Asian countries, the resident Chinese population controlled a disproportionate percentage of the wealth of Indonesia and during most of the twentieth century had sent remittances worth millions of dollars to mainland China. Funds thus received from the overseas Chinese had come to play an important role in China's foreign-exchange position. The desire to ensure the continued flow of remittances and deposits from overseas Chinese to the mainland—if possible, in increased amounts —must have been one of the key reasons Peking wanted to displace her Taipei rival in southeast Asia as soon as possible.

Because of the nature of the goals and interests of mainland China, it was unlikely that Peking and Djakarta would have the same view of the proper role of Chinese representatives in Indonesia. The Chinese government clearly regarded the main tasks of its future diplomatic mission in Indonesia to be extending the CPR's influence in the Chinese community, defeating the KMT organizations, extracting remittances, and, almost certainly,

---

1954), considered all overseas Chinese to be CPR citizens. It declared that Peking would "adopt the measures necessary . . . to facilitate remittances from overseas Chinese" (Article 37) and "do its utmost to protect the proper rights and interests of the Chinese residing abroad" (Article 58). Later, Article 23 of the Electoral Law of March 1, 1953, would provide that "the overseas Chinese shall elect 30 deputies to the All China [National] People's Congress."

developing a variety of contacts with the Indonesian communists. These objectives were not basically different in kind from the goals of other foreign powers in Indonesia, except in scale. No Indonesian government with the power to do otherwise could possibly permit the CPR to make contact with some three million people it claimed were nationals of China—particularly in light of the economic influence the resident Chinese exerted on the country and in view of Djakarta's anxiety about any potential foreign-directed subversive elements. The fundamentally conflicting objectives of Peking and Djakarta quickly surfaced when the question of consular representation arose.

Ambassador Wang Jen-shu began negotiations with the Indonesian government on this matter in October 1950. The talks dragged on for five months. An agreement was finally reached in March 1951 which permitted the CPR to open consulates in Djakarta (in Java), Medan (Sumatra), Bandjarmasin (Indonesian Borneo), and Makassar (Celebes).[30] Since Peking's original request had been for permission to reopen the seven consulates Nationalist China had operated prior to April 1950, it was clear that, for China, the principal outcome of the negotiations constituted a setback.

The talks were marked by a basic conflict on two points: the jurisdiction of the Chinese consulates; and the date the consulates would open. At first, Djakarta held that no consulates should be established until the status of the Chinese born in Indonesia had been clarified in accordance with the provisions governing the division of citizenship in the Round Table Conference Agreements.[31] These agreements provided that Indonesian-born Chinese who had been formerly assimilated under Dutch law as Netherlands subjects would acquire Indonesian

[30] *Pengumuman Kementerian Luar Negri* (Announcement of the Ministry of Foreign Affairs), March 16, 1951. Indonesia did not open a consulate in China until 1957. See NCNA (Peking), August 21, 1957.

[31] Statement by the Indonesian Minister of Information, M. A. Pellaupessy, reported by Antara (Indonesian News Agency), Nov. 2, 1950.

citizenship within two years of December 27, 1949, unless they made a declaration to the contrary during this period. Those who took the trouble to reject Indonesian citizenship formally were to be considered nationals of China. A few Chinese in either category might opt for Dutch citizenship or, by making no option, be regarded as stateless.[32] In effect, therefore, most locally born Chinese could acquire Indonesian citizenship "passively." The Indonesian government argued that because the total number of alien Chinese could not be determined before December 27, 1951, the end of the option period, no CPR consulates should be opened prior to that date.

The Chinese negotiators argued that since, under Chinese law, the Chinese born in either Indonesia or China were considered subjects of mainland China, there could be no unilateral Indonesian determination of their citizenship. The Indonesian government's stand was criticized openly as having "no legal basis" and as being "completely contrary to the wishes of the majority of the Chinese people." According to a clarification released by the Chinese embassy, overseas Chinese, in order to acquire Indonesian citizenship, would be required to obtain "letters of explanation" from the Chinese government. The issuance of such letters, the Chinese negotiators maintained, would necessitate the opening of CPR consulates before December 1951.[33]

[32] United Nations Commission for Indonesia, appendixes to *Special Report to the Security Council on the Round Table Conference* (United Nations Security Council publication, S/1417/Add. 1, Nov. 14, 1949), p. 84. For further discussion of Chinese citizenship status at this time, see Donald E. Willmott, *The National Status of the Chinese in Indonesia, 1900–1958* (Ithaca: Cornell Modern Indonesia Project, Monograph Series, 1961), p. 29.

[33] *Keterangan Dari Pihak Ambassade Republik Rakjat Tionghwa Mengenai Soal Pembukaan Konsulat-Konsulat* (Statement by the Embassy of the People's Republic of China on the Question of Opening Consulates), Djakarta, Nov. 18, 1950; reported in *Indonesia Merdeka* (Free Indonesia), Nov. 18, 1950.

Naturally, Djakarta feared that any CPR consulates opened early might be used by Peking to encourage Chinese born in Indonesia to reject Indonesian citizenship. While the Indonesians were focusing attention on the need to prevent this possibility, they lost sight of a more important implication of the Chinese embassy's statement. Clearly, the phrase "letters of explanation" indicated that, as early as 1951, Peking was prepared, in principle, to renounce claims on some overseas Chinese, provided she could do so on the basis of formal negotiations between the concerned parties, not unilaterally or under duress. Ultimately, an accommodation was reached; the four CPR consulates were allowed to open in April 1951 instead of in the following December. But since there would be only one CPR consulate on each of the main Indonesian islands, it did not seem that the degree of political influence Peking would exert on the Indonesian Chinese community prior to the end of the citizenship-option period would be very great.

Like the decision to establish diplomatic relations with Peking, the consular agreement had far from unanimous support within the Indonesian government. Some members of the cabinet opposed granting the CPR any consular representation, on the ground that to do so would inevitably strengthen the orientation of local Chinese toward the mainland, and unwanted political repercussions might follow. In the opinion of the government headed by Prime Minister Natsir, which negotiated the agreement, this risk had to be weighed against a compelling argument. To deny the CPR any consular representation would not inspire the Chinese community to cooperate with Djakarta or enhance its loyalty to Indonesia but would, instead, arouse its resentment. Hence a complete rebuff of Peking was not regarded as a likely means of avoiding the adverse political consequences the dissenters in the government were concerned about but, rather, it might magnify them.[34]

[34] Interview with Muhammad Roem (former foreign minister in Natsir's cabinet), June 13, 1961; also interview with Hatta, June 8, 1961.

The majority in the government also assumed that the anticapitalist creed of the CPR would not strike a responsive chord in the Indonesian Chinese, of whom an overwhelming percentage were engaged in commercial enterprises. Nor did the government believe at the time that the presence of CPR consulates would decisively affect the choice of citizenship by the Indonesia-born Chinese.[35] Fragmentary data available in early 1950 indicated that only about 10 percent of the Chinese would actually go to the trouble to reject Indonesia.[36] On the strength of the trend evident early in the option period, allowing the CPR to open four consulates did not seem to endanger any government attempt to curb Peking's influence on the Chinese community. The government's analysis of the situation proved, however, to be quite wrong.

Under Wang Jen-shu,[37] the Chinese embassy lost no time in developing an extensive campaign to bring the Indonesian Chinese into the orbit of the Peking government's policies and programs. The embassy and consulates began to register Chinese families—no matter where their members were born—to solicit funds for various embassy-sponsored activities, to provide pro-Peking instructors and teaching materials in Chinese schools, and to set up a new system of CPR-oriented community associations to compete with the long-established KMT organizations.

[35] *Ibid.*

[36] An early report from East Java indicated that only 39 of 411 Chinese had taken the trouble to reject Indonesian citizenship (*Shen Huo Pao* [Surabaja], June 12, 1950).

[37] Wang had lived in Medan, Sumatra, before 1947, when he was deported by the Dutch. While in Indonesia he taught in a teachers' training school and was active as a leftist in the revolutionary movement. Following his expulsion Wang returned to China and in 1949 published a book entitled *The Country of the Indonesian Archipelago,* in which he accused Hatta of treason (Dunning Idle, "Indonesia's Independent and Active Foreign Policy," Ph.D. dissertation, Yale University, 1955–1956, pp. 26–27). According to Hatta, he was unaware of Wang's background until after he was appointed ambassador; otherwise he would not have accepted his appointment (interview, June 8, 1961).

The result was a small-scale but intensely bitter struggle between the rival Chinese factions in Indonesia.[38] Peking won a major victory early, when the Bank of China, the most powerful Chinese financial institution in Indonesia, broke its ties with Taiwan and went over to the CPR. This event caused many wealthy and influential Chinese to follow suit. Another consequence was the strengthening of the Chinese embassy's economic and political power throughout the country. Having lost substantial sources of financial support, demoralized adherents of the KMT became more dependent on their natural ally in Indonesia, the American embassy. The resulting collaboration took a variety of overt and covert forms[39] and no doubt played a role in the 1958 decision Djakarta made to crush the KMT organizations altogether.

Although Djakarta objected to many of the Chinese embassy's political activities, particularly in the Chinese schools, the developing Chinese mini-civil war between KMT and CCP supporters was of some advantage to the Indonesian government. While the Chinese fought among themselves there was no

[38] For a discussion of the political situation in the Indonesian Chinese community about this time see G. William Skinner, *Report on the Chinese in Southeast Asia* (Ithaca: Cornell Southeast Asia Program, 1950), especially pp. 67–73. For useful data on various aspects of CPR policies toward the overseas Chinese in Indonesia and other Southeast Asian countries at this time see Lu Yu-san, *Programs of Communist China for Overseas Chinese* (Hong Kong: Union Research Institute, 1956), pp. 1–82.

[39] Sympathizers of the Nationalist Chinese told this writer that Nationalist Chinese overseas organizations and leaders maintained close contacts with the United States embassy and consulates in Indonesia after Djakarta established relations with Peking. They also said (documentation is unavailable) that money from the embassy found its way into various KMT activities, particularly to such pro-Taipei newspapers as *Keng Po* and to the Nationalist Chinese school system before it was closed down in 1958.

possibility that anyone would dominate the community, which was what the Indonesian leaders feared most. Moreover, much useful intelligence about the activities of both factions and their external allies reached various government departments. Presumably this information helped Djakarta to decide what countermeasures were necessary. In one respect, however, the government's information about the affairs of the Chinese community was quite faulty. Djakarta greatly underestimated the number of local-born Chinese who actually would go to the trouble to opt for Peking citizenship despite the fact that most Chinese had a petty-capitalist background and could easily acquire Indonesian citizenship by simply remaining silent.

When the option period ended in December 1951, Djakarta's inadequate administrative agencies still had only a fraction of the information they needed to ascertain what the final outcome was. But by 1953 the government was startled to learn that between 600,000 and 700,000—or approximately 40 percent—of the local-born Chinese had formally rejected Indonesian citizenship.[40] Since nearly another million Chinese were foreign-born and were thus already considered CPR nationals, about half the entire Chinese population now had to be considered mainland citizens according to the provisions of the Round Table Conference. This result had not been anticipated, and it raised grave doubts about the genuineness of the loyalty of the other half of the Chinese population, who had simply said nothing.[41] As the implications of this situation began to sink in, Djakarta became increasingly apprehensive about the impact the Chinese embassy was having on Indonesia's domestic affairs. Moreover, the rejection of Indonesia by so many Chinese created serious disenchantment with the whole Round Table formula for dealing with the citizenship issue. To many, both inside and outside

[40] Interview with representative of Indonesian Department of Justice, Djakarta, Aug. 21, 1961.
[41] Ibid.

the government, it had now become clear that the 1949 citizenship agreements had raised more problems than they had solved.

The Crackdown on the Chinese Embassy

Djakarta could not do much, in the short run, to reverse the rising tide of pro-Peking sympathy that developed in the Chinese community after 1950. The government had created many of the problems, inescapably, by agreeing to the citizenship-option formula of 1949, establishing diplomatic relations with Peking, and deciding to permit the CPR to open consulates. These actions naturally encouraged many Chinese to assume that contact with the Chinese embassy was quite appropriate. On the other hand, the government moved decisively to curb the more controversial political activities of Ambassador Wang Jen-shu and the Chinese embassy. Wang began quite early to deliver speeches attacking "U.S. imperialism." Aside from the fact that Djakarta did not then share his view of American policy, Wang's attacks were in violation of accepted diplomatic norms. On several occasions in 1950 and 1951 the Indonesian government warned the Chinese ambassador to stop giving anti-American speeches and used these opportunities to insist that the Chinese embassy confine its activities to normal diplomatic functions and discontinue its contacts with those local-born Chinese whom Djakarta regarded as Indonesian subjects.[42]

It appears, however, that these admonishments failed to produce the desired response from Peking and the issue soon came to a head. A minor diplomatic rift with Peking in mid-1951 was effectively used by Djakarta to drive home a political lesson. On July 22, CPR Consul General Ho Ying arrived in Indonesia accompanied by nineteen other newly appointed members of the diplomatic staff. Sixteen of these were refused entry by the Indonesian authorities, although apparently all of them had official entry visas that had been duly approved by the Indonesian

[42] Interviews with Hatta, June 8, 1961, and Roem, June 13, 1961.

embassy in Peking.[43] According to the Indonesian Foreign Ministry, this action had been taken because, for the third time, Peking had failed to give adequate "prior notification" of the arrival of new embassy personnel and had thus committed a "breach of diplomatic courtesy."[44] Peking immediately protested, charging that advance notification had been given and that the Indonesian action was evidence of an "unreasonable and unfriendly attitude."[45] The CPR protest was rejected, however, and the diplomatic personnel in question were obliged to return to China.

The real issue Djakarta raised apparently had very little relationship to the question of adequate "prior notification." What disturbed the Indonesian government was the unacceptable activities of the Chinese embassy, a symptom of which, in Djakarta's view, was the unnecessarily large and growing Chinese diplomatic staff. In limiting Peking to four consulates Djakarta's intention had been to reduce sharply the CPR's contact with the Indonesia Chinese minority. That objective was being partially circumvented, the government in Djakarta believed, by the dispatch from China of unexpectedly large numbers of diplomatic personnel to staff the embassy and consulates in Indonesia. According to Indonesian informants, many of the Chinese personnel coming into the country, though officially designated as clerical and maintenance assistants, in fact were specialists in political education and overseas Chinese affairs.[46] It therefore appears that Djakarta alleged the infraction of "diplomatic courtesy" in order

[43] NCNA (Peking), July 25, 1951.

[44] Statement by Indonesian Foreign Ministry spokesman, Darmaesetiawan, in Antara, July 26, 1951. The statement charged that on previous occasions Peking failed to notify the Indonesian government of the arrival in Djakarta of the CPR consul general and two military attachés.

[45] Statement of the CPR Foreign Ministry, July 26, 1951, in NCNA (Peking), Aug. 11, 1951.

[46] Interviews with Hatta, June 8, 1961, and Roem, June 13, 1961.

to show Peking that she would not permit her purpose in originally limiting the CPR to four consulates to be undermined. China had been served fair warning that her efforts to increase contacts with the Indonesian Chinese would be successfully opposed and that her attempt to circumvent this could prove diplomatically embarrassing.

Not unreasonably, the CPR must have questioned the real motivations behind Indonesia's offensive treatment of Chinese diplomatic personnel. For example, the staff of the United States embassy and the number of its consulates (eight) were larger than those of China, though the number of American citizens in Indonesia was quite small. American intelligence agents also masqueraded as "foreign service officers" and "technical assistance" personnel. One reason Djakarta cracked down on Peking but not on Washington was that the Hatta and Natsir governments favored a strong anticommunist policy.

Peking no doubt thought the Hatta and Natsir governments were simply doing the bidding of their imperialist master—which was true to an extent—but she was to see in the successor cabinet headed by Dr. Sukiman what a truly anticommunist Indonesian government looked like.[47] The Sukiman cabinet was dominated by the Moslem Masjumi party, the strongest anticommunist force in the country except for the army. It followed a foreign policy more closely identified with that of the United States than had any of its predecessors—and the identification was very close indeed, given the fact that Indonesia's "neutral" position in the Cold War had been substantially more reliant on the West than, for example, that of India and Burma. Sukiman's government decided to align Indonesia even more closely with Washington by accepting aid under the United States Mutual Security Act— a device to set up *de facto* military anticommunist alliances in instances where formal NATO- or ANZUS-type treaties between

[47] For an analysis of the Sukiman cabinet's policies see Herbert Feith, *The Decline of Constitutional Democracy in Indonesia*, pp. 177–224.

other countries and the United States might not be politically feasible because of internal opposition to entering into Cold War pacts. Sukiman also decided to crack down on the PKI and the Chinese embassy. That this move was also inspired by the American embassy seems likely but has not yet been proved.

On the basis of an alleged communist plot to overthrow the government, in August 1951 the Sukiman cabinet suddenly launched a series of massive arrests that netted more than fifteen thousand persons, including PKI leaders and several hundred resident Chinese.[48] The fact that many of those arrested were neither Indonesian nor Chinese communists but political enemies of Dr. Sukiman stamped the "August Raid" as something less than a bona fide defensive measure to protect the country from subversion. Nevertheless, the raid struck hard at people and groups Peking regarded as communist, progressive, and anti-imperialist. That the Chinese government was prepared to identify itself with Sukiman's targets was indicated when the Chinese embassy granted asylum to Alimin, a prominent leader of the Indonesian Communist party.[49] That event alone was enough to give anticommunists a basis, otherwise lacking, for suggesting that Peking and the Chinese in Indonesia were implicated in an alleged plot to overthrow the government. In the end the Sukiman government was unable to convince parliament that there had been any threat to the state and, eventually, it was forced to release those it had arrested.

The "August Raid" was another in a series of events which had demonstrated the readiness of the Indonesian government to risk—indeed to provoke—diplomatic ruptures with Peking. Though Djakarta had not been very successful before 1951 in curbing CPR influence on Chinese in Indonesia, other political activities undertaken by the Chinese embassy had been put under tighter control and surveillance. All this must have seemed pre-

[48] *Ibid.*, pp. 187–192.
[49] Aneta, Aug. 16, 1951.

dictable but nevertheless disturbing to policy makers in Peking, especially in light of the ascendance of the Sukiman government and the intensified anticommunist foreign and domestic policies it pursued. Sukiman's government seemed plainly bent, not only on again suppressing the Indonesian communists—then just beginning to reorganize themselves after the Madiun disaster—but also on pressing conflicts with China. More important to the Chinese, American influence in Indonesia was then at its peak.

By mid-1951 it was becoming clear that Peking's assertive actions in Indonesia had reached a dead end. They had been viable and even logical as long as the ideologically derived assumption on which they were based bore some relationship to the actual situation. As it became evident, however, that China lacked the power or influence to back up such a policy in the face of mounting resistance from Djakarta, conditions seemed to call for a revamping. Further confrontations could only serve the interests of the reactionary forces in Indonesia and their foreign imperialist supporters. But the decisive factor that was soon to cause a reassessment by Peking was not the dawning recognition that an impasse had been reached in Indonesia. As the next chapter attempts to demonstrate, the ultimate reason for a shift in policy was less the recent failures in Indonesia than the new Chinese analysis of the whole international situation. By mid-1951, Peking was beginning to see that the attitudes and actions formed in the period of the Cominform's two-camp doctrine no longer reflected Asian or global realities.

4

Toward Peaceful Coexistence: Emergence of the United-Front-from-Above Strategy

The Peace Offensive

The CPR's estimate of the international situation was still optimistic when the Soviet-backed North Korean army struck across the thirty-eighth parallel on June 25, 1950. What first appeared to be another triumph for communist revolution soon developed into a strategic reversal, following the defeat of the North Korean army and the advance of United Nations forces to the Yalu River. To prevent the liquidation of the North Korean regime and the consequent deployment of American military power on her border, Chinese forces intervened and successfully checked General Douglas MacArthur's advance. The resultant military stalemate, as well as the heavy costs inflicted on the CPR to maintain it, was a major factor prompting the Chinese leadership to reappraise the international situation.

As a consequence of the Korean conflict China and the entire socialist camp found themselves in a defensive military and diplomatic position. For the war spurred the United States to reverse its post-1949 policy of disengagement from the affairs of the Chinese mainland and added fuel to its efforts to organize the rest of the Asian states into a military bloc opposed to the CPR. The nations Washington could not persuade to take up arms against China in Korea she tried to draw into collective-security pacts intended to provide the United States with military bases and to develop local anticommunist armed forces. In an attempt further to isolate and punish China, Washington succeeded in forcing through the United Nations resolutions condemning the CPR as an aggressor and imposing a trade embargo against her. By placing the Seventh Fleet in the Taiwan Straits and undertaking to revitalize the Nationalist Chinese army and government, the United States precluded any possibility that the Chinese communists would soon be able to settle the Chinese civil war on their terms. Indeed, American revitalization efforts in Taiwan were accompanied by official declarations of support for the KMT's proclaimed goal of eventually retaking the mainland. Far from driving imperialism from East Asia, the Korean War had the undesired effect of producing a vast American political, military, and economic build up in the region—a development that threatened every conceivable Chinese interest.

In the early 1950's there was not much on the revolutionary side of the ledger to offset these adverse trends. Asian communist parties that had attempted to generate armed struggles had suffered crushing defeats everywhere except in Vietnam. Partly in response to this situation, from early in 1951 onward the communist parties in key Asian states—Japan, India, and Indonesia—began to reject violent struggle, which had resulted only in their own weakening or destruction. These parties shifted to parliamentary strategies in order to build up bases of popular support and political organization which, as the preceding insurrectionary period had shown, the communists did not have. As the major communist powers became more aware of the real conditions prevailing in Asia, their general foreign-policy lines began to reflect their interest in defending rather than advancing the cause of socialism in the Far East. The tactical result of this shift from the Cominform's two-camp doctrine was the gradual adoption by Russia and China of foreign policies enabling them to enlist the support of various international political elements that were willing to remain neutral or to oppose American policy.

The Asian neutrals could, in light of this shift, be regarded as potential candidates for inclusion in an enlarged antiimperialist united front, since, contrary to the two-camp doctrine, they did not prove to be flunkies of the United States. India and Burma, in particular, opposed the U.N. resolutions branding China an aggressor and declaring a trade embargo against her. Even the more American-oriented Indonesian government would not go along with U.S. policy on these issues, in spite of its own frictions with Peking, and abstained from voting on the U.N. condemnation of the CPR.[1] But if the independence of the neutral countries was to be encouraged and their separation from the American sphere of influence completed, the communist powers needed to overhaul their previous attitude toward the leaders of the developing countries, who were still being depicted, in 1950 and 1951, as mere representatives of the Western powers.

The shift in communist attitudes toward the Afro-Asian nationalist regimes was reflected first not in Soviet but in Chinese policies, since Chinese interests were most adversely affected by the situation growing out of the Korean War. As early as June 1951, more than a year before Moscow took similar steps, authoritative CPR spokesmen began to endorse the need for coexistence between socialist and nonsocialist states for the purpose of thwarting the alleged plans of the imperialists to start a new world war.[2] In an important foreign-policy speech in October 1951, Chou En-lai explicitly stated that "countries of diverse social systems all over the world can exist peacefully side by side." China, he said, had "never thought of threatening or invading

[1] For the official Indonesian position on the United Nations' sanctions against China see Indonesian Ministry of Information, *Report on Indonesia*, January 31, February 9, May 25, and June 7, 1951.

[2] The first indication by a leading figure in the Peking government that its foreign policy had shifted was the speech by Soong Ching-ling, "On Peaceful Coexistence," *People's China* (Peking: Foreign Languages Press; bimonthly current-affairs journal beginning 1950, superseded by *Peking Review* after 1957), 2 (June 1, 1951), 1–6.

anyone," but neither would she tolerate "threats and aggressions" directed against her by others.[3]

Well before the end of the Korean War, therefore, Peking began to conceptualize the political and class basis of a conciliatory policy toward those Asian governments with which, because they had not tied themselves to the United States, she could enter into an entirely different relationship than with those states which chose to remain American clients. In order to explore the possibilities China sponsored the Asian and Pacific Peace Conference in May 1952.[4] By this time her former straightforward revolutionary line had given way to a "people's diplomacy" aimed at organizing a broad multiclass "peace" front. Virtually all progressive elements in the Asian countries that might actively oppose United States policies and espouse peace and friendship with China were targets of her appeal. At the formal diplomatic level the new policy found expression, beginning in 1951, in the improved relations Peking was able to develop with India, Burma, and Ceylon.

Failure of the Peace Offensive in Indonesia

The tension between Peking and Djakarta that had resulted from the Chinese embassy's provocative activities in 1950 and early 1951 was clearly not in keeping with the CPR's new appreciation of the need to develop better relations with her Asian neighbors. Isak Mahdi, Indonesia's chargé d'affaires in Peking at this time noted that a decidedly more friendly attitude was dis-

---

[3] Chou En-lai, "Political Report to the Third Session of the First National Committee of the Chinese People's Political Consultative Conference," Oct. 23, 1951; in *New China Forges Ahead* (Peking: Foreign Languages Press, 1952), p. 12.

[4] See the collection of documents published in *Ya-chou t'ai-p'ing-yang chu-yu ho-p'ing hui-i chung-yao pao-kao chi chueh-i* (*Important Reports and Resolutions of the Peace Conference of the Asian-Pacific Region*) (Peking: n.p., 1952).

played by Chinese officials after mid-1951 than when he first arrived in Peking, in spite of the hostility of the Sukiman government toward China.[5] Further evidence of change was Peking's sudden withdrawal late in 1951, of the main symbol of her theretofore unfriendly attitude toward Indonesia: Ambassador Wang Jen-shu.[6] In retrospect—it was not so regarded at the time—his recall was the first clear indication of the end of Peking's hard line in Indonesia and the beginning of a more conciliatory approach.

The chief obstacle to an early improvement in the situation was the political orientation of the Sukiman government, which was not interested in loosening its ties to the United States in order to win the approval of the CPR. It was not even greatly interested in normalizing its strained relationship with China. On the other hand, bringing pressure to bear on the Dutch, who continued to hold the territory of West Irian, did interest the Sukiman cabinet, but to pursue this end Djakarta needed the diplomatic and economic support of the United States.

The Indonesians had hoped to negotiate the transfer of sovereignty over this irredenta by 1951, in accordance with their interpretation of the Round Table Conference Agreements' provisions governing this matter. When, however, negotiations broke down, Djakarta turned to the United States for support. Though

[5] Interviews with former chargé d'affaires Isak Mahdi, Feb. 18 and June 5, 1961. According to Mahdi, the very cool treatment he and other Southeast Asian diplomats had initially received in Peking began to change sometime before Wang Jen-shu was recalled, or about the time the Korean War reached a stalemate. Thereafter, cordial contacts with the CPR Foreign Ministry were frequent. Mahdi also recalled that the Chinese seemed very anxious to normalize relations with Indonesia from 1952 on, and that they also wanted to settle the overseas Chinese nationality question. This testimony suggests that Peking was by no means as reluctant to relinquish claims on the overseas Chinese as is commonly supposed.

[6] Reported in Antara, Dec. 26, 1951.

Indonesia depended on the United States to further her West Irian policy, she did not completely support American Far Eastern policy. But the dependence did lead Sukiman to follow Washington's initiative on two policy matters that fundamentally compromised Indonesia's declared neutrality in the Cold War.[7]

First, the Sukiman governments, in September 1951, signed the Japanese Peace Treaty, a document which, Peking charged—with considerable justification—the United States had "compelled a group of satellite countries to sign."[8] That group obviously included Indonesia. There was strong opposition in the Indonesian parliament to Sukiman's endorsement of this treaty (for this reason ratification was delayed until 1958), but the government was able to ride out the storm. The second compromising action of the Sukiman cabinet was its decision in February 1952 to accept American aid under the 1951 Mutual Security Act. This move precipitated a far more serious political crisis and ended with Sukiman's resignation the following month.[9] The MSA crisis marked the passing from the scene of the last flagrantly pro-America government Indonesia was to have until the overthrow of Sukarno in 1966.

The successor cabinet headed by Wilopo has rightly been called a turning point in Indonesia's postindependence history.[10] During its tenure (March 1952 to June 1953) Indonesia made a transition from the anticommunist, Western-oriented foreign policies that had been dominant since 1950 to a greater degree of autonomy in foreign affairs. Wilopo's cabinet prepared the way,

[7] On the politics and policies of the Sukiman cabinet see Feith, *Decline of Constitutional Democracy in Indonesia*, pp. 177–224.

[8] Chou En-lai, "Political Report," p. 15, *Jen-min Jih-pao*, Sept. 10, 1951.

[9] The details of the crisis are in Feith, pp. 198–207.

[10] For the best analysis of this period see Herbert Feith, *The Wilopo Cabinet, 1952–1953: A Turning Point in Post-Revolutionary Indonesia* (Ithaca: Cornell Modern Indonesia Project, 1958).

as it were, for the changes that by 1954 would result in the complete normalization of Indonesia's relations with the communist states and the first assertions of Djakarta's later nationalistic diplomacy.

In a certain sense the Wilopo government, though it changed foreign policy, did not itself have one. If one existed, it was well concealed. Because this government's support in parliament was fragile, it tried to avoid controversial foreign-policy decisions. As a result, no new attempts were made to conclude agreements for American military, economic, or technical assistance. Plans to reopen the West Irian question with the Dutch were also abandoned. On the other hand, the substance of Wilopo's policies toward the communist states did not differ radically from that of Hatta's and Natsir's. The running argument with the Chinese embassy was dropped, but Wilopo did not attempt to normalize relations with the CPR. No effort was made to fill the still vacant ambassadorial post in Peking; nor did Wilopo press for the establishment of diplomatic relations with the Soviet Union.[11]

The foreign policy of the Wilopo government thus gave little positive encouragement to the development of a thaw in Sino-Indonesian relations. This posture contrasted with that of other Asian neutrals, which were improving their relations with Peking at this time. On the other hand, important changes were occurring in Indonesia's internal political situation that could not have

[11] The Wilopo cabinet's foreign minister, Mukarto, had initially stated that it was not possible to delay any longer the establishment of diplomatic relations with the Soviet Union (Antara, April 24, 1952). In July, the cabinet approved, in principle, a decision to send an ambassador to Peking (Antara, July 2, 1952). This followed a suggestion by Indonesian chargé d'affaires Isak Mahdi that an ambassador was required in Peking in view of China's importance in the world (Indonesian Ministry of Information, *Report on Indonesia,* June 30, 1952, p. 3). Again, however, opposition from the Masjumi party obliged the Wilopo government to shelve any plans for proceeding with the normalization of relations with China and the Soviet Union.

escaped Peking's attention, though they did not immediately affect Peking's policy toward Djakarta. An important factor in Chinese planning for the future must have been the fact that the Wilopo cabinet was the first to receive the support of the PKI in parliament. This support symbolized a reversal of the political line and strategy of the Indonesian communists and could not fail to give Peking an added incentive to improve relations with the Indonesian government as soon as conditions would permit.

Since 1950 the PKI had been allowed to exist as a legal party and had been allotted sixteen seats in the provisional parliament. But the Indonesian communists had stood in opposition to every government since the first Hatta cabinet, and they still bore an antinationalist stigma because of the Mediun uprising. Until mid-1951 the party's attempts to instigate labor strikes and other disturbances served only to re-enforce this image, while Sukiman's 1951 August raids further weakened and discredited the PKI. It was not until his government fell that the PKI's new leadership, under Dipta Nusantara Aidit, was in a position to shift the party's line.[12] In March 1952 the PKI made the shift, announcing that it would support the Wilopo cabinet, provided that the latter's policies were "progressive and national."[13]

The decision to give the PKI's parliamentary support to the Wilopo cabinet was a consequence of the party's change to a domestic united-front line emphasizing political-legal struggle and the avoidance of discredited agitational tactics. In this way

[12] On the history of the PKI during this period, and the events leading up to its change in strategy, see Donald Hindley, *The Communist Party of Indonesia* (Berkeley: University of California Press, 1964), pp. 22–26; and Justus van der Kroef, *The Communist Party of Indonesia* (Vancouver: University of British Columbia Publications Centre, 1965), pp. 44–53.

[13] Statement of the PKI Central Committee, *Harian Rakjat* (People's Daily), March 26, 1952.

the party hoped to build mass popular support and strong labor unions and to focus its attack on imperialist and feudalist elements and their domestic supporters. The tactical objectives of the new united-front policy were to exploit the serious frictions that had begun to develop between the PNI and Masjumi parties and to align the PKI squarely behind the nationalist goal of liberating West Irian. The claim to the Irian territory had become the central concern of Indonesian foreign policy by 1952, and the party believed that the nationalistic, anti-imperialist feelings this issue evoked among nearly all Indonesians could be transformed into domestic political radicalism that would help to restore popular confidence in the communists.

Although based on a tenuous parliamentary coalition composed of PNI, Masjumi, and PSI (Indonesian Socialist party) factions, Wilopo's cabinet was the first since independence to be led by the PNI. Wilopo was no radical on either foreign or domestic issues. His government found favor with the PKI because the conservative anticommunists who had been dominant in past cabinets were momentarily eclipsed. Therefore, the Indonesian communists had a strong interest in helping to sustain Wilopo and in cooperating with some of the other political parties which, for one reason or another, could be considered useful to the PKI in keeping the anticommunist factions out of the government.

It thus becomes clear that the Aidit shift to a united-front policy accorded with the international united-front line Peking initiated in 1951. On the other hand, it does not seem very likely that Chinese communist influence prompted the 1952 shift in the PKI's domestic strategy. For the essential element in the new Indonesian communist line was its concentration on legal, parliamentary struggle, to the exclusion of radical social-economic programs in the countryside or even a pronounced emphasis on political work among the peasantry—the central focus of Chinese theories on revolution and party-building. Actually, of course, the low priority the PKI assigned the peasantry, rather than the party's "parliamentary road," from the beginning stamped the Aidit leadership as a non-Maoist group. It is also difficult to see Chinese influence behind the PKI's shift if we look more closely at Peking's diplomatic behavior toward Indonesia at this time.

It was eight months after the PKI shift had occurred, and ten months after the recall of Wang Jen-shu, before Peking made any conciliatory overtures toward the Wilopo government. In view of the important role the new cabinet played in the Indonesian communists' attempt to make a political comeback, this seems a strangely long delay if Peking was, in fact, attempting to exert influence on the PKI to bring its policies into line with China's. In October 1952, the Chinese embassy proposed discussions with Djakarta concerning the establishment of trade relations between the two countries.[14] Previous trade deals with India and Ceylon in 1951 had been preceded by such an overture. Because of Indonesia's decision to honor, even though she had not signed, the U.N. embargo against the CPR, this initiative appeared to be an effort on the part of Peking to see whether Djakarta's policy had changed in any significant way since the overthrow of the Sukiman government. The door was quickly closed, however, when the Wilopo cabinet failed to show any serious interest in discussions with Peking concerning trade, and the Indonesians allowed the whole matter to drop.

Even so mild a rebuff as Djakarta's disinterest in trade talks was sufficient to deter the Chinese from using other diplomatic gestures to signal a desire for improved relations. If the concern to coordinate tactics with the PKI had been a major factor in Chinese policy at this time, other means of wooing the Indonesian government were available, such as appointing a new ambassador to Djakarta. This would have indicated, quite openly, a Chinese desire to terminate the era of bad feelings created by Wang Jen-shu and the Sukiman cabinet. Evidently Peking did not intend to

[14] Reported in Antara, Oct. 27, Nov. 5, 1952

give any more friendly signals to Djakarta until there was some concrete gesture by the Indonesian government indicating that it was prepared to improve relations with the CPR. Thus matters stood for the duration of the Wilopo cabinet.

The Normalization of Peking-Djakarta Relations

Favorable opportunities for Peking to improve relations with Djakarta began to emerge after June 1953, following the formation of a new cabinet headed by Ali Sastroamidjojo.[15] Unlike previous Indonesian governments, Ali's cabinet was actually dependent on the parliamentary support of the PKI for its majority. The PKI was able to play this key role because Ali's government was based on a weak coalition led by the left wing of the PNI. The latter, in order to hold a working majority which excluded the conservative Moslem parties, required parliamentary support from the extreme left, and this could only be provided by the PKI. Although the PKI was not invited to join the cabinet —Ali's "left-wing" PNI faction intended no program of serious reforms—it was amply rewarded for its support. As a parliamentary ally of the government of the day, PKI regained its former nationalist credentials. Moreover, the support given to Ali helped the party to develop its campaign to build mass organizations, and thus to isolate the Moslem anticommunists.

Peking was encouraged by the Ali cabinet's commitment to an anticolonialist foreign policy and by its decision to attempt to normalize relations with the communist states. On most Cold War issues Ali adopted a position parallel to that of Burma and India. Moreover, during this government's tenure a resolution of the West Irian issue and the assertion of a leadership role in the Afro-Asian world became dominant objectives of Indonesia's foreign policy. Eventually, the pursuit of these aims would result in the reversal by Djakarta of policies that had led to *de facto*

[15] For an analysis of the Ali cabinet see Feith, *Decline of Constitutional Democracy in Indonesia*, pp. 331–413.

alignment with the American camp, and thus open the way for a more active relationship with the communist powers.

The first step the cabinet took to improve relations with China was to send to Peking, in October 1953, a well-known member of the Indonesian elite, Arnold Mononutu, as Indonesia's first ambassador.[16] Possible economic contacts were next explored, and in December 1953 a Sino-Indonesian two-year barter-trade agreement was signed.[17] The Ali cabinet's program also called for the establishment of diplomatic relations with the Soviet Union.[18] Negotiations were successfully completed in Moscow, and a Russian embassy was opened in Djakarta in March 1954.

Peking responded to these encouraging developments in November 1954 by sending, as her new ambassador to Djakarta, Huang Chen,[19] a senior diplomatic officer previously posted in Eastern Europe—a man quite the opposite of the bombastic, nonprofessional Wang Jen-shu. By late 1954 full diplomatic relations had been achieved. The moment was ripe for the two powers to consider substantive political problems they heretofore had been unable to discuss, much less negotiate.

The Sino-Indonesian Dual Nationality Treaty

An important domestic policy consideration had been among the factors prompting the Ali government to normalize relations with the CPR. The program Ali had placed before parliament in 1953 included proposals for a new law on Indonesian citizenship which would affect the legal status of overseas Chinese. A draft was completed in February 1954.[20] However, before the law

[16] *Jen-min Jih-pao,* Oct. 19, 1953.

[17] Antara, Jan. 16, 1954.

[18] Ministry of Information, *Keterangan dan Djawaban Pemerintah atas Program Kabinet Ali Sastroamidjojo* (Government Statement and Replies on the Program of the Ali Sastroamidjojo Cabinet) (Djakarta, 1953).

[19] NCNA (Peking), Nov. 22, 1954.

[20] Feith, *Decline of Constitutional Democracy in Indonesia,* p. 385.

could be enacted there would have to be negotiations with China about certain aspects of the proposed legislation, since, as a result of the 1949–1951 option, many local-born Chinese were claimed as nationals by both Indonesia and the CPR. The 1954 draft law was the outgrowth of Djakarta's mounting dissatisfaction with the results of the Round Table Conference formula. Prior to the time of the Ali cabinet, no Indonesian government had been prepared to grapple with this thorny issue, and during the period when relations with China were strained a negotiated settlement was out of the question. Ali concluded that conditions were now quite favorable for a settlement.

The basic policy of the CPR toward the overseas Chinese populations in Southeast Asia in 1954 was still based on the 1949 Common Program and the 1953 Electoral Law. These documents plainly regarded foreign-domiciled Chinese as mainland citizens and, in effect, seemed to express Peking's intention to strengthen, not weaken, the CPR's ties with the overseas Chinese. On the other hand, by 1954 this stance was clearly becoming incompatible with Peking's emerging policy of peaceful coexistence, which required the elimination of potential sources of friction with the Southeast Asian neutrals. And anti-imperialist united-front cooperation certainly could not become the basis of China's relations with these countries so long as Peking's insistence that local Chinese were citizens of the CPR continued to alarm her neighbors.

Whether expansionist Chinese nationalism or a desire for peaceful coexistence actually determined Peking's policies was, from the perspective of several Southeast Asian countries, a question that would largely be answered by evidence of the mainland's readiness to modify its citizenship claims on the overseas Chinese. If Peking would not make substantial concessions on this issue, there was little prospect of improving her relations with these countries to any significant degree. On the other hand,

Peking might turn the vexing problem posed by this minority to her diplomatic advantage in the region if she could hold out the possibility of renouncing her claims on the foreign-born Chinese as an inducement to certain Southeast Asian governments to improve their relations with the CPR.

Ambassador Mononutu raised the question of settling the Chinese citizenship issue soon after his arrival in Peking, and he found Chou En-lai receptive to the idea. According to Mononutu, the Chinese leader emphasized that agreeing to negotiate this matter was a major departure from China's traditional policy, and that his government would regard any conclusion of a treaty with Djakarta as a test case which, if successful, might be extended to other countries on a bilateral basis.[21] Following this initial meeting of minds, the first phase of serious, unpublicized negotiations got underway in Djakarta between Indonesian representatives and members of the Chinese embassy. Shortly thereafter a special Indonesian team was sent to Peking, where the second and more formal series were conducted, between November 4 and December 23, 1954. A third and final phase of negotiations took place in Djakarta and Bandung from March 29 to April 20, 1955; they concluded with a formal agreement of April 22 just in time for the Asian-African Conference.[22]

The basic terms of the 1955 Sino-Indonesian Dual Nationality Treaty provided that those overseas Chinese designated as simultaneously possessing both CPR and Indonesian nationality would formally choose the nationality of one country within two years after the treaty had been ratified. The citizenship of those who failed to choose would be determined by the nationality of their fathers.[23]

[21] Interview with Mononutu, former Indonesian ambassador to China, Aug. 4, 1961.

[22] Interviews with a member of the Indonesian team which negotiated the Dual Nationality Treaty, July 11, 12, Aug. 30, 1961.

[23] For the complete text of the Dual Nationality Treaty see Willmott, *The National Status of the Chinese in Indonesia*, pp. 130–134.

In addition to these provisions, the treaty incorporated important political pledges and understandings that both sides wished to see reflected in the document. Peking pledged that those Chinese who remained CPR nationals would "abide by the laws and customs" of Indonesia and "not . . . participate in political activities."[24] These two provisions, which were stated in general terms rather than as specific principles, enabled the treaty, in effect, to record Peking's public renunciation of any attempt to interfere in Indonesia's internal affairs by influencing the Chinese minority. This, of course, was a major objective of the Indonesian government.

For her part Djakarta pledged "to protect the proper rights and interests" of those Chinese who remained CPR nationals. Naturally, this was the provision Peking most wanted to be explicitly stated in the treaty as a restraint on discriminatory Indonesian economic or civil regulations affecting Chinese nationals.[25] From the text of the treaty it appears that China had acquired another important safeguard. There were also provisions for an "exchange of minds" and for "negotiations" between the two parties in the event of differences of "interpretation" that might result from "implementation" of the agreements.[26] Strictly interpreted, these provisions could serve as the legal basis for Peking's challenging or delaying the enforcement of Indonesian regulations affecting Chinese nationals which, in the CPR's judgment, contravened the treaty.

The major Indonesian objective in these negotiations was to undo the results of the citizenship-option period carried out in accordance with the provisions of the Round Table Conference Agreements. A second objective was to secure Peking's renunciation of legal claims on the local-born Chinese before they were

---

[24] Dual Nationality Treaty, Article XI, par. 1, *ibid.*
[25] *Ibid.*, par. 2.
[26] *Ibid.*, Articles XII, XIII.

offered a new option of taking Indonesian citizenship. They could no longer acquire it "passively"; they would have to make formal application and undergo an irritating bureaucratic process (involving fees, proofs, forms, and so forth) which would test how genuinely they wanted Indonesian citizenship.

That China was willing to accept Djakarta's determination of those who had to choose and those who did not was conclusively demonstrated not only by the 1955 treaty's provisions but also by supplemental agreements. In June 1955, Chou En-lai agreed to recognize as Indonesian nationals an additional category of Chinese, not explicitly covered by the treaty, whom Djakarta regarded as already having implicitly opted for Indonesia by virtue of "their political and social status."[27] Depending on how meticulous the Indonesian government wanted to be about the documentation the Chinese would have to present in order to establish proof of birth in Indonesia—thousands of Chinese had never conceived it would be necessary to do this—Djakarta could make the choice of Indonesian citizenship very easy or very hard. Although the treaty said nothing specific about provisions for implementation, the basic principles of the agreement indicated that China had accepted Indonesia's right to determine the number of local-born Chinese who would be eligible to choose Indonesian citizenship.

Whether large numbers of such Chinese should be encouraged to take Indonesian citizenship or prevented from doing so was a decision Djakarta had not incorporated in any statutory law at the time the treaty was concluded. Since the Indonesian leaders had gone to the trouble of negotiating an agreement wherein Peking renounced claims on the Chinese in Indonesia, the logical

[27] "Note of Prime Minister Chou En-lai's to Prime Minister Ali Sastroamidjojo on the Implementation of the Dual Nationality Treaty," June 3, 1955 (full text issued by the Cultural and Information Office, Embassy of the People's Republic of China, Djakarta, 1955).

assumption is that Djakarta must have wanted large numbers of them to opt for Indonesian citizenship. In fact, however, opinion on this matter in the government was sharply divided. It appears instead that what Djakarta wanted in 1955 was not a definitive, spelled-out settlement but only the removal of Peking's claim on the local-born Chinese. Indonesia could thus reserve the option of carrying out either a broad or a narrow assimilation policy toward the resident Chinese in the future. Djakarta's interpretation of the Dual Nationality Treaty satisfied this objective, but as later events proved, it certainly did not accord with Peking's conception of the meaning of the agreements.

Peking's interests also seemed to be well-served by her interpretation of the treaty. Its provisions enabled her to renounce honorably a previous nationalistic policy without abandoning the remaining China-born Chinese who would automatically be regarded as CPR citizens, and those Indonesia-born overseas Chinese who might opt to remain CPR citizens, to a potentially hostile environment. As subsequent anti-Chinese outbursts in Indonesia demonstrated, China's fears of what might happen to her nationals were completely justified. But in April 1955 there were more reasons for hope than fear. Peking-Djakarta relations were improving rapidly, and there were grounds for hoping that the conciliatory position China had taken on the citizenship issue would be reciprocated by Djakarta's restraint in applying economic regulations against the Chinese nationals. Peking probably also calculated that her concessions strengthened the hand of a moderate government which would be more likely to protect the Chinese from the more openly hostile anti-Chinese elements in the country.

The treaty's provision that Indonesia would protect the "rights and interests" of the Chinese nationals was phrased in very general terms, indicating that the negotiators actually had been quite far apart in their interpretations of the meaning of this concept. According to Indonesian informants who were members of Djakarta's negotiating team, Peking had pressed for a specific understanding by the two sides that "rights and interests" meant all rights and interests, including economic ones. The Indonesian negotiators, on the other hand, insisted that the phrase should mean only "legal" rights and interests—that is, whatever Indonesian law said those rights and interests were. Inasmuch as the language adopted in the treaty was quite unspecific, the final provision was closer to the Indonesian than the Chinese conception. Thus the fundamental conflict of interests over the economic position of the Chinese in Indonesia was not resolved but merely papered over in the treaty.

The importance of this failure to reach a clear understanding on the "rights and interests" issue was not fully understood at the time. It became of utmost significance four years later, in 1959, when Djakarta suddenly placed drastic restrictions on Chinese traders in the villages, thereby precipitating a major diplomatic rupture with Peking. But the atmosphere in 1955 was quite different. There were some problems relating to aspects of the treaty, but the larger domestic and foreign interests of the two governments were propelling them toward a period of very cooperative relations. Potential conflicts over what the treaty's provisions meant must have seemed insignificant and very far away.

Bandung and the Peaceful-Coexistence Strategy

The conclusion of the Dual Nationality Treaty with Indonesia was an important element in the pattern of new Chinese diplomatic initiatives after 1954. Agreements such as those that resulted in the treaty made it possible for Peking to improve her relations with Southeast Asia and thus to begin to transform the basic political alignments in the entire Far East. As a consequence of her diplomatic triumphs of 1954–1955 the CPR seemed on the verge of breaking out of the isolated and defensive position that had been forced on her by the Korean conflict and interventionist American policies in the area.

Four factors were primarily responsible for the CPR's new diplomatic flexibility: (1) Stalin's death in 1953 and the subsequent leadership struggle in the Soviet Communist party greatly weakened the presumption of Moscow's leadership of the Sino-Soviet alliance—a process that probably began as a result of dissatisfactions relating to the Korean War. Peking's readiness to take independent foreign-policy initiatives even before Stalin's death had already become apparent, but his passing from the scene—leaving no one in the communist movement really comparable to Mao Tse-tung in stature—must have increased assertive tendencies in the Chinese leadership. (2) The unwillingness of the Asian neutrals to support American foreign-policy objectives and the possibility that China might even unite with them to oppose the United States had made it much easier for Peking to discontinue ideological attacks on the bourgeois nationalist regimes and to settle outstanding questions that remained from the colonial period. (3) To an increasing number of Asian governments, including such allies of the United States as Japan, Thailand, and Pakistan, Peking's demonstrated moderation had largely disproved American charges that she was an aggressive power. By concluding a treaty with India on the status of Tibet (April 1954), by playing a major role in bringing the Indochina War to an end (July 1954), and by joining with India and Burma to proclaim the Five Principles of Peaceful Coexistence (June 1954), the CPR had indicated that she was prepared to live at peace with her neighbors. (4) For their part, the Asian neutrals had correctly gauged the implications of the important shift that had occurred in the foreign policies of the communist powers about 1954, and they were consequently unable to accept the American thesis that the pattern of Cold War alignments reflected in the European situation should be transferred to East Asia. At a time when intraregional conflicts spawned during the preceding colonial era seemed amenable to solution on the basis of cooperation and negotiations with the CPR, the American thesis that anticommunist military pacts were necessary to save this area from a Chinese menace had a hollow ring.

Nowhere was China's diplomatic breakout more effectively and dramatically exploited than at the meeting of the twenty-nine Asian and African leaders at Bandung, Indonesia, in April 1955. The domestic as well as foreign interests that might be served by such a conference were in the minds of leaders like Nehru, Ali, and other statesmen who called it. And there was genuine concern among the Afro-Asian states that the time had come to discuss their own problems and to act in concert to prevent their countries from becoming ever more entangled in the Cold War rivalries.

Most of the delegates attending the historic meeting were convinced by Chou En-lai's presentation of China's desire to see the principles of peaceful coexistence become the basis of relations among all the non-Western states.[28] These nations, he said, had fundamentally the same interests, despite their differing social systems, and China had "no intention whatsoever to subvert the governments of its neighboring countries." Openly declaring Peking's renunciation of any attempt to use her overseas Chinese communities or to influence foreign communist parties to subvert her neighbors, Chou proclaimed, "If nations gave assurances not to interfere in each others' internal affairs, it [would] then be possible for the people of these countries to choose their own political system and way of life in accordance with their own will." Henceforth, any provable charges of Chinese subversion or interference on behalf of revolutionaries in newly independent states would certainly expose the Peking government before the

[28] For the full text of Chou En-lai's three speeches at the conference see *China and the Asian-African Conference* (Peking: Foreign Languages Press, 1955), pp. 9–27 and 29–31 (documents).

entire Asian-African community as a leadership whose words did not match its deeds. Even those leaders at the conference who doubted the sincerity of China's pledge to pursue a peaceful-coexistence policy were unable during the ten years that followed Bandung to present a valid instance in which Peking broke this pledge. By 1965, of course, American intervention in Southeast Asia, especially in the Vietnamese civil war, had effectively destroyed the prospect of peaceful coexistence.

The obstacle to friendly relations between China and the Afro-Asian countries, Chou En-lai argued, was not the social system or foreign policy of the CPR but the actions of the United States, which continued "to create tensions in the Taiwan area" and was "establishing more and more military bases in Asian and African countries." Although the Chinese premier acknowledged that many countries had become independent, he insisted that "the rule of colonialism was not dead . . . and new colonialists [were] attempting to take the place of the old ones." Hence, the main basis for "unity" and "common ground" among all the Asian-African countries was their mutual interest in ending "the suffering and calamities under colonialism." If this goal were achieved, Chou declared, "it [would] be very easy for us to have mutual understanding and respect, mutual sympathy and support instead of mutual suspicion and fear, mutual exclusion and antagonism."

A number of pro-Western leaders at Bandung still had doubts about how far Peking was prepared to carry the peaceful-coexistence doctrine. In a separate statement issued immediately after the conference the Chinese premier offered to "enter into negotiations with the United States Government to discuss the question of relaxing tensions in the Far East, and especially the question of relaxing tensions in the Taiwan area."[29] This offer

[29] *Ibid.*, p. 28.

almost, but not quite, amounted to an implication that peaceful coexistence might even be possible with the leader of the imperialist camp itself if Washington ceased its interference in China's internal affairs and was prepared to withdraw American military power from other areas. Although this initiative led to the commencement of Sino-American talks in Geneva later in 1955 but no resolution of the issues, its immediate political impact was to strengthen further the CPR image among the Afro-Asian neutrals as a state ready to abide by the principles of peaceful coexistence.

The proposals for Afro-Asian cooperation which Chou En-lai announced at Bandung showed the extent of the transformation that had occurred in China's foreign-policy strategy by 1955. What the Chinese leader said and pledged amounted to a replacement of the 1949 to 1950 Mao-Liu call for a revolutionary united front from below by a call for a united front from above. Peking's new allies could be the bourgeois governments of newly independent Afro-Asian states which might, for reasons of their own, share China's interest in banding together to prevent the United States from dragging the Third World into the Cold War.

Indonesia certainly seemed a prime candidate for membership in the new coalition China was proposing. The issue of Chinese domiciled in Indonesia appeared to be settled or at least was no longer a major source of tension. Peking's renunciation of the Mao-Liu revolutionary line also helped to defuse potential conflicts that might arise from her fraternal ties to the PKI, especially since the latter was itself already committed to peaceful parliamentary struggle and a policy of united-front cooperation with the same elements of the Indonesian bourgeois elite who favored friendly relations with the CPR. Indeed, the PKI's domestic policy was completely in accord with the Chinese leaders' global united-front strategy, and vice versa. Now that the issues of Chinese residents of Indonesia and subversion had seemingly been laid to rest the obvious similarity between Chinese and

Indonesian foreign-policy interests might become apparent: the similar irrendentist struggles of Peking for the recovery of Taiwan and of Djakarta for the recovery of West Irian—territories that were symbols of incomplete sovereignty forced on both countries by imperialist intervention.

5

Militant Anti-Imperialism: A Modified
United-Front-from-Above Strategy

The major foreign-policy initiative China took at the Bandung Conference was based on two assumptions: that Sino-Soviet unity would continue and that there would be an increased scope for the application of the peaceful-coexistence doctrine. If the Chinese assumptions were correct, the combined effect of the Soviet-Chinese alliance and the improvement of relations between Peking and her neighbors would be to expand the basis for a united-front strategy of opposition to the American presence in Asia. These expectations, however, soon proved to be unrealistic. After Bandung the hoped-for possibility of a united front did not materialize and, in fact, China, rather than the imperialists, became increasingly isolated and thrown on the defensive. To grasp the nature of the pressures that prompted the shift in Chinese strategy after 1958, and the effect this shift had on the developing pattern of Sino-Indonesian relations, it is necessary to analyze briefly the factors that caused the breakdown of the Bandung policy.

Estrangement from Moscow

The Chinese Communist party claims that the rift with Moscow began at the Twentieth Congress of the CPSU in 1956, when Khrushchev denounced Stalin and advanced proposals for dealing with the United States that Peking could not accept. The controversy had actually begun to take shape before this event.[1] The Soviet Union chose to de-emphasize the significance of the Bandung Conference, especially the implication Peking derived from it: that the communist bloc should concentrate its strategy on the Afro-Asian states, to the end of exploiting their differences with the imperialist powers. It was already clear from the Soviet's participation in the Big Four talks on Berlin and disarmament at the July 1955 Geneva Conference that Moscow's primary attention would remain focused on the Atlantic theater and, consequently, that she did not welcome pre-emptive Chinese moves to redirect the efforts of the socialist camp elsewhere. That Moscow was, in fact, interested in the relaxation of tensions with the United States in the Far East, on the basis of accepting the status quo, was revealed in the October 1956 Soviet decision to establish diplomatic relations with Japan. Though unprotested by Peking, this move implicitly undermined the 1950 Sino-Soviet Treaty of Friendship and Alliance, under which both powers had theretofore followed a common policy of refusing to normalize ties with Tokyo (both had rejected the 1951 Japanese Peace Treaty), pending Japan's withdrawal from her military alliance with the United States, severance of ties with Nationalist China, and recognition of the CPR.

The main political effect of the Soviet resumption of ties with Japan was to encourage conservative circles in the Japanese and in other Asian governments in the belief that a "two-Chinas" policy was possible. The Russian action also suggested that the communist powers' militance toward imperialism was weakening and that they might eventually become reconciled to the continuance of military pacts between Asian nations and the United

[1] "The Origins and Development of the Differences between the Leadership of the CPSU and Ourselves: Comment on the Open Letter of the Central Committee of the CPSU" (July 14, 1963), dated Sept. 6, 1963; in *The Polemic on the General Line of the International Communist Movement*, pp. 59–67.

States. This was certainly not the message Peking was trying to convey by its consistent policy of resolute, united opposition to the military pacts of the United States, nor was it the objective China had in proposing the Bandung formula. Given Moscow's disinterest in a clear anti-imperialist line in Asia, the Chinese now had to reappraise the implications of the Russians' post-1956 diplomatic and economic campaigns in India, Burma, and Indonesia. Was it clear after 1956 that these Soviet initiatives were for the purpose of countering American policy or was their real intention to curb China's growing influence in the region?

Heightened Tensions between China and the United States

Accumulating evidence of divergent Soviet and Chinese policies in Asia necessarily had the effect of undermining China's position in the contest with America in East Asia. The Sino-American talks on relaxing tensions in the Taiwan Straits area, which began in 1955, revealed from the beginning that Washington would not agree to remove her military presence unless Peking was prepared to recognize the American-created status quo, that is, the perpetuation of the Nationalist Chinese regime. While these talks continued, the United States proceeded with the training and rearmament of the Nationalist armies. Further evidence of the real American intention was the steady rearmament of Japan and the development of Okinawa into the most powerful air, naval, and nuclear-weapons base in the Pacific. Since these efforts proceeded apace, despite the moderate and restrained foreign policy of the CPR at this time, Peking had to conclude that the American camp did not want a relaxation of tensions in Northeast Asia. Any possibility that the Bandung policy might have been the basis for a whole new approach toward the United States—faintly implied by Chou En-lai's offer to talk with Washington—rather than a bid for organizing a broader united front against her, was quickly dashed by the concerted American Far Eastern policy after 1954, which aimed at organizing Asia into a political-military system directed against China.

In Southeast Asia the tenuous political-military arrangement that had been worked out at the Geneva Conference was, by 1955, also being rapidly undermined by the United States, which had decided to overturn the 1954 Indochina settlement. The first consequence of this decision was the Southeast Asia Treaty Organization (SEATO), established by a security treaty (September 1954), dealing with Laos and Cambodia, in which an umbrella clause permitted the signatory powers—but actually the United States—to intervene in these countries in the event of "aggression"—despite the plain language of the Geneva Agreements, which explicitly called for the neutralization of these two states. As the French withdrew from South Vietnam, the United States undertook to create a regime in Saigon under Ngo Dinh Diem; the aim was the permanent division of Vietnam into communist and anticommunist zones—similar to the Korean division—again in violation of the 1954 Geneva Agreements. Under the SEATO treaty Thailand and the Philippines would serve as the flanks buttressing the main American bastion being created in South Vietnam. By 1956, Washington was already developing a pattern of covert diplomacy and intervention in Laos—which was extended to Cambodia in 1958 and to other Southeast Asian countries—designed to strengthen the remaining weak links in the chain that the United States was forging to "contain" communist China.

During this same period the United States made a massive effort (matched by the Soviet Union, which thus indirectly supported American aims) to underwrite the Indian five-year plans, a development that was evidently an attempt by Washington (and Moscow) to strengthen New Delhi as a counterweight to China in Asia. Elsewhere, in 1957 and 1958, rightist military coups were carried out in Burma, Pakistan, Laos, and Thailand, and the army became the dominant political influence in Indonesia. Although evidence of covert American intervention on behalf of the military in this region at that time has been documented only with respect to South Vietnam, Laos, and Indonesia, it is clear that the policy of Secretary of State John Foster Dulles welcomed the coming to power of army-controlled regimes which might be more easily influenced to develop less moderate attitudes toward China than those of the previous civilian leadership. To Peking, therefore, it must have seemed that in the period between 1955 and 1958 the United States was engaged in a new drive to dominate Southeast Asia and to sabotage the Bandung formula. The success of this American effort to "roll back" China had a great influence on the subsequent policy shift Peking was forced to make.

Defection of the Neutrals from the United Front

The Bandung policy of promoting common unity and support among Asian-African states on the basis of resistance to imperialism notably failed to inspire most of the parties to whom it was directed. Overall, the Afro-Asian states seemed to interpret the Chinese assertions to mean acceptance of the status quo, not a call to resist American policies. In other words, peaceful coexistence meant only live and let live. This was not an unreasonable inference, since Chou En-lai's statements at Bandung had stressed the point that all the new countries should concentrate on national economic construction, and such a focus was not exactly consistent with the diversion of energies to confrontations with the colonial and imperialist powers. Had not China also said that peaceful coexistence was possible even with the Asian military allies of the United States—Japan, Thailand, and Pakistan? And if Peking could offer to sit down to talk with the imperialists themselves after Bandung, on what basis could China logically object to the Asian neutrals' adopting a nonmilitant posture toward the United States?

It was not clear in 1955, however—as it became after 1956—

that the Bandung policy was not going to deter the United States from intensifying its containment strategy in Asia. Moreover, it turned out that the conciliatory position Peking adopted toward her neighbors did not garner her much support from other powers, notably Russia and India, to offset the adverse effect of American efforts to promote an anticommunist rollback. In this situation, the Bandung policy could not remain viable unless Peking succeeded in infusing it with a stronger anti-imperialist motif. To do this China needed to organize much stronger regional and international support to undermine American policy. Strategically, Peking needed to turn the thrust of the communist-led international united front to Asia to defend threatened Chinese interests.

Sino-Soviet Differences Regarding Peaceful Coexistence

It was primarily because the Bandung policy failed to deter the American rollback campaign in Asia that China became alarmed at the main foreign-policy theses Khrushchev announced at the CPSU Twentieth Party Congress.[2] He interpreted peaceful coexistence to mean, essentially, nuclear coexistence with the United States, and thus clearly implied that the Soviet Union was willing to accept not only the status quo imposed by the United States in Asia but also American actions designed to roll back communism and neutralism. In Moscow's view, the pursuit of an active anti-imperialist strategy by the socialist powers to counter the American offensive strategy in Asia was unacceptably dangerous, since it might lead to general war. Instead, Khrushchev held that the dislodgement of the imperialists from the

---

[2] For analyses of Khrushchev's theses, see Donald S. Zagoria, *The Sino-Soviet Conflict, 1956–1961* (Princeton: Princeton University Press, 1962), pp. 39–42; and Richard Lowenthal, *World Communism: The Disintegration of a Secular Faith* (New York: Oxford University Press, 1966), pp. 39–69. An English-language text of Khrushchev's speech appears in the Soviet Tass dispatch, February 14, 1956.

colonies and the newly independent countries must be achieved primarily by strengthening the socialist camp. Khrushchev asserted that growing strength, as well as the bright prospects for communist parties' winning victories through legal parliamentary struggle in the industrialized European countries, would lead to the advance of socialism in the West and eventually be of decisive assistance to the national liberation movements in Asia, Africa, and Latin America.

From this argument it was clear what the priorities of the socialist camp should be. China and other countries at odds with the imperialists would have to wait until the Soviet Union had prevailed over the West after prolonged, essentially economic competition in the West. Khrushchev's assertion that peaceful coexistence should be "the general line" of the foreign policies of all communist parties really meant that Moscow would formulate the strategy the world movement should follow, and this strategy would be determined by the overriding factor of Soviet-American nuclear rivalry.

In 1956 and the years thereafter, the doctrine of peaceful coexistence between states with different social systems was not contrary to earlier Chinese foreign policy. Peking had advanced peaceful coexistence as a basic, but not the only, principle of her foreign policy several years before Khrushchev suddenly became attached to the concept. Since 1954 it had been the basis of China's relations with friendly Asian states. But she disagreed with Khrushchev's idea that peaceful coexistence should also apply to U.S. imperialism, which was pursuing rollback, anticommunist policies in Asia inimical to Chinese interests. Acceptance of Khrushchev's definition of peaceful coexistence would mean that Peking could not actively oppose the enlargement and the consolidation of the American sphere in Asia until the balance of power in the West had decisively shifted in favor of the Soviet Union. But in view of Soviet policies in Asia after

1956, the Chinese were entitled to wonder how soon, if ever, they would receive Moscow's support. Khrushchev's ideas about "peaceful transition" were also unpalatable to the Chinese. For if the main task of communist parties in the colonial and newly independent countries was to wait for the victory of socialism in the West to weaken imperialism, then revolutionary struggles were not only unnecessary but could, in fact, be avoided. As the colonial world became more aware of the socialist system's high levels of production, Khrushchev argued, more people would flock to the banners of the communist parties in distant lands, enabling them to participate in governments controlled by bourgeois nationalists. Khrushchev envisioned the colonial world as gradually moving toward a "noncapitalist road of development" or toward "national democratic states," which would evolve into socialist states as they entered the orbit of Soviet power. In other words, there would be no need for strong, independent communist parties and national united fronts—certainly not for independent communist military forces—and probably no need for a dictatorship of the proletariat at the time the bourgeois system was peacefully overthrown.

Khrushchev's program for the Afro-Asian world thus repudiated the basic core of Chinese revolutionary theory and doctrine as well as the interests of the Chinese state. If accepted without alteration there could be no serious pressure exerted by local communist parties on their governments to pursue anti-imperialist foreign policies. In the Chinese view, such parties could not build the kind of strength or militancy they would need to win power by political means or by armed struggle when the eventual showdown came. They could not be "self-reliant," as the Chinese insisted they must be, because their success or survival would essentially depend on Moscow's handling of the world struggle and the Soviet's ability to prevent the unreliable bourgeois-nationalist governments from suppressing local communist parties.

With respect to the second condition, all past experience had shown that an attempt by the bourgeoisie to suppress the communists would occur at some stage during the anti-imperialist phase of a national revolution, and that communist aid from outside the country could not prevent this from happening.

China Calls for an Anti-Imperialist Strategy

Concern about the possible effects of Khrushchev's proposals led China, in 1957, to call for the socialist camp to take a militant stance toward the United States. The call reflected not only China's anxiety about her endangered national interests but also her deepening lack of confidence in the Soviet leadership's global objectives and its long-range intentions respecting the CPR. The call to action came from Mao Tse-tung himself in the famous "East Wind over West Wind" speech delivered at the 1957 Moscow Conference.[3] His basic thesis—that the total strength of the forces of socialism had surpassed that of the imperialists—was actually a reiteration of the view he and other Chinese leaders had asserted since 1946:[4] that the Soviet victory over the Axis powers and the victory of the CCP over the KMT in China had shifted the world balance of forces in favor of the communist camp. Mao's analysis of the balance of forces stressed ideological, political, and economic factors, not only military ones. Because this affirmation of the supremacy of the socialist bloc coincided with the launching of the first Soviet sputnik, most foreign observers misinterpreted Mao's speech and subsequent Chinese

[3] Excerpts from Mao's speech are in *Comrade Mao Tse-tung on "Imperialism and All Reactionaries Are Paper Tigers"* (Peking: Foreign Languages Press, 1963), p. 35.

[4] Cf. "Talk with the American Correspondent Anna Louise Strong," in *Selected Readings from the Works of Mao Tse-tung*, pp. 281–284; also Mao's speech and that of Chou En-lai at the Third Session of the First National Committee of the Chinese People's Political Consultative Conference, Oct. 23, 1951, in *New China Forges Ahead*, pp. 4–5 and especially p. 11.

pronouncements on the same theme. It was commonly assumed that the Chinese were demanding Soviet adoption of a strategy of military force against the imperialists, and that Peking indiscriminately advocated communist-led revolutionary struggles in the colonial and newly independent countries of Asia, Africa, and Latin America.[5]

Subsequent Chinese actions and statements proved that Peking was, indeed, urging a more militant strategy to counter the American attempt to destroy neutralism and to reverse communist gains in the Afro-Asian countries. Nor was there much doubt that the Chinese tried to force the Soviets to adopt a strategy which would concentrate the efforts of the socialist camp to support the crumbling CPR position in Asia. The Chinese urged that this struggle should not take the form of war initiated by the socialist countries but a determined readiness to oppose the Americans when they intervened in the internal affairs of socialist states (for example, in China's relations with Taiwan and Tibet) or independent countries or when they attempted to suppress national liberation movements in the colonial world. From the Chinese viewpoint, the motivation behind the call to action was defensive, not offensive; the major power which was making it perfectly clear it would not accept peaceful coexistence, neutralism, or noninterference in the affairs of other countries was none other than the United States.

On the question of peaceful coexistence, therefore, the dispute with Moscow was essentially over the Chinese insistence that this principle could not be applied to relations between "oppressed and oppressors" (that is, to liberation movements struggling against imperialism). Nor could the doctrine become the "general line" of all communist parties, irrespective of national conditions or arrival at the stage of violent conflict with the capitalist order.

[5] Zagoria, pp. 152–171; Alice L. Hsieh, *Communist China's Strategy in the Nuclear Era* (Englewood Cliffs, N.J.: Prentice-Hall, 1962); A. M. Halpern, "Communist China and Peaceful Coexistence," *China Quarterly*, 2 (July–Sept. 1960), 16–31.

On the other hand, Peking made no calls for revolution in countries which were friendly to China, including some of the capitalist partners of the United States.

Peking temporarily accepted the Soviet definition of peaceful coexistence, which became the version stated in the 1957 Moscow Declaration. She did this only because that version also reaffirmed the principles China had earlier pledged would govern her relations with Asian-African states.[6] Indeed, if the genuineness of the communist states' commitment to peaceful coexistence was in doubt in late 1957, it was owing to Soviet intervention in Hungary and Poland, not to aggressive actions taken by China. Peking's principal external activity in 1956 and 1957 was the development of a diplomacy of friendship and negotiation with neutralist Asian neighbors, most of which were dominated by military elites—hardly the behavior of a reckless or revolutionary radical.

For the sake of Sino-Soviet unity, which might yet be preserved through future negotiations, the basic issues that had been raised in 1956 and 1957 were papered over with formulas intended to conceal Moscow's and Peking's increasingly divergent foreign policies. After the Moscow Conference, however, China attempted to alter the course on which the Soviet Union was set by proceeding down a different path herself. In effect, Peking tried to redirect the communist powers' international line.

China's own policies after 1957 made it clear that she welcomed collaboration with bourgeois states and leaders who actively opposed the United States. Peaceful coexistence with all

[6] However, in a November 10, 1957, memorandum circulated to communist delegations at the conference, the Chinese objected to the declaration's emphasizing only the possibility of peaceful transition rather than a formula admitting the possibility of both violent and peaceful seizure of powers. The Chinese contended that thus the communist parties would retain flexibility. See "Outline of Views on the Question of Peaceful Transition," in *The Polemic*, pp. 105–108.

friendly or neutral states was still highly desirable, and genuine neutralism in the Cold War would be respected. And there was no call for revolution by Peking in independent countries clearly outside the American-controlled orbit. But China did try to heighten the militancy of the communist states and parties by increasingly more verbal encouragement of all types of struggles she asserted to be anti-imperialist. On the state-to-state level, more emphasis was put on strengthening political ties with any of those states which, like China, were threatened by, or opposed to, United States policies. Post-1957 Indonesia was a prime target for China's new attempt to revise the socialist camp's international aims and commitments. A major political upheaval was taking place in Indonesia about this time. The course of its development soon led to a closer identification of foreign-policy interests by Peking and Djakarta.

The 1958 Indonesian Rebellion

In February 1958 dissident military commanders in Sumatra and Sulawesi (Celebes) rebelled against the central government of Indonesia.[7] The rebellions followed a series of internal crises that started late in 1956, which demonstrated Djakarta's inability to control regional insubordination. The usurption of authority by certain regional military commanders was motivated by local opposition to Djakarta's policies toward the outer islands. To a lesser, but not unimportant, extent the rebellions stemmed from mounting fears among conservative Moslem and army circles over the Ali cabinet's friendly ties with the PKI, Russia, and China. As a result of its inability to assert control over the rebels, the Ali government resigned in March 1957. It was the end of

[7] A good account of the 1958 regional rebellions is in James Mossman, *Rebels in Paradise: Indonesia's Civil War* (London: Jonathan Cape, 1961); also Herbert Feith's chapter "Indonesia" in George McT. Kahin, ed., *Governments and Politics of Southeast Asia* (Ithaca: Cornell University Press, 1964), pp. 262–265.

Indonesia's ill-fated attempt to deal with the condition of the country's sprawling regions and to unite divisive political forces by means of borrowed but inapplicable Western institutions.

The collapse of the parliamentary order quickly led to political chaos. President Sukarno filled the void, backed up by the army, which, in March 1957, he endowed with martial law authority. Under the previous regime the Masjumi and PSI parties had attempted to shunt Sukarno aside as a figurehead president. He had always rejected this conception of his presidential role, however, and continued to use his great prestige and influence with the elite and the masses to force the political parties to take him into account; on occasion he decided major policy issues by directly intervening in the political process.

Sukarno had never been enthusiastic about the parliamentary system, believing it to be unsuited to Indonesian conditions and characteristics. Hence he was not sorry to see the experiment in democratic government fail. As early as 1956 he had begun to call for a different form of democracy, *demokrasi terpimpin* (democracy with leadership, or "guided democracy") and to argue that it was time "to bury the political parties" whose idea of "fifty-percent plus one democracy" was not in harmony with traditional Indonesian methods of decision-making.[8] These traditions, which Sukarno excelled at manipulating, tended to emphasize mutual help (*gotong-rojong*), consensus (*mufakat*), and collective deliberations (*musjawarat*). On the other hand, these methods were inappropriate for the highly contentious style of combat Sukarno perceived to be characteristic of Western democratic processes.

Despite his antipathy toward the parliamentary system, Sukarno, like many others in the Indonesian elite—including

[8] See Sukarno's speeches of October 28 and 30, 1956, in Antara, same dates, and Ministry of Information, *Indonesia, Pilihlah Demokrasimu jang Sedjati* (Indonesia, Choose Your Own True Democracy) (Djakarta, 1956).

many members of the officer corps who shared his views—went along with the experiment in parliamentary democracy. He took a stand against the 1952 "October 17 Affair," an attempt by dissident army officers to win his support in a coup to topple the Wilopo cabinet, and he backed the anticommunist policies of the earlier Hatta and Sukiman cabinets.[9] But he began to withdraw his support from the parliamentary system when it became clear that the wrangling political parties were going to reject his ideas and leadership but were themselves unable to galvanize the nation for a campaign to force the Dutch out of West Irian.

Ever since negotiations with the Netherlands broke down on this issue, in late 1951, Sukarno had repeatedly insisted that Indonesia's energies must be focused on the struggle for West Irian. He had supported the pro-American Sukiman government largely because its policies emphasized this struggle, even though Sukarno's own anti-imperialist ideology favored a neutralist Indonesian position on Cold War issues. Except for the left wing of the PNI, the only political party which shared his conception of national priorities was the PKI, and this fact heavily influenced the post-1952 rapprochement between Sukarno and the Indonesian communists. After 1956 the PKI was also the only major party which supported his call for a new political system to replace Indonesia's discredited constitutional democracy.[10]

In backing Sukarno, the PKI hoped to gain greater influence within his government and, ultimately, to improve its long-range

[9] Feith, *Wilopo Cabinet*, pp. 109–136, and *Decline of Constitutional Democracy*, pp. 46–224.

[10] On Sukarno's relations with the Indonesian communists, see Donald Hindley, "President Sukarno and the Communists: The Politics of Domestication," *American Political Science Review*, 56 (Dec. 1962), 915–926; Herbert Feith, "Dynamics of Guided Democracy," in Ruth T. McVey, ed., *Indonesia*, pp. 336–342; and Ruth T. McVey, "Indonesian Communism and the Transition to Guided Democracy," in A. Doak Barnett, ed., *Communist Strategies in Asia: A Comparative Analysis of Governments and Parties* (New York: Praeger, 1963), pp. 148–198.

prospects for taking power. These prospects, of course, most alarmed the other political parties and the anticommunist circles in the country. On one hand, these elements were not themselves greatly grieved to see the parliamentary order collapse, since the electoral route to power for the PKI was now clearly foreclosed. On the other hand, once many of the lucrative spoils of office were lost, the corrupt and poorly organized noncommunist parties would be at a serious disadvantage vis-à-vis the PKI. Unlike its rivals, the PKI was not dependent on the spoils system that Indonesia's parliamentary democracy provided to mobilize political supporters. There was, therefore, great fear among domestic and foreign anticommunist circles that the Indonesian communists would be the principal beneficiaries of guided democracy, unless the PKI could somehow be excluded from, or contained within, the new political order. While Sukarno was negotiating with other political leaders how to keep the PKI from becoming too powerful in a government under guided democracy, two events occurred which profoundly altered the course of Indonesia's internal political evolution and Sukarno's attitude toward the great powers.

On November 30, 1957, Moslem fanatics, who appear to have been associated with dissident army officers and Masjumi leaders, attempted to assassinate Sukarno.[11] When, two months later, the outer-island rebellions erupted and their leaders sought assistance from the West, Sukarno drew the not unnatural conclusion that some sort of conspiracy existed between certain Western countries and the rebels to depose or kill him.[12] Much under-

[11] For the factors and events leading up to the rebellion, see George McT. Kahin's chapter on Indonesia's postrevolutionary government, in Kahin, ed., *Major Governments of Asia* (Ithaca: Cornell University Press, 1958), pp. 557–572; and Daniel S. Lev, *The Transition to Guided Democracy: Indonesian Politics, 1957–1959* (Ithaca: Cornell Modern Indonesia Project, 1966), pp. 11–43.

[12] See, for example, Sukarno's speech of April 3, 1958, which ex-

emphasized by most commentators on the Sukarno era, these two events played a critical role in generating the deepening suspicion and hostility the Indonesian president subsequently displayed toward the West, especially the United States and Britain. The rebellion and assassination attempt also played an important part in the genesis of Sukarno's decision to seek the support of the PKI for his internal policies while he turned to the Soviet Union and China for the aid he needed to carry out an independent, nationalistic foreign policy.

The day before the assassination attempt the United Nations General Assembly voted to reject Indonesia's petition asking that the Netherlands be called upon to negotiate the status of West Irian. Sukarno carried out his threat to take "dramatic action" if the United Nations failed to act. In mid-December he ordered the seizure of Dutch property in Indonesia and expelled the more than forty thousand Dutch nationals in the country. The resulting political situation was of enormous advantage to the PKI. It responded to the crisis by staging mass demonstrations and by joining with PNI-dominated labor unions to seize Dutch property, thus pressuring the government to put nationalization measures into effect.[13] The PKI at last had the issue it desperately needed to become the mobilizing force behind Sukarno's militant policies and, in playing this role, ultimately to capture the leadership of Indonesia's resurgent anti-Western nationalism.

The anticommunists made their countermove on February 15, 1958, by forming a rival government on Sumatra. This action split Indonesia into two hostile camps. Although the army shared the rebels' concern about the alarming growth and influence of the PKI and Sukarno's apparent willingness to treat the communists as a bona fide nationalist party, it was not prepared to

---

plicitly connects the rebellions with foreign powers, in Ministry of Information, *Indonesian Students Meet the Challenge of the Times* (Djakarta, 1958).

[13] Kahin, *Major Governments of Asia*, p. 570.

side with dissident brother officers in actions that could destroy the country. Evidently, the rebels—and the American and Nationalist Chinese intelligence services which gave assistance to them—assumed that by raising the charge of growing communist influence on the government, the central military commanders in Djakarta would force Sukarno's downfall or at least a reversal of his policies. This assumption might have proved correct if it had not been for the fact that once the external powers behind the rebels had been exposed the army high command saw the possibility of intervention by Western capitalist nations as a more immediate threat to the state than were the Indonesian communists.[14]

Officially, the United States announced that it had adopted a "neutral" position on the Indonesian civil war. From the beginning, however, Secretary of State Dulles made it quite clear that Washington's sympathies lay with the rebels.[15] In

[14] In 1956, the United States declined to sell the Ali government arms and munitions it had requested in order to be able to deal more firmly with internal-security problems. Fear that the arms might be used to promote Dutch withdrawal from West Irian was the official United States explanation for this decision, but many Indonesians believed that the United States possibly did not want the government equipped to crush rebellions. This suspicion was heightened when the 1958 rebellion occurred; many of those involved were anticommunists desirous of closer ties to the United States.

[15] Speaking before the House Foreign Affairs Committee, Dulles said there was "a fair chance" that the Indonesian rebellion would bring a "curtailment of the trend toward Communism." He commented, "We [the United States] would be very happy to see the non-Communist elements who are really in the majority . . . exert a greater influence" in Indonesia. Sukarno's "so-called guided democracy theory," Dulles said, was a "nice sounding name for what I fear would end up to be a Communist despotism" (New York Times, March 9, 1958). For statements affirming the neutrality of the United States, see Secretary Dulles' press conference statements of February 11, April 18, May 1, and May 20, 1958; texts in Department of State, Bulletin, May 3, 1958, p. 334; April 28, 1958, pp. 684–685; May 19, 1958, p. 808; June 9, 1958, p. 946.

early March 1958, American ambassador to Indonesia John Allison, a man moderately disposed toward Sukarno, was replaced—apparently because he disagreed with the emerging American plan to aid, covertly, the rebellion. As soon became evident, what Secretary Dulles meant by "neutrality" was, in fact, public encouragement by the United States of the rebels' efforts to unseat Sukarno. A March 13, 1958, SEATO Council communiqué, obviously pointing to the events in Indonesia, referred to the "particular danger arising from some noncommunist governments' failing to distinguish between the aims and ideals of the free world and the purposes of international Communism."[16] Shortly thereafter, as the Indonesian army began to send forces to put down the rebels in Sumatra, units of the United States Seventh Fleet arrived off the coast, ostensibly to stand by to protect any American nationals and property which might be threatened by the civil war. To many Indonesians, however, the presence of the United States Navy smacked of "gunboat diplomacy"[17] and a veiled threat of possible intervention in their domestic affairs.

That threat became a reality when Chinese Nationalist arms were flown to the rebels via American bases in the Philippines. One of the rebels' aircraft, an American-made B-26, was later shot down and its American pilot, Allan Pope, was captured, complete with papers and documents connecting him with the United States military command on Okinawa. Washington's complicity in the rebellion not only became an international news item; it completely backfired when the Indonesian army failed to turn against Sukarno, as the United States had hoped it would.

[16] SEATO Council final communiqué, in Department of State, *Bulletin*, March 21, 1958, p. 504.

[17] This phrase was frequently used by Indonesian government officials and political leaders interviewed by the writer in 1961. Even then, three years after American intervention had ceased, the incident was well remembered and evoked strong feelings.

In the light of this failure the United States was obliged to withdraw its support of the rebels, for it had become clear that the intervention was undermining American relations with the army, the major political force Washington had decided to back in Indonesia. Although the outer-island revolt did not completely end until 1961,[18] the withdrawal of American support, moral and material, quickly sealed the fate of the resistance. The United States did not thereafter seriously attempt to mend relations with Sukarno. Rather, Washington continued to regard and to aid, openly and covertly, the Indonesian army as the main force that could be relied on to curb the PKI's influence and prevent the implementation of Sukarno's nationalistic policies. Consequently the intervention of the United States in the civil war did not have the therapeutic effect it might otherwise have had on American policy in Indonesia. And, of course, the failure of the United States to make amends reinforced Sukarno's suspicion that Washington still had not abandoned the aim of eventually overthrowing him.

China's Response to the Rebellion

The 1958 Indonesian rebellion thus not only hurt American policy but also put Peking in a position, for the first time, to invite active Sino-Indonesian cooperation in the struggle against American imperialism. The failure of the rebellion dealt a heavy blow to the anticommunist elements in Indonesia, and it brought to the fore, in the person of Sukarno, the leading exponent of militant struggle against the Dutch for control of West Irian. This issue could now be linked to China's own struggle for the removal of the American presence in Taiwan. American intervention in the Indonesian rebellion had created a real imperialist threat that Djakarta could see for herself.

[18] On the collapse of the rebels' cause, and the Indonesian army's skillful efforts to bring them back into the republic, see Herbert Feith and Dan S. Lev, "The End of the Indonesian Rebellion," *Pacific Affairs,* 36 (Spring 1963), 32–46.

China's response to the Indonesian crisis took the form of timely diplomatic and material support to Sukarno. She promptly condemned the March 13 SEATO communiqué as an attempt by the "Manila bloc" to interfere in Indonesia's internal affairs.[19] In an exchange of notes on April 17, 1958, Chinese political support was backed up by a sixteen-million-dollar credit to Djakarta for rice and textiles.[20] On May 15, a CPR government statement directly linked American intervention in Indonesia to the major theme of Peking's policy toward Djakarta, the need to heighten anti-imperialist unity between the two countries. The May 15 statement drew attention to the fact that "China's territory of Taiwan" was being used by the United States and her agents "the Chiang Kai-shek clique" to sustain the rebellion in North Sulawesi (the rebels' position in Sumatra had collapsed earlier). This American-directed activity was seen as designed "to subvert the lawful Indonesian government . . . to suppress the Indonesian peoples' movement in defense of their national independence and against imperialism and thus to shackle the Indonesian people again with colonial rule." Moreover, the broader aim of the United States was "to deal a blow to the resurgent national independence movements in Asia and Africa." Such action "not only constitute[d] an open provocation to the Indonesian people but also a serious challenge to the principles adopted by the Bandung Conference."

In an effort to stress the parallel interests of China and Indonesia, the May 15 statement said it was now necessary "to emphasize the gravity of the situation" resulting from the U.S. use of Taiwan to conduct "interference in Indonesia" and that the continuance of this development "will inevitably give rise to very dangerous consequences." The statement pledged "further assistance . . . as may be requested by the Indonesian government" and called for "the support of the Asian and African

[19] "CPR Government Statement on the SEATO Council Session," March 10, 1958; *Peking Review*, 1 (March 18, 1958), 22–23.

[20] NCNA (Peking), March 25, 1958, April 17, 1958.

peoples and all countries and peoples . . . " to aid the Indonesians in their defense of "national independence and against
U.S. intervention."[21]

Although not evidently reported at the time, the present
writer was told by Indonesian Foreign Ministry officials that
Peking also offered to send "volunteers" at Djakarta's request.[22]
If true, Peking was no doubt aware that giving this kind of
assistance was not really feasible, as it involved transport over
waters controlled by the United States Seventh Fleet. Since it
also seems clear that Djakarta certainly would have had no need
or intention of asking for Chinese military assistance, the purpose
behind the Chinese gesture, if it was made at all, must have
been largely to demonstrate solidarity with Sukarno. Its possible
impact is hard to calculate. At the least it must have been sin-
cerely appreciated by a leader who believed that the world's
strongest power, the United States, was trying to depose him.

Peking and Sukarno

An important precondition for the later alliance with Sukarno
was thus established by Peking's support during the critical period
of the Indonesian rebellion. In the years since 1949 communist
China's evaluation of the Indonesian president had undergone a
complete transformation. Because of his role in suppressing the
PKI at Madiun and because he was a member of the leadership
that had accepted Indonesian independence under the Nether-

[21] "CPR Government Statement on United States Intervention in
Indonesia," Peking Review, 1 (May 20, 1958), 19–20.

[22] Interviews with representatives of Indonesian Foreign Ministry,
June–July 1961. The offer was made in order to deter further Taiwan
intervention and, therefore, in the expectation that Washington might
also rethink its policy toward Djakarta if Peking would gain from an
unsuccessful rebellion. Chou En-lai reportedly reiterated the offer of
"volunteers" in August 1958 at a reception in the Indonesian embassy
(Asian Recorder, 3 [Aug. 17, 1958], 2225).

lands-Indonesian Union, Sukarno was initially regarded as a "lackey of imperialism." He had been a major factor in the rise of the Sukiman cabinet, and he had made no effort to obstruct the latter's anticommunist campaign or its feud with the Chinese embassy.

During the years immediately following Indonesia's achievement of independence Sukarno had also warned the local Chinese not to side with the communists, for the very sound reason that if a social revolution ever took place in the country, it would immediately become a racial conflict as well.[23] As later events were to demonstrate, he proved to be quite accurate in that prediction. Despite his anticommunist record Sukarno was never afflicted with the racist attitudes toward the local Chinese commonly shared by nearly all segments of the Indonesian elite. And it evidently took the leaders in Peking several years to understand that most Chinese in Indonesia regarded him as the leading, perhaps the only, source of protection in an otherwise hostile environment.[24]

Sukarno displayed other characteristics which did not easily fit into the communist stereotype of bourgeois-democratic man. Although he had already shown by his handling of the Madiun uprising that he would crush the communists if they threatened the republic, he regarded the major Western powers as the most serious and immediate external threats to Indonesia's independence. Nor could his opposition to colonialism be readily explained in Marxist terms—that is, as a function of his bourgeois class background, which made him, ultimately, an agent of aspir-

[23] For examples of Sukarno's early speeches warning the communists and the local Chinese, see Antara, November 10, 1951, and Aneta, August 20, 1951.

[24] This feeling was expressed in all the interviews the writer had with local Chinese, irrespective of their political views, wealth, or status. It was even true of KMT supporters who much disliked the trends in Indonesia and blamed Sukarno for many of them, but did not associate him with the racist attitudes expressed by others in the native elite.

ing native capitalism. Sukarno's deep belief in the need for harmony among Indonesia's diverse peoples placed him squarely in opposition to any notions of violent class struggle, but he was far from being an admirer or advocate of capitalism. If he ever actually had a coherent economic ideology, it was probably a concept of a form of welfare-state socialism—which should evolve slowly and protect the class status of the Indonesian feudal elite.[25]

In any event the main problems that concerned Sukarno were not economic but political: how to solidify the Indonesian nation, focus attention on the West Irian issue, and contain the destructive rivalry among the Islamic, communist, and secular nationalist political parties. He welcomed the PKI's support of his stand on the Irian question, and he was not alarmed by the prospect that the communists might be strengthened by his association with them. A single speech by him in September 1948 had brought down on the PKI a massacre of such proportions that the communist movement was virtually exterminated. And he was well aware that all the guns in Indonesia were in the hands of an army that would cheerfully exterminate the PKI again whenever he gave the word. In effect, he knew he held the Indonesian communists' death sentence in his pocket[26]—and so did they. The possibility that the PKI might again attempt to seize power during his lifetime appears never to have figured prominently in Sukarno's worries. His troubles, as he saw them, derived from the need to deal with the anticommunists who had all those guns, who doubted the wisdom of his attempt to fuse nationalism, Islam, and communism, and who had powerful friends in the West anxious to see that Sukarno's ideas failed.

[25] See the "Political Manifesto," speech of August 17, 1959, in Ministry of Information, *Political Manifesto, Republic of Indonesia* (Djakarta, 1959), pp. 27–85; and his *Marhaen and Proletarian* speech of July 3, 1957, trans. Claire Holt (Ithaca: Cornell Modern Indonesia Project, 1960).

[26] This was the impression George Kahin received during interviews with Sukarno in 1954 and 1955 (*Major Governments of Asia*, p. 541).

Exactly when Sukarno's potential as a progressive anti-imperialist nationalist began to play a prominent role in Chinese policy toward Indonesia is difficult to determine. The PKI clearly realized the significance of the positions Sukarno was taking on both foreign and domestic affairs as early as 1952, for from that time on the party aligned itself squarely behind him.[27] The fact that China did not publicly give any attention to Sukarno before 1956 may have been owing to the expressed wish of the PKI, which may have believed that for China to do so might tarnish the image Aidit was carefully trying to create of the PKI as a genuinely national communist party completely independent of the Soviet Union and China. But it is more likely that Peking's belated appreciation of Sukarno's potential in Indonesia and in the Afro-Asian world developed only after it became clear that his power was increasing, and only after Peking—not the PKI—was prepared to believe he would try to assert Indonesia's independence from the United States. There is some indication that Peking first began to take Sukarno seriously shortly before the 1955 Bandung Conference. After a visit of CPR Vice-Chairman Soong Ching-ling to Indonesia, Peking invited Sukarno to make an official state visit to the CPR.

The context of his October 1956 visit to China appears to explain much of its impact on Sukarno. It took place during a world tour which first included visits to the United States and the Soviet Union. By neither country was he particularly well received or favorably impressed. The timing of the China trip was politically significant, too, because the decline of Indonesia's constitutional system was by then far advanced, and Sukarno was already acting like a powerful president rather than a figurehead. Shortly before arriving in Peking he demonstrated his increasing sense of power by single-handedly negotiating an aid

[27] Donald Hindley, *The Communist Party of Indonesia, 1951–1963,* pp. 255–274; McVey, "Indonesian Communism and the Transition to Guided Democracy," pp. 162–180.

agreement with the Soviet Union without the prior approval of the Ali cabinet, the formal repository of such authority at that time.[28]

In press statements before his arrival, Peking credited Sukarno, in somewhat exaggerated terms, with a major part in "all the important achievements of Indonesia."[29] She praised him "for promoting peace in the Asian and African regions," for making "outstanding contributions to the victorious struggle of the Indonesian people against colonial rule," and for his "determined stand to maintain national solidarity." Singled out for emphasis was a speech Sukarno had made earlier that year in the United States, where he had said, "We will labor in our land and jungles with bare hands rather than exchange any part of our freedom for any aid."[30] Peking evidently considered this an indication that Sukarno was serious about insisting on Indonesia's independence from the United States. Because of his recent record, it was not surprising that his visit was hailed in Peking as "an event of paramount importance in the friendly relations and cooperation between China and Indonesia."[31]

The visit to China had a profound effect on Sukarno, much greater than the Chinese leaders might reasonably have expected. What he observed in China reinforced his beliefs that parliamentary democracy was wrong for Indonesia and that it was

[28] Indonesian-Soviet joint statement, Sept. 10, 1956. See Willard A. Hanna, "Moscow Comes to Bung Karno—and So Does Peking," *Newsletter of the American University Field Staff,* 5 (Nov. 30, 1956).

[29] Shortly before his arrival, Peking announced the publication in Chinese of Sukarno's selected speeches that had emphasized themes of anti-imperialism and Afro-Asian solidarity. This indicated the CPR's recognition of his growing importance as an anti-Western leader (NCNA [Peking], Sept. 26, 1956). No other Indonesian leader of that time, not even PKI chairman D. N. Aidit, had been accorded similar recognition.

[30] *Ibid.*

[31] *Jen-min Jih-pao,* Sept. 30, 1956.

possible, as China had shown, to achieve national unity and economic progress and stability. These dominant impressions were evident in a statement he made to correspondents accompanying him on the tour. Obviously thinking about the Indonesian domestic situation, he said that in China he had seen the practice of "democracy under leadership" and that only this form of leadership could "bring the people a real, just and prosperous new world."[32]

Such observations seemed to imply that to modernize Indonesia it might be desirable to adapt some of the techniques and methods Sukarno had seen in the CPR. Of course, since "every nation had its own special features, its own characteristics, its own orbit and its own individuality," Sukarno felt constrained to say also that he saw his country moving toward "socialism corresponding to the national characteristics of Indonesia."[33] There was not much doubt, then or later, that the Indonesian "socialism" he envisaged did not provide for a dictatorship of the proletariat or the overthrow of the native bourgeois elite. Nevertheless, Sukarno seems to have been genuinely impressed by the possibility that the techniques of mass mobilization on behalf of constructing a nation and achieving unity that he had seen in China might somehow be adapted to a noncommunist Indonesia.

When Sukarno unveiled his conception of guided democracy a few months later, in February 1957, he seemed to be consciously striving to articulate his idea of the role he could perform in Indonesia's modernization equivalent to that of the Chinese Communist party—a combination of leader, energizer, and organizer of a society in revolution. An essential difference, of course, was that Sukarno hoped to perform this role by relying

[32] *Harian Rakjat,* Oct. 17, 1956.
[33] Speech by Sukarno at the Joint Session of the Standing Committee of the National People's Congress and the National Committee of the Chinese People's Political Consultative Conference, Peking, Oct. 4, 1956 (NCNA [Peking], Oct. 5, 1956).

on traditional Indonesian methods of persuasion and compromise, rather than on the highly structured and disciplined controls employed by the Chinese Communist party. The most notable proposals Sukarno made in his 1957 guided-democracy formula—inclusion of the PKI in the cabinet and the formation of an advisory national council composed of various functional groups[34]—were for an amalgamation of heterogeneous elements that would result in a structure altogether different from the "people's dictatorship" under the leadership of the CCP. But the form of the new institutions he proposed may very well have been influenced by his earlier impressions of democracy-with-order in China.

Well before the train of events set in motion by the 1958 Indonesian rebellion, therefore, a convergence of interests and attitudes was gradually developing in the relationship between Peking and the Indonesian president. Whether on foreign or domestic issues, the stands Sukarno was taking after 1957 were the kind the Chinese leaders had hoped the Bandung policy would help the noncommunist leadership of the Afro-Asian states to develop. Indeed, post-1957 Indonesia, under Sukarno's leadership, seemed like one of the few bright prospects for building an anti-imperialist united front anywhere in the Third World.

In their subsequent eagerness to support Sukarno's nationalistic foreign policy, however, it is not at all clear that the Chinese sufficiently realized the political obstacles to any alignment between Indonesia and the CPR. Djakarta's conflicts with the Western powers were certainly propelling the two powers together on anti-imperialist issues; but domestic trends in Indonesia after 1958 were pushing them in opposite directions. The reemergence of the thorny issue of the Chinese resident in Indonesia and the rising powers of the Indonesian army were manifestations of the actual fragility of the Peking-Sukarno relationship.

[34] See Feith, "Dynamics of Guided Democracy," pp. 319–320.

One of the important political dividends Peking received from the 1958 rebellion was the total destruction of the Kuomintang position in the Indonesian Chinese community, a victory for Peking that her own efforts theretofore had been unable to achieve. As a consequence of Nationalist China's assistance to the rebels in 1958, Djakarta banned all pro-Taiwan Chinese newspapers and associations, confiscated the commercial enterprises and banks run by Taiwan supporters, and arrested or deported many Chinese known to be or suspected of being Kuomintang sympathizers.[35] These actions left Peking the only source of external protection to which the Chinese in Indonesia could turn. On the other hand, the crushing of the KMT supporters created a precedent for similar measures against the pro-Peking Chinese in Indonesia. Since 1956 the indigenous native entrepreneurial class had been demanding that the government take stronger measures to break the hold of the Chinese traders, and few Indonesian merchants made any distinction between the Peking- and Taipei-oriented Chinese.[36] These demands had such widespread popular support that it was by no means certain that Sukarno could politically afford to resist calls for nationalization measures against the CPR nationals, even if he was otherwise inclined.

[35] A general discussion of these events is V. Hanssens, "The Campaign against the Nationalist Chinese in Indonesia," in B. H. M. Vlekke, ed., *Indonesia's Struggle, 1957–1958* (The Hague: Netherlands Institute of International Affairs, 1959), pp. 56–76.

[36] This has been called the "Assaat Movement." Assaat was a former Minister of the Interior in the Natsir cabinet who had a prestigious political background. Actually, the main force behind these economic demands was the All-Indonesian Congress of National Importers (KENSI), at whose 1956 convention in Surabaja Assaat delivered a bluntly anti-Chinese keynote address. For details, see Feith, *Decline of Constitutional Democracy in Indonesia*, pp. 481–487. To capture the real flavor of Indonesian anti-Chinese racism, however, it is necessary to read A. J. Muaja's pamphlet, *The Chinese Problem in Indonesia* (Djakarta: New Nusantara, 1958).

The political class which benefited most from the suppression of the Nationalist Chinese followers was not, however, the native capitalists but the Indonesian army. As in the case of the earlier confiscation of Dutch assets, the nationalization of KMT-Chinese property actually resulted in bureaucratic capitalism for the domestic officer class. The army managed nearly all the larger enterprises which had been seized, and it had the determining voice in deciding who should run many of the smaller ones as well. This practice, common during the period after 1957 when the army had martial-law powers, expanded during the later period of the so-called guided economy. The resulting spoils-through-nationalization which accrued to politically well-placed army officers—confiscated homes, extorted money, "managerial" salaries, automobiles—were among the main economic lubricants of the system created by Sukarno's radical nationalism and the army's power.

As the principal beneficiary of Indonesia's groping search for state capitalism, the army naturally had a strong interest in the early confiscation of the as yet untouched assets of the Peking-oriented Chinese. The fulfillment of its desire awaited only the appropriate pretext for action. Again, owing to the delicate nature of Sukarno's political relations with his generals, it was by no means certain that he could prevent, or would necessarily want to prevent, them from taking over the remaining Chinese enterprises in order to advance their own economic interests. Any future threat to the economic position of the CPR Chinese was, therefore, certain to strain the Peking-Sukarno relationship unless communist China was prepared to acquiesce in the kind of mistreatment of her own nationals that had been inflicted on those of Nationalist China and the Netherlands.

Nor was it entirely clear that China's developing policy of support for Sukarno was advantageous to the Indonesian communists. So long as Sukarno needed the PKI as an instrument to arouse the masses and counterbalance the real repository of power in the country, the army, the communists might be allowed to expand their organizations. The PKI could expand, however, only if it made no demands which seriously challenged the regime's authority and programs. Guided democracy was not intended, by either Sukarno or the army, to lead to radical reforms or to a social revolution but, rather, to shore up the existing system and to restrain and suppress any forces advocating fundamental changes harmful to the vested interests of the conservative Indonesian elite.[37] Because of the power realities of the situation, the PKI had no real alternative, other than a suicidal one, to going along with Sukarno's makeshift bourgeois-feudal system, meanwhile hoping and working for political opportunities that might somehow enable the communists to capture the leadership of the Indonesian nationalist movement somewhere down the road.[38]

The similarities between the position of the PKI under Sukarno after the 1958 rebellion and that of the CCP during the 1923 to 1927 period of collaboration with the KMT are obvious. And, from the record after 1958, it is equally obvious that by this time Peking had made an appraisal of the Indonesian situation that was similar to Stalin's appraisal of China in the mid-1920's: the PKI was not yet a strong force; the Indonesian revolution was still in an early bourgeois-democratic stage. Hence the correct line for the PKI was a policy of collaboration with the anti-imperialist Indonesian elements (for example, Sukarno) for the purpose of acquiring leadership of the national united front. This was the only realistic course of action open to the PKI at the time. It also complemented China's post-1957 foreign-policy strategy, which centered on efforts to create an anti-imperialist united front between communism and nationalism in the Third World. To

[37] The theme of the Indonesian elite's interest in Sukarno's system is developed in Lev, *The Transition to Guided Democracy.*

[38] McVey, "Indonesian Communism and the Transition to Guided Democracy," pp. 167–189.

further this policy, friendship and support for the anti-Western, nationalist regime of Sukarno were regarded by Peking as necessary and possible. Whether this analysis could be the basis for a viable Chinese policy in Indonesia was soon to be severely tested.

6

Chinese Policy at the Crossroads: The Overseas Chinese Dispute and Sino-Soviet Rivalry in Indonesia

Because of the promising developments that had occurred between 1955 and 1958, the course of China's relations with Indonesia appeared to be headed toward an era of growing cooperation and harmony. Although the political stability of Sukarno's new regime was by no means assured, it had put down a foreign-backed anticommunist rebellion and had evidenced no inclination to drive the PKI underground. No issues had yet arisen to threaten the increasingly cordial diplomatic ties between the two states; indeed, Djakarta seemed bent on expanding contacts with all the socialist countries. The essentially fragile nature of the Sino-Indonesian relationship, however, became all too apparent in the three years after 1959. During this period several basic aims and interests of the two powers came into sharp conflict; consequently, the central premise of China's diplomacy—that her policy should be based on continuing collaboration with the Sukarno regime—was questioned.

The most serious and immediate source of conflict was the sudden re-emergence of a dispute over the legal and economic status of the Indonesian Chinese minority—an issue which had seemingly been resolved by the 1955 treaty on dual citizenship. Relations between Peking and Djakarta were also strained, though more subtly and in a manner not so easily documented, by

Moscow's bid for influence in Indonesia, which began to unfold in 1960 and led to massive Soviet military aid in support of Sukarno's campaign to dislodge the Dutch from the disputed West Irian territory. Both developments resulted in a general rise in American and Soviet influence and the consequent near-collapse of Chinese influence in Indonesia. As a whole, the period between 1959 and 1962 was to demonstrate, beyond any reasonable doubt, that the guided-democracy system included powerful anti-Chinese and anticommunist groups which were largely beyond Sukarno's control and eager to destroy the developing pattern of Sino-Indonesian accord. Despite his anti-imperialist credentials, even Sukarno was to show that he was quite willing to curry favor with Russia and America in order to attain his domestic and foreign goals, although such manipulations might adversely affect the prospects for close ties with Peking. Overall, during this period, China's diplomacy in Indonesia was very much thrown on the defensive.

The events examined in this chapter constitute a major turning point in the evolution of Chinese policy. The analysis focuses on the interplay of two themes: (1) how the dispute over the Chinese minority and the rise of Soviet influence nearly destroyed Peking's position in Indonesia; and (2) how the adjustments China was obliged to make in order to salvage her influence affected the subsequent direction of her policies.

The Ban on the Chinese Traders

Two Indonesian government decrees in May 1959 precipitated the first major crisis in Sino-Indonesian relations: a Ministry of Trade regulation revoking the trading licenses of aliens in the rural areas by December 1959,[1] and a decree by the central army headquarters empowering regional military commanders to remove aliens from their places of residence for "security reasons."[2]

[1] SK Menteri Perdagangan Tanggal 14 Mei, 1959, No. 2933/M (Ministry of Trade Decree, May 14, 1959) (Djakarta, 1959).

[2] Pengumuman Penguasa Perang Pusat, No. Prt/Peperpu/039/1959

On the basis of the army decree, the military comander in West Java, Colonel Kosasih, issued a separate decree in August ordering all aliens in his district to evacuate the villages and move to towns and cities by December 1959.[3]

These measures appeared, in part at least, to reflect a concerted drive by the Indonesian government to use a sweeping economic reorganization program as the pretext for eliminating the local Chinese traders. In a major policy speech of August 17, 1959, Sukarno called for a complete "re-tooling" of the national economy. He announced that "all funds and all forces which have proved to be progressive," including "non-native forces and funds which have already settled in Indonesia," would be given "an appropriate place and opportunity" in the economy. On the other hand, "vulture capitalists of our own nation" and "foreign non-Dutch capital [which] illegally gives support to contra-revolution . . . or carries out acts of economic sabotage" would be crushed. The continuance of permission for the use of nonnative funds and forces, Sukarno insisted, was contingent on absolute obedience to Indonesian laws and regulations.[4]

This declaration indicated, beyond any doubt, that Sukarno intended or had agreed to make substantial changes in the economic position of the Chinese traders and that the May retail-trade ban had his approval. Unless Peking was prepared to rupture her carefully nourished relations with him she had not much scope for an effective policy of opposition on this issue

---

(Central War Administrator's Announcement, No. 039, May 12, 1959) (Djakarta, 1959).

[3] *Keputusan Penguasa Perang Daerah Swatara I Djawa Barat,* No. KPTS. 70/8/PPD/1959 (West Java War Administrator's Decree, No. 70), Aug. 28, 1959.

[4] "The Rediscovery of Our Revolution," address by Sukarno on Aug. 17, 1959, the anniversary of the proclamation of Indonesian independence. This speech became known as the "Political Manifesto," the major philosophical and ideological foundation of Indonesia's guided democracy (in Ministry of Information, *Political Manifesto, Republic of Indonesia,* pp. 27–85).

once Sukarno had publicly committed the government to this course of action. But the August 17 *Manipol* speech had given no indication that the residence of foreign-born Chinese might be the subject of arbitrary regulations. Hence the West Java commander's residence ban appeared to be, if not in flat contradiction to, clearly well beyond, the general guidelines Sukarno had laid down.

If implemented, the economic ban alone would completely nullify the Chinese interpretation of the 1955 treaty under which Indonesia had pledged to "protect the rights and interests" of the Chinese nationals. Implementation would also mean that Djakarta intended to take such measures without holding "consultations" with Peking, as provided for in the Dual Nationality Treaty. Thus the unresolved differences about the interpretation of Chinese "rights and interests" had at length come to the surface, with all the potential for conflict Peking and Djakarta had tried to paper over in the 1955 formula.

The decrees affecting the local Chinese were clearly an exercise of Indonesia's sovereignty in internal matters which the Chinese government could not legally contest. Moreover, when the measures were announced Djakarta was not bound, in any contractual sense, by the terms of the Dual Nationality Treaty, since that document was not yet a valid legal instrument. The CPR had ratified the 1955 treaty on December 7, 1957.[5] But at the time of the 1959 bans the Indonesian parliament had not ratified it; hence, the treaty was not in force. The reasons for this Indonesian delay explain a great deal about the origins of the dispute over the status of the Chinese living in Indonesia and Peking's role in it.

Although it had gone to the trouble of negotiating the treaty, after 1955 the Indonesian government began to have second thoughts about the wisdom of the decision. Except for the Ali

[5] Announced in *Jen-min Jih-pao*, Dec. 7, 1957.

cabinet, which was removed from the scene early in 1957, the treaty had very few supporters. Conservative elements in the political parties raised numerous objections to it, mainly on the grounds that, if its provisions were carried out, there would still exist an overly large alien minority in Indonesia and, consequently, that Peking's unwanted influence in the country was likely to increase.[6]

More important opposition to the treaty came from native capitalists, who in 1956 began a major campaign demanding discriminatory legislative measures against the Chinese traders. Naturally, the native entrepreneurial class did not want a treaty that would create legal obstacles to future attempts to weaken the economic position of alien competitors.[7] Its views had powerful support in the government after 1957 since, in the era of "guided economy," civilian and military bureaucrats alike were well disposed toward the idea of nationalizing and expropriating foreign assets in the country. For these elements the problem was that in 1959 Djakarta was encumbered by a treaty which, in principle but not in law, pledged Indonesia to protect the interests of the alien Chinese minority. Indonesia wanted to rid herself of the consequences of that pledge. The retail-trade ban, therefore, was Djakarta's first step toward unilaterally scrapping the 1955 treaty with China so that she might be free to attack the economic position of the resident Chinese.

Implications of the Anti-Chinese Measures for Peking's Policy

The Peking government was not only in a poor position to argue that a valid treaty had been violated; it was also hard put

---

[6] For an analysis of Indonesian reactions to the treaty see Willmott, *The National Status of the Chinese in Indonesia*, pp. 48–50.

[7] The relevant historical data on the increasingly strong anti-Chinese activities among the native entrepreneurial class after 1956 is examined by Feith, *The Decline of Constitutional Democracy in Indonesia*, pp. 481–487.

to defend the interests of petty capitalists in Indonesia, because of the fate of private enterprise in People's China. For a brief period Peking did try to circumvent the logic of her own socialistic programs by arguing that, unlike the big foreign oil companies—which Djakarta's decrees did not touch—the Chinese traders in Indonesia were a progressive economic force in the country. But it soon became clear that the defense of overseas Chinese capitalism was only a secondary objective of the Chinese leaders' decision to risk a rupture of relations with Djakarta over the status of their nationals.

The real irritant was the West Java commander's residence ban, which, if carried out under the umbrella of restricting alien domination of retail trade, would result in the uprooting of tens of thousands of Chinese from their homes and their moving to towns and cities, where taking up a new life would be a very painful experience. Moreover, the army's ban served a broader and distinctly anticommunist purpose. In May 1959 the army had begun to harass various PKI organizational activities in a search for pretexts to prevent or disrupt the party's forthcoming Sixth National Congress.[8] It was apparent to Peking that certain elements in the army—encouraged by the Americans—hoped to pick a quarrel with China over the Chinese minority in Indonesia which could be turned to the army's advantage in the domestic political struggle with the Indonesian communists. The army also did not like Sukarno's growing friendship with Peking and, by provoking an anti-Chinese campaign, hoped to create frictions between the two.[9] Obviously, more significant issues were im-

---

[8] On the army-PKI rivalry during this period see McVey, "Indonesian Communist and the Transition to Guided Democracy," in Barnett, ed., *Communist Strategies in Asia,* pp. 168–170.

[9] This appraisal of the army's intentions was frequently brought up by a number of knowledgeable Indonesian political observers in the course of interviews with the author in 1961.

plicit in the anti-Chinese measures than a rampant demand by the indigenous capitalist class for the elimination of alien domination over the rural economy. The Indonesian anticommunists actually were spoiling for an issue that could be turned, with a little luck, into a campaign leading to the suppression of the PKI, the abandonment of Sukarno's policies toward the communist powers, and the return of Indonesia to the Western capitalist fold.

The anti-Chinese bans had other threatening implications, but none of these dangers could really be avoided, or made to disappear, by adopting either of the two basic policy options open to Peking. Passive acceptance of the Indonesian decrees might avert an immediate rupture with Djakarta and might temporarily deprive the Indonesian army of the fight it was looking for. But would not the anticommunists create another incident? The other alternative was not much better. Since the West Java commander's ban exceeded the guidelines of Sukarno's generally more modest statement on nationalization policy, it was conceivable that a firm protest by Peking might produce a split in the Indonesian government that would end in the dropping or modifying of the residence decree. On the other hand, it was equally likely that outside pressure by Peking would have the effect of driving the army and Sukarno closer together.

A spirited defense of the Chinese living in Indonesia was almost certain to place many of them in a very difficult, possibly precarious, position; but to abandon them was tantamount to surrendering any future Peking claim to represent their interests and would be unacceptable on purely nationalistic grounds. The international consequences of a potential rupture with Indonesia could not have come at a more inopportune moment. The Sino-Soviet dispute was just becoming an open rivalry for power, with each contestant seeking the support and favor of the Afro-Asian states. China's ability to compete in this theatre of the struggle with Moscow had already been compromised by the

CPR's border conflict with India. An additional dispute with Indonesia was certain to undermine the whole concept of Afro-Asian unity against the West and to raise serious doubts, however unfounded, in the neutralist countries about the sincerity of China's commitment to peaceful coexistence and the Bandung principles.

By no means, however, would China's basic international interests be best served by a retreat in the face of Djakarta's blatantly discriminatory and humiliating measures. Peking certainly had not meant to convey at Bandung, or by her policy of accommodation and friendship with the Afro-Asian states, that agreements between her and any of them could be broken at will or that, merely to stay on good terms with her neighbors, she would not defend her national interests by protecting overseas Chinese. It was, in truth, by no means clear that retreat was the best way to prevent the issues raised in Indonesia from resulting in a conflict that would benefit the Indonesian anticommunists and Washington and Moscow as well.

Diplomacy and Intervention

The initial phase of the dispute was characterized by Chinese diplomatic efforts to secure the abandonment of the anti-Chinese measures before a crisis erupted. From the outset this attempt failed. More important, the behavior of the Chinese government revealed that the Peking leadership apparently did not see that it was faced with nothing less than an agonizing, unavoidable decision to sacrifice the overseas Chinese for the sake of larger policy interests. Because Peking tried to avoid making this choice, the dispute did indeed explode and nearly led to a complete diplomatic break.

On September 7, 1959, shortly after the West Java residence ban and Sukarno's *Manipol* speech, Peking privately protested the anti-Chinese measures and, at the same time, suggested that the two governments hold discussions as soon as possible.[10] Evidently, by means of "quiet diplomacy" Peking not only hoped to head off a rupture but also to conceal the seriousness of the issues involved from international attention. Indonesian Foreign Minister Subandrio flew to Peking, where he held talks with Chou En-lai and Chen Yi beginning October 7. At the conclusion of these talks a joint communiqué, issued October 11, suggested that the impending clash had been averted. Its key paragraph stated that both parties agreed that the "economic position of the Chinese nationals . . . may be affected in some ways" and that "an appropriate way should be sought [to solve the question] . . . in the interests of the economic development of Indonesia . . . and the proper rights and interests of the Chinese nationals [which] will be respected."[11]

Since, however, the communiqué in no way directly dealt with the main issue—what was to be done about the army's residence ban—it was clear that nothing substantive had been accomplished. In fact, Subandrio's visit had added more fuel to the fire. It was soon learned that he had been subjected to an intimidating session with an enraged Chinese leadership. According to George Kahin's interviews with Indonesian officials who had attended the meetings, Peking threatened, if Djakarta carried out the anti-Chinese decrees, to punish her by calling on Singapore's communist-dominated dock workers to boycott the handling of goods bound to or from Indonesian ports.[12] Subandrio

[10] The text of this note was never released, but a reference to it appears in Chen Yi's protest note of December 9, 1959. Officials of the Indonesian Foreign Ministry also confirmed to this writer that a note to this effect had been received and that it prompted Subandrio's mission to Peking.

[11] Joint Communiqué of Foreign Minister Subandrio and Foreign Minister Chen Yi, Oct. 11, 1959; in Indonesia Ministry of Information, *Special Release on Current Indonesian Affairs*, No. 80 (Djakarta, 1959).

[12] George McT. Kahin, "Malaysia and Indonesia," *Pacific Affairs*, 37 (Fall 1964), 253–270. See also the article by Dennis Bloodworth, who

made no concessions, as the communiqué's language confirmed, and returned to Djakarta to report the failure of his mission.

Peking's rough handling of Subandrio only strengthened Djakarta's determination to deal firmly with China, but the Sukarno government still hoped to avoid a showdown, though doubtless the army favored confrontation. Sukarno's desire to conciliate Peking, but without compromising the principle of internal sovereignty, was shown by the modified form in which the trade ban finally appeared. The version of the decree which became law November 16, 1959, exempted sixteen categories of Chinese traders or provided alternatives to outright confiscation.[13] Neither of these options had been provided for in the original May regulation. Similarly, Sukarno apparently exerted pressure on the West Java commander to modify the residence ban, for the final form of this ban when it was implemented, issued November 11, exempted those Chinese aliens who had applied for Indonesian citizenship before May 4, 1959.[14] Despite the failure of Subandrio's efforts in Peking it still seemed possible to avoid a major rift over the Chinese traders.

That slim hope vanished when, immediately after the Novem-

---

interviewed members of the Subandrio delegation shortly after their return from China, in *The Observer* (London), November 1, 1959.

[13] *Peraturan Pemerintah* (Government Regulation), No. 10, 1959 (Djakarta, 1959). The final version exempted those firms engaged in service trade and those which included one or more Indonesian partners. There were several alternatives to outright confiscation: compensation was promised; the firms could be transferred to cooperatives, sold to Indonesian nationals, or the entrepreneur could relocate his business in a town or city with the permission of the Ministry of Trade. Finally, the December 1, 1959, deadline was postponed to an indefinite time in 1960 to permit the Chinese sufficient time to make the necessary arrangements. See the statement by Prime Minister Djuanda, reported in *PIA* (Djakarta), November 24, 1959.

[14] Statement of the West Java War Administrator's Office, reported in Aneta, Nov. 11, 1959.

ber 11 modification of the army's residence ban, Colonel Kosasih began to expel forcibly all the Chinese traders in the villages of West Java. Even before it was amended, the original decree of the West Java commander had given the Chinese until December 29, 1959, to move out of the villages. The modified version of the residence ban said that they should prepare to leave, presumably before the December deadline. But Kosasih ordered them to evacuate at once, frequently with only overnight notice. When compliance was not immediate, the army personnel in charge of the operations literally threw hundreds of Chinese families into trucks and took them to hastily constructed relocation camps. Not infrequently, resistance met with harsh treatment.

Kosasih's forced-removal campaign openly contradicted the conciliatory gestures the civilian government had made toward Peking in modifying the retail-trade ban, and thus smacked strongly of an effort by the army high command to ignite a conflict with China. Apparently because of such an appraisal of the situation, Peking decided to respond by intervening directly. It must have hoped to force Sukarno to bridle his recalcitrant officers. Presumably, Peking reasoned that his interests were not served by the army's blatant provocation and that he was aware that the army's real game was, if possible, to turn the whole affair into a campaign against the PKI. Since the success of this provocative venture could only weaken the political balance between the anticommunists and the PKI which was the basis of Sukarno's power, Peking apparently thought the Indonesian president would have to oppose his generals.

As the only political group which had consistently opposed the main stream of Indonesian antipathy toward the resident Chinese,[15] the PKI was certain to be hurt by the dispute, whether

[15] For a general discussion of the historical and political factors behind the PKI's attitude toward the local Chinese minority, see Ruth McVey, "Indonesian Communism and China," in Tang Tsou and Ho P'ing-ti,

it decided to defend this minority—thereby isolating itself on an issue which had widespread popular support—or whether it abandoned the Chinese to racist forces—thereby causing a split between itself and the CPR. The Indonesian army evidently expected that Peking or the PKI would, by taking a stand in defense of the local Chinese, create an issue of alleged communist subversion which could be used as a pretext to ban the PKI. Since only Sukarno could overrule the generals, forcing his immediate intervention in the crisis necessarily had to be the main objective of Chinese policy.

As soon as the army's forcible removal of Chinese traders began, the Chinese embassy in Djakarta launched an extensive program of obstructive acts. Embassy personnel engaged in a series of forays into the West Java countryside, interposing themselves between the Chinese and the army officials at places where the evictions were being carried out. Meetings were arranged with local Chinese organizations, during which embassy personnel even went so far as to instruct Chinese nationals to disobey the army's orders. Printed instructions, evidently drawn up by the embassy, were sent to villages, ordering the local Chinese to stay in their places of residence until Peking could "solve the problem."[16]

These actions, of course, played directly into the army's hands.

---

ed., *China in Crisis* (Chicago: University of Chicago Press, 1968), II, 357–366.

[16] A copy of one such instruction fell into the army's hands, and it was promptly released to the news media. It read, in part: "If the fundamental human rights are violated and the personal property of the Overseas Chinese are confiscated, then the Chinese Government will protect the Chinese with all its power. So in this regard it is expected that the Overseas Chinese should not feel disturbed and remain in their places, because the Chinese Government will try to solve the problem with the Indonesian Government in a friendly way" (*New York Times*, Nov. 18, 1959).

The West Java commander promptly responded with a November 20 decree forbidding all members of the Chinese embassy to enter or stay in the region until further notice.[17] He released detailed reports to the Indonesian press of the Chinese embassy's interference, including documents the Chinese officials had issued instructing the Chinese residents to disobey the army's orders.[18] A number of Chinese nationals were arrested, and the army intensified its forced-removal campaign against the settlers.

The first phase of the confrontation had not resulted in Sukarno's intervention against the army. On December 9, 1959, Chen Yi appealed directly to the Indonesian government, urging "immediate consultations" to work out a settlement. To this end, he advanced a three-point proposal: (1) immediate ratification and implementation of the Dual Nationality Treaty so that those Chinese opting for Indonesian citizenship would be "entitled to the civil rights of Indonesia without discrimination"; (2) protection of Chinese nationals' "rights and interests"; and (3) assurance that Djakarta would permit the voluntary repatriation of those Chinese who now wished to return to China and would allow them "to sell their properties" and make other necessary arrangements for departure.[19]

The Chinese government, Chen Yi said, was particularly disturbed by the passive attitude of Djakarta toward the "forces bent on sabotaging the friendship between our two countries." He openly solicited Sukarno's intervention by stressing the contradiction between the Indonesian president's "repeatedly proclaimed policy of friendship toward China" and the provocative

---

[17] Text in Antara, Nov. 20, 1959.

[18] For details of the West Java War Administrator's reports on the Chinese embassy activity, see PIA, November 19, 21, and December 9, and Indonesian Observer, December 10, 1959.

[19] Full text in Peking Review, 2 (Dec. 15, 1959), 6–7, and Jen-min Jih-pao, Dec. 10, 1959.

acts of "some influential forces [i.e., the army] which dared so wildly to carry on disruptive activities against the friendship of our two countries."[20] From the contents of his note it was evident that Peking's basic grievance was not the retail-trade ban—Chen Yi did not demand that it be rescinded—but, rather, the army's forced removals of Chinese and its campaign to impair Sino-Indonesian relations. The note also showed that Peking hoped to protect some of her nationals by winning Indonesia's early agreement to ratify the 1955 treaty and that she was prepared to bring home those who no longer wished to stay in Indonesia. Thus a negotiating position had been staked out offering Sukarno a settlement on the terms he had stated in the *Manipol* speech, if only he would rein in the army which was making a compromise on the issues impossible.

Subandrio's reply of December 11 ended any hope that Sukarno would attempt to override the army. The Indonesian foreign minister agreed to an early ratification and implementation of the Dual Nationality Treaty and to assist the departure of those Chinese who wanted to leave the country. An accord on these questions, however, was not regarded as eliminating "the obstacles standing in the way of the realization of the [retail-trade ban] Presidential Decree No. 10/1959." Only if Peking would accede to this decree "could [Indonesia] protect without discrimination the rights and interests of the overseas Chinese."[21]

Subandrio was careful to avoid coming to grips with the real issue raised by Peking—the army's enforcement of the removal decree and its fanning of an anti-Chinese, anti-Peking campaign. His contention that acceptance of Decree No. 10 by China would provide the basis for a settlement could only have been a straw man, since he knew perfectly well that Peking was not using the Chinese embassy to obstruct the retail-trade ban, which applied

[20] *Peking Review,* 2 (Dec. 15, 1959), 7.

[21] Ministry of Foreign Affairs, Press Release No. P/52/59, Djakarta, Dec. 13, 1959.

throughout Indonesia, but only to oppose the army's forcible removal of Chinese families from West Java. The real, though unstated, message in Subandrio's note was that Sukarno would not be coerced by Peking into an open dispute with his generals over behavior that had widespread popular support. At this point it should have become apparent to Peking that the political repercussions of a potential confrontation with the army were more threatening to Sukarno's vital interests than was the deterioration of his relations with China.

Peking Calls the Overseas Chinese Home

After the failure of her attempt to force Sukarno's intervention on her behalf nothing further was to be gained by a policy of confrontation. A diplomatic retreat was now inevitable, since further friction could only harm Peking's overall position in Indonesia, endanger the Chinese community and the PKI, and benefit the Indonesian anticommunists. But the Chinese leadership evidently did not regard the situation as hopeless. Instead, it attempted to use what economic leverage it had to punish the Indonesian government, apparently believing that this would force Sukarno's hand.

On December 10, 1959, Peking launched a campaign to call the overseas Chinese back to the mainland. For several weeks thereafter Radio Peking beamed daily broadcasts urging the Chinese to return to the "warm bosom of the motherland," where they would have "excellent opportunities" for taking part in "socialist construction."[22] Fang Fang, vice-chairman of the Overseas Chinese Affairs Commission, declared that the CPR welcomed, not only those affected by the discriminatory Indonesian decrees, "but also all overseas Chinese who had difficulties or for some reason did not want to stay overseas." "We want none

[22] Radio Peking broadcast to Indonesia, Dec. 10, 1959. These exhortations to the overseas Chinese to return to the mainland continued for two weeks.

of our dear ones to suffer in foreign lands," he said, "and it [is] our hope that they will all come back to the arms of the motherland." He further declared that "the Chinese Government has decided to receive all returned overseas Chinese whether they were half a million, a million or several million."[23]

Although this call made no distinction between those who were affected by the 1959 decrees and those who were not, the Chinese embassy and consulates in Indonesia were instructed to do their recruiting primarily among those Chinese who had skills or trades useful for building socialism on the mainland. The departure of persons in this category would also do the most damage to the already shaky Indonesian economy. In a short time hundreds of Chinese carpenters, mechanics, electricians, teachers, and other skilled or semiskilled workers were induced to return to the mainland. The recruitment campaign was not limited to foreign-born (totok) Chinese but also extended to local-born (peranakan) Chinese with dual nationality, who otherwise might be eligible to take Indonesian citizenship.[24] Peking evidently wanted to demonstrate that she too could violate the 1955 treaty—whose provisions prohibited her from trying to influence Chinese who were Indonesian citizens—if Djakarta was prepared to act without regard to the spirit of the agreements.

As thousands of Chinese made ready to leave Indonesia, severe inflation struck the economy. Fearing the possibility of a general pogrom, members of the Chinese community began to hoard scarce consumer goods and to trade their local currency on the

[23] "Report on the Current Situation and Overseas Chinese Affairs at the Fourth Plenum of the First Committee of the All-China Federation of Returned Overseas Chinese," Ta Kung Pao, Dec. 20, 1959; trans. in Survey of China Mainland Press (SCMP), No. 2164 (Dec. 28, 1959), 13–15.

[24] A number of overseas Chinese, both supporters and detractors of the Peking government, told the writer this was the policy of the CPR embassy during the early phase of the dispute.

black market for foreign exchange deposited in Singapore and Hong Kong. A steep rise in the price of all locally available goods was the immediate effect; this harmed the native Indonesians much more severely than the Chinese.[25]

Toward a Settlement of the Overseas Chinese Dispute

From the course of the dispute until late December 1959 two facts had become clear. Djakarta had shown she could disregard Peking's objections and ruthlessly uproot the Chinese minority from their homes and deprive them of their livelihood in the villages. On the other hand, Peking was proving that simply by calling home certain elements of the Chinese community she could inflict serious damage on the Indonesian economy. It seems that the Chinese hoped this war of attrition would soon cause Djakarta to modify her stand. Evidence of this hope is the fact that Chen Yi, in a note of December 24, 1959, again indicated China's desire to settle the dispute by compromise.

[25] There has been a popular conviction in Indonesia, shared by every government since independence, that the Chinese community's role in the economy is wholly an exploitive one. Like the Dutch, however, the Chinese performed many crucial economic functions the Indonesians had not learned, and showed no particular interest in learning, to perform themselves. Because skilled Chinese played a key role in the processing and marketing of Indonesia's exports, notably rubber, tin, oil, and copra, their departure was a heavy blow to the foreign-exchange-earning capabilities of the economy. After 1960, a major reason why Indonesia's foreign exports continued to decline steadily was the loss of these skilled Chinese. Similarly, the small Chinese traders were the basic source of credit for the farmers in the villages and provided the only efficient mechanism whereby the produce of the countryside reached the cities and consumer goods flowed back to the villages. Some Indonesians hoped the 1959 decrees would replace this system with local cooperatives. But after the Chinese were driven out the cooperative movement never got off the ground. Where cooperatives were established they did not prove to be efficient or to result in higher prices for the farmer's produce or lower prices for what he had to buy.

In this note the Chinese foreign minister called on Djakarta to join in establishing a joint committee to negotiate the various problems involved in the repatriation of the Chinese nationals and to implement the Dual Nationality Treaty speedily.[26] Indonesia responded favorably to these proposals, and on January 20, 1960, instruments of ratification were exchanged in Peking, bringing the treaty into force.[27] A joint committee was established to work out methods of implementing the treaty.[28] However, no compromise was reached on the principles that would govern the repatriation of the Chinese who wished to leave Indonesia. Instead Peking was again forced to accept Djakarta's very harsh terms. The Indonesian government flatly rejected any notion of negotiations with the CPR on the terms of repatriation, holding that Chinese would be permitted to leave solely in accordance with Indonesian laws and regulations.[29] The practical effect of this ruling was that those who departed did so virtually penniless. Djakarta denied them compensation for their confiscated property and prevented them from leaving the country with their capital and personal belongings.[30]

[26] Complete text in NCNA (Peking), Dec. 25, 1959.

[27] *Jen-min Jih-pao,* Jan. 20, 1960.

[28] *Ibid.*

[29] Letter of Foreign Minister Subandrio to Chinese Foreign Minister Chen Yi, Jan. 23, 1960 (*PIA,* Jan. 27, 1960). The CPR's proposals for settling the repatriation questions appear in Chen Yi's notes to Subandrio, in NCNA (Peking), Dec. 25, 1959; and *Jen-min Jih-pao,* Dec. 28, 1959, March 17, 1960. For Indonesia's negative response, see text of Subandrio's replies in Antara, January 27 and March 30, 1960.

[30] The departing Chinese found Indonesian exit regulations exceedingly harsh. They were allowed to take with them such clothing and household belongings as they could carry by hand and no more than thirty dollars per person in foreign exchange. An exception was made in the case of those leaving by commercial ships; they were permitted to purchase foreign-exchange currency up to the amount of their fare (interviews at Indonesian Ministry of Foreign Affairs, Aug. 21, Sept. 3, 1961).

By May 1960 some 40,000 Chinese were gathered in Indonesian ports awaiting passage to China.[31] Before the dispute ended the total number who ultimately left swelled to 119,000.[32] Four ships of the CPR's very small merchant fleet plied back and forth between the mainland and the islands in the unprofitable trade of bringing the Chinese home.[33] Although several thousand returnees had useful skills, the vast majority were old or middle-aged and usually had a background in trade; they would be of little economic use and could not easily accommodate themselves to social conditions in mainland China. Since the recruitment campaign by Peking had been directed toward enlisting the young and the skilled or semiskilled, it seems reasonable to assume that the huge numbers of older and nonskilled working people who applied for repatriation were both unexpected and unwanted. In any event, by early 1960 it was becoming clear that the effort to punish Indonesia was also involving prohibitively high economic and social costs for the CPR. About April 1960 the Chinese embassy dropped the recruitment campaign and quietly began to urge other potential repatriates to stay in Indonesia.[34]

[31] NCNA (Canton), June 9, 1960.

[32] Interviews at Indonesian Department of Immigration, June 23, 1961. According to these sources, approximately another seventeen thousand repatriated to Taiwan.

[33] Most of the departees, however, bought passage on commercial ships to Hong Kong. There they were put on trains and transported to the CPR.

[34] This was freely admitted by a number of Chinese nationals oriented toward Peking whom this writer interviewed in 1961. According to them, Chinese families and friends in Indonesia began to receive letters from the newly arrived repatriates in China urging those still in Indonesia to postpone any plans they had to return to China, because the situation was not yet favorable for them to return, and they should remain in Indonesia unless this was really impossible. Similar appeals came from the Chinese embassy through the local overseas-Chinese associations. The embassy let it be known that it preferred the Chinese to stay in Indo-

The fact that Peking was belatedly reversing her stand was officially conveyed by Chou En-lai's report to the second session of the National Peoples' Congress on April 10, 1960. Peking's premier placed the dispute with Indonesia in a broad political context that included much more than the immediate difficulties. He said that China's peaceful foreign policy had "stood the test of time" despite the schemes of "U.S. imperialism" in conjunction with "reactionaries, revisionists and their followers in various countries [which were] causing temporary commotion." The efforts of these elements to "prevent the spread of China's influence and to isolate China in international affairs" had failed, however. Referring to the specific case of Indonesia, Chou En-lai declared that a "good start" had been made in solving the repatriation problem—although of course it had not—and that now "a reasonable all-around settlement of the overseas Chinese question [could] be arrived at."[35]

The continuing obstacle to an early settlement of the dispute was much more candidly identified by another speaker at the congress, the Overseas Chinese Affairs Commission's vice-chairman, Fang Fang. He depicted the anti-Chinese movement in Indonesia as "part of the Cold War scheme by U.S. imperialism . . . to infiltrate the countries of Southeast Asia and strangle the national democratic movement in the area; a handful of bourgeois elements" (i.e., the Indonesian army) was using anti-Chinese measures "to undermine the patriotic democratic forces in their own country [i.e., Sukarno and the PKI] to pave the way for achieving military dictatorship."[36] There was little of the con-

---

nesia until better conditions obtained on the mainland. At the same time, the Chinese were told that one day the CPR would make a home for all of them.

[35] "On the Current International Situation and China's Foreign Relations," *Peking Review,* 3 (April 12, 1960), 7–9.

[36] NCNA (Peking), April 10, 1960.

ciliatory spirit in this speech that had characterized Chou En-lai's remarks, but the two speeches made reasonably clear what Peking was trying to say to Djakarta and to whom the message was directed. In effect, Sukarno was being told that by quietly backing down on all the major issues, Peking was trying to settle the dispute, and that if the conflict was not speedily brought to an end, only his generals, and the Americans who were behind them, would profit from continuing Sino-Indonesian discord.

Far from helping to end the dispute, Fang Fang's scarcely veiled attack on the Indonesian army added more fuel to the fire. A strong protest note from the Indonesian embassy in Peking promptly followed his speech.[37] The Indonesian army, for its part, began to step up the campaign to remove the Chinese settlers from West Java, thus reviving the main issue, which had subsided somewhat after the negotiations on implementing the Dual Nationality Treaty earlier in January. Two other regional army commanders on April 27 forcibly evicted the Chinese consuls in Selatpandjang (Sumatra) and Samarinda (Borneo) for allegedly interfering in the army's handling of the Chinese who were being repatriated from these areas. After a strong Chinese protest on May 13 against these acts,[38] the Indonesian government backed up the army by demanding the recall of the two consular officials.[39] There was another strong protest from Peking. By this time the dispute appeared to be fully heated up, and the two nations seemed on the verge of an open diplomatic break.

Despite the unintended assistance it was receiving from Peking,

[37] Antara, April 13, 1960.
[38] "Chung-hua jen-min kung-ho kuo ta-shih-kuan shou-yin-jen te sheng-ming" ("Statement by the Spokesman of the Embassy of the People's Republic of China"), May 13, 1960; English text in Antara, May 13, 1960.
[39] Text of Indonesian protest notes in Ministry of Foreign Affairs, Press Release No. P/27/60, Djakarta, May 19, 1960.

the Indonesian army's efforts to inflame the dispute—now clearly successful—suddenly collapsed as a result of its own overzealous enthusiasm. On July 3, 1960, two Chinese women in Tjimahi (West Java) were killed by soldiers when they resisted being forcefully evicted from their homes.[40] This time the West Java command had gone too far. Provoking the CPR as part of the anticommunist game was one thing; wantonly killing innocent Chinese citizens was an entirely different matter. The long and futile effort of Peking to force Sukarno's hand finally achieved its goal as a result of the actions of the Indonesian army itself. No official document exists which indicates exactly when and how Sukarno overruled the generals, but the cessation of forced removals soon after the "Tjimahi Affair" could not have been the work of anyone else.[41] Characteristically, the rebuke to the army was delivered with the subtle, indirect Sukarno touch: Colonel Kosasih, the commander in West Java and the main instrument in the army's (and probably the Americans') campaign to rupture relations with China, was soon transferred to Central Sumatra—but he was later promoted to general.

Although Sukarno had no intention of criticizing the army in public, after Tjimahi he left no doubt that he wanted an immediate end to the rift with the local Chinese and Peking. In his address to the nation August 17, 1960, Sukarno again declared that all "non-native funds and forces" would be given an appropriate place in Indonesia, provided they served a "progressive" purpose that was in conformity with the government's program. But he now urged that for the sake of the national economic pro-

[40] Text of CPR protest note in *News Bulletin,* No. 43/1960 (Djakarta: Cultural and Information Office of the Embassy of the People's Republic of China in Indonesia, July 4, 1960).

[41] This was the construction placed on the episode by most Indonesians the writer interviewed in 1961. The Indonesian specialist Herbert Feith has reached the same conclusion. See his chapter "Indonesia" in George McT. Kahin, editor, *Governments and Politics of Southeast Asia,* p. 267.

gram no groups in the country should do anything to harm "an atmosphere of cooperation."[42] Although the previous atmosphere of Sino-Indonesian diplomatic concord was not formally restored until Foreign Minister Chen Yi visited Indonesia in April 1961, nine months later, by August 1960 the overseas-Chinese issue was dead.

In view of the great political damage, as well as human suffering, the Chinese might have incurred if the anticommunist elements in Indonesia had won their game, Peking's losses in the conflict were comparatively small. Though her position was weak throughout the dispute, her policy in Indonesia was not crippled in 1959 and 1960. The rift did not become a completely disastrous diplomatic rupture for two reasons: China steadily retreated on all the major points at issue; and the army eventually so overplayed its hand that Sukarno was compelled to intervene. Peking did not win the struggle for Sukarno's support; the anticommunists lost it.

Although the dispute did not come to an end until July 1960, following Sukarno's response to the Tjimahi killings, it is clear that Peking had already decided the previous April to shift from confrontation to accommodation. The evidence supporting this conclusion is quite strong: first, the steps taken by the Chinese embassy to discourage further repatriation; and second, Chou En-lai's conciliatory statements at the National People's Congress indicating that China's stance of peaceful coexistence had withstood the temporary disturbances in relations with Indonesia caused by the imperialists and their reactionary followers. These occurrences of April 1960 seemed to be the result of an attitude that was in marked contrast to the posture of confrontation Peking had adopted prior to that time. While the change in the Chinese attitude undoubtedly reflected hopes for a smooth repa-

[42] *Like an Angel That Strikes from the Skies: The March of Our Revolution* (Djakarta: Ministry of Information, 1960), p. 30.

triation process and a speedy implementation of the dual-citizenship treaty, these hopes were not the ultimate source of the shift in Peking's policy toward Djakarta in April 1960. A close examination of other issues confronting Chinese policy makers at this time indicates that Peking altered her stand on the overseas-Chinese dispute primarily because it had come into conflict with more important objectives in Indonesia.

Peking-Moscow Rivalry and the Sino-Indonesian Dispute

Because the costs of protecting the overseas Chinese were at the expense of achieving other goals, there was ample reason why Peking should have abandoned her defense of them well before April 1960. It had been clear since December 1959 that the Chinese embassy's interventionist and obstructive tactics would not force Sukarno to bridle the army but would only drive the two together. Moreover, in failing to stop anti-Chinese repression by exerting extreme diplomatic and economic pressure, Peking showed how really weak her leverage was in Indonesia. The long-term effect of this test of strength would, naturally, be to encourage the Indonesian anticommunists and their American backers to believe that provoking China was politically safe and profitable.

Peking's militant defense of the overseas Chinese also certainly worked to the disadvantage of the Indonesian communists, and presumably she did not wish to compromise or antagonize them. Whatever the amount of contributions by local Chinese to the PKI's coffers,[43] they were not likely to increase or to be freely

---

[43] Donald Hindley, who has done the most extensive analysis on this question, concludes that the local Chinese business community was the "main source" of nonparty contributions (*The Communist Party of Indonesia,* pp. 117–118). Kahin and Feith, leading scholars on Indonesia, agree. See Kahin's chapter, "Indonesia," in his *Major Governments of Asia,* p. 599; and Herbert Feith, *The Indonesian Elections of 1955* (Ithaca: Cornell Modern Indonesia Project, 1957), pp. 27–28.

given in the future once it was clear, as the dispute was proving, that any ties the Chinese in Indonesia might have with communism on the mainland were potentially quite dangerous. Furthermore, the inflation and commodity shortages that resulted when Peking called home the overseas Chinese hurt the PKI's worker and peasant supporters far more than other classes; indeed, the whole affair was advantageous only to the Indonesian army.

There is some evidence that the PKI and Peking differed on the principles involved in the dispute over the Chinese residents of Indonesia and on how it should be handled. The PKI Politbureau's carefully worded statement of November 22, 1959, had taken a position midway between those of Peking and Djakarta. It strongly protested the army's forced removal of Chinese in West Java, charging that such action was in violation of the guidelines Sukarno had presented in the *Manipol* speech, and it asserted that right-wing elements were attempting to destroy Sino-Indonesian friendship. But the Politburo had accepted without question the right of the Indonesian government to implement the retail-trade ban, and it did not echo the Chinese allegation that both measures violated the 1955 treaty's provisions concerning prior consultations with Peking.[44] Because the Indonesian army's anti-Chinese campaign presented Peking and the PKI with an essentially common danger, the possibility that they differed over how to respond to it should not be blown out of proportion. It is important to bear in mind, however, that although the PKI repeatedly criticized the army's behavior after November 1959 and, editorially at least, befriended the local Chinese, it did not defend Peking's attempted intervention by means of the Chinese embassy or endorse her proposals for resolving the crisis.

Logically, since the PKI was the real target of the army's provocations, its leaders had a very strong desire for an early

---

[44] Text in *Review of Indonesia*, Nov.–Dec. 1959, pp. 3–5.

termination of the dispute, even at the expense of the local Chinese and injury to Peking's prestige. It seems equally clear that in deciding to press the defense of their nationals in Indonesia, the Chinese leaders were willing to risk the prospect that the PKI might, as a result, be seriously harmed. That Peking would assign the PKI this low priority reveals a great deal about the primary objectives of Chinese policy at this time and the basic assumptions underlying it.

From whatever standpoint Peking chose to view the matter, the welfare of the Indonesian Communist party in 1959–1960 could only be a distinctly secondary consideration in the formulation of Chinese policy. That party had, in fact, become an increasingly less important political force as a result of its steady domestication under the Sukarno regime.[45] His government, by canceling the general elections scheduled for 1959, had simply destroyed the PKI's excellent prospect of becoming the largest party in parliament and thereby exerting some influence on the government. Thereafter the Sukarno regime demanded that all demonstrations and other political activities in support of radical causes be channeled through officially sponsored agencies, which were almost exclusively presided over by the Indonesian army.

The PKI's collaboration with the Sukarno regime certainly found no critics in Peking, which was doing precisely the same thing. Insofar as tactics were concerned, discord between the Indonesian and Chinese parties probably stemmed from the Indonesian comrades' ideas and programs for building a domestic united front. PKI policy on these issues must have raised serious doubts in the Chinese leaders' minds about this party's ability to become a genuinely strong political force in Indonesia in the near future. By 1958 the PKI's electoral strength approximated

---

[45] On the increasingly narrow scope for PKI activities during the early years of Guided Democracy see Ruth McVey's excellent analysis in "Indonesian Communism and the Transition to Guided Democracy," pp. 148–195.

that of each of the rival PNI and Moslem parties, and its labor, youth, and women's organizations were already large and rapidly expanding.[46] But the party remained essentially an urban-based organization dominated by intellectuals and trade-union members. Primarily because the Sukarno government, in effect, co-opted many of their political and organizational activities in the cities, the Indonesian communist leadership did not make a serious effort to organize in the countryside until late in 1959.[47] This delay must have been regarded as a cardinal error by the Chinese communists, who believe that the mobilization of peasant support is the decisive precondition for the survival and expansion of a revolutionary movement in colonial and semicolonial countries. The PKI's failure to attempt to mobilize the peasantry before 1959 was not entirely the result of necessity. Basically, the PKI opted to concentrate in the cities on the false assumption that legal-political struggle would be permitted by the bourgeois regime if the party acted according to the rules of parliamentary democracy. In following this strategy consistently from 1951 on, the PKI showed quite clearly that it was not much impressed by the relevance of Chinese theories and experience to the Indonesian situation.

While it is reasonable to assume that the Chinese communists thoroughly disagreed with the rationale behind their Indonesian comrades' slighting of the peasantry, this issue, by itself, was unlikely to strain relations between the two parties greatly. Other considerations apart, urban-oriented communist parties following the peaceful "parliamentary-road" strategy had no difficulty staying on good terms with Peking. In any event, China was in no position to insist that these groups should adopt a Maoist-type program if it was not suitable, since to do so would

[46] For details of the organizational growth and structure of the PKI from 1951 to 1960 see Hindley, pp. 61–230.
[47] McVey, "Indonesian Communism and the Transition to Guided Democracy," pp. 177–179.

have weakened her own contention that there should be no "great-nation chauvinism" in the movement. A stronger source of CCP disenchantment was the PKI's drift toward the Soviet camp and its endorsement of Soviet policies in Indonesia—policies which increasingly appeared to be motivated by the desire to undermine the CPR.

As the leading specialists on Indonesian communism have pointed out, after 1956 the Aidit group skillfully used the Sino-Soviet dispute to assert the autonomy and influence of their own party in the international communist movement. However, on the key issues raised in the polemics before 1963, the PKI's position was much closer to that of Moscow than of Peking.[48] There were very good reasons why the Indonesian communists should have been favorably disposed toward Soviet policy, despite its increasingly anti-Chinese overtones. Since 1956, Djakarta had been receiving sizable Soviet economic aid, and prospects were very bright that even more would be available in the future. Soviet assistance to a regime might be useful to local communist parties, because in some instances it acted as a deterrent to the suppression of leftists by the recipient government, while it also served to bolster the national prestige of communist parties. In January 1960, at the height of the Peking-Djakarta dispute, Khrushchev visited Indonesia and extended a $250,000,000 credit to the Sukarno government. This action, warmly applauded by the PKI, greatly helped to shore up Djakarta's economic position at the very moment of the dispute over the Chinese residents of Indonesia when Peking was trying to weaken it.

Actually, the 1960 aid deal was only the first step in a bold Soviet bid to displace Peking and Washington from their faltering positions. It heralded a new phase of great-power competition

---

[48] See the discussion of the PKI's position in the Sino-Soviet dispute in Donald Hindley, "The Indonesian Communists and the CPSU Twenty-second Congress," *Asian Survey*, 2 (March 1962), 20–27; and McVey, "Indonesian Communism and China," pp. 369–377.

in Indonesia, set in motion by a massive Soviet military-aid program in support of Sukarno's campaign to wrest West Irian from the Dutch. The PKI was enthusiastic about Moscow's post-1960 bid to establish a political-military beachhead in Indonesia; moreover, its pro-Soviet stance in the communist movement suggested that it did not disapprove of the main objective of Soviet policy in Indonesia: to undermine the influence of China.

In light of this background of a developing Soviet challenge and considerable evidence of the PKI's tacit support of it, the fundamental reasons for Peking's April 1960 shift to an accommodation with Djakarta on the issue of the Chinese in Indonesia becomes more intelligible. The sequence of events suggests that China's sudden retreat was motivated less by a realization that she could not prevail than by her appreciation of the important international threat to her interests posed by the Soviet Union. If Peking was to find a way to check the alarming growth of Moscow's influence on Djakarta, a speedy termination of the overseas-Chinese conflict was essential. This interpretation is supported by the fact that Chou En-lai had explicitly mentioned the "revisionist" (i.e., Soviet) plots to undermine Sino-Indonesian relations in his conciliatory statements of April 10. But more revealing, on April 16, Peking released "Long Live Leninism!"; this major ideological broadside precipitated the phase of open rivalry with Moscow for leadership of the communist parties and for influence in the Afro-Asian anti-imperialist movements.[49] The decision to fling an open challenge to the Soviet Union led to the subordination of a bilateral Chinese policy in Indonesia to the broader policy required by the struggle among the great powers.

When Sukarno finally brought his generals under control in July 1960, the stage seemed to be set for the improvement of relations between Peking and Djakarta. But this development

[49] *Hung-ch'i*, 8 (April 16, 1960).

did not immediately help to curb the threat to China of rising Soviet influence in Indonesia. Actually, the end of the dispute with China freed Sukarno to announce, on August 17, 1960, his campaign to seize West Irian.[50] It later became clear that he was determined to engage in this venture with Moscow's military aid unless the Dutch yielded to Indonesia or were induced to yield by Washington's diplomatic pressure. In 1961 and 1962 over a billion dollars' worth of Russian arms, including modern aircraft and warships, were delivered to Indonesia. Indonesia thereby became the strongest indigenous military power in Southeast Asia at that time, while the Soviet Union, by virtue of the extensive training programs and advisory missions it set up, was in a position to exert further influence on the Sukarno regime. The Soviet Union, whatever its motives—to forestall suppression of the PKI, to turn Indonesia against both China and the United States, or eventually to create forward military bases in the Pacific—seemed to be encouraged by Sukarno's West Irian campaign to attempt a limited but nonetheless provocative strategy in Southeast Asia. This interpretation gains plausibility when it is recalled that the Soviet arms deal with Indonesia resembled Russian maneuvers in the Middle East and Latin America at this time.[51]

In the end Sukarno did not have to put his Russian-equipped forces to the acid test of carrying out an attack against the Dutch —a showdown it was by no means certain the Indonesians could have won. The United States, as alarmed as China by the Soviet penetration of Indonesia, exerted diplomatic pressure on the Netherlands to accept a face-saving formula that gave West Irian to Djakarta as 1962 drew to a close. Unlike its predecessors, the Kennedy administration could see that Indonesia's incorporation

[50] *Like an Angel That Strikes from the Skies*, pp. 38–46.

[51] For details of the arms deal and an interpretation of Soviet intentions in Indonesia during this period see Guy J. Pauker, "The Soviet Challenge in Indonesia," *Foreign Affairs*, 15 (July 1962), 612–626.

of the disputed territory was in the long-term interest of the United States, especially since American policies aimed at strengthening anticommunist elements abroad and protecting American businesses and investments. Thus the timely diplomatic pressure that the United States brought to bear on the Dutch not only checked Djakarta's dependence on the Soviet Union but also helped to increase the good will many Indonesian leaders, including Sukarno, still felt for the United States despite its blunders in the 1950's.

The emergence of Moscow and Washington as the principal beneficiaries of the resolution of the West Irian dispute did not severely set back Peking's position in Indonesia, though it appeared to at the time. It was true that the Moscow-Djakarta weapons deal greatly strengthened an Indonesian army that had already shown its eagerness to provoke Peking and the PKI, and consequently the Indonesian right-wing elements might in the future feel more emboldened to launch an anticommunist campaign or even to depose Sukarno. On the other hand, most of the new Soviet weapons went to Indonesia's navy and air force, which were actually more amenable to Sukarno's influence than was the army. Among the most important, though long-range, political consequences of the arms deal, therefore, were a further diffusion of power and a magnification of frictions within the Indonesian military establishment. Presumably, Peking understood that the weapons Indonesia had acquired also made her an anti-imperialist force to be reckoned with, particularly if Sukarno's radical anti-Western brand of nationalism continued to hold sway in the country. For the Chinese leaders, therefore, much depended on how Sukarno would use his new military power and whether the possession of these arms would weaken or strengthen his independence of Moscow and Washington.

The evidence points to the conclusion that Peking decided Sukarno would not allow himself to become a client of either the United States or Russia and, therefore, that it was possible

Chinese Policy toward Indonesia

to improve relations with him, even at the very height of Djakarta's rapprochement with China's enemies. Foreign Minister Chen Yi's visit to Indonesia in April 1961 thus seems to mark the onset of yet another Peking effort to woo Sukarno. He officially expressed China's satisfaction with the joint committee's formula for implementing the Dual Nationality Treaty, invited Sukarno to visit the CPR, and offered to supply economic aid for the new Indonesian development plan.[52]

During Sukarno's second visit to Peking in June 1961, Chinese newspapers hailed the "heartening developments [that] have taken place in the friendly relationship between our two countries."[53] CPR Chairman Liu Shao-ch'i went out of his way to express strong confidence in Sukarno, saluting him as having "all along been devoted to the great project of the bridge of friendship between China and Indonesia."[54] China's confidence in the Indonesian leader soon proved to be well justified. At the Belgrade conference of nonaligned nations in September 1961, Sukarno advanced the doctrine of the struggle between the "newly emerging" and "old-established" forces, an idea almost identical to that expressed in Peking's call for the Afro-Asian countries to unite against the big industrialized Western powers. The Indonesian president was praised by the Chinese for his strong anti-imperialist stance on most of the international issues raised at the conference, particularly for his opposition to Nehru's attempt to dampen criticism of the Western powers.[55] Although

[52] "Chen Yi fu tsung-li wai-chiao pu-chang tsai kao-pieh yen-hui shang ti chiang-hua" (Speech at Farewell Banquet for Vice Premier and Minister of Foreign Affairs Chen Yi), Djakarta, March 31, 1961, in *News Bulletin*, Special Issue, April 20, 1961, p. 13. See also *Jen-min Jih-pao*, April 4, 1961, and *Peking Review*, 4 (April 7, 1961), 6–10.

[53] *Ta Kung Pao* (Peking), June 13, 1961.

[54] Speech welcoming Sukarno to China, June 13, 1961; in NCNA (Peking), June 13, 1961.

[55] For example, see the Chinese article in NCNA (Djakarta), Septem-

this conference was held well before the renewal of heavy fighting between China and India on their common frontier, it had already become clear that Sukarno's was the voice Peking wanted to hear in the Afro-Asian world. In October 1961, the CPR extended Indonesia a credit of thirty million dollars for machinery and technical assistance in building textile mills and factories[56]— evidence that Peking regarded Sukarno as an anti-imperialist in good standing and, in view of his Belgrade declaration, considered his rapprochement with the Soviet Union and the United States by no means stable or permanent.

While the relationship with Sukarno had improved by 1962, the distance between Peking and the PKI had, if anything, grown wider. Throughout the period in which Russian arms were fueling the West Irian campaign, the Aidit leadership continued to take an essentially pro-Soviet position regarding the widening ideological rift in the international communist movement.[57] The PKI did not join Moscow in the condemnation of Albania at the CPSU Twenty-second Congress in October 1961, but that was because it perceived this issue as one that affected the national autonomy and self-determination of communist parties rather than one that required being pro-Moscow or pro-Peking. On the other hand, at the same congress the PKI praised the Russian party's "Program for the Development of Communism," a document the Chinese ridiculed as sheer "revisionism."[58] When Stalin was vilified at the congress, Aidit upheld the right of the Soviet communists to "do whatever they wished with their

ber 5, 1961, hailing Sukarno's speech at the conference, "Indonesia Differs with Nehru's Stand."

[56] The agreement on economic and technical cooperation was signed in Peking, October 11, 1961 (NCNA [Peking], Oct. 11, 1961).

[57] Hindley, "The Indonesian Communists and the CPSU Twenty-second Congress," pp. 20–27.

[58] *Ibid.*

former leader";[59] his contention was a far cry from China's defense of Stalin's historical role as a staunch anti-imperialist leader. As to who was entitled to lead the international communist movement, the PKI's position could not have been stated more unequivocally than when Aidit told the Third Plenum of the party Central Committee in December 1961, "There is only one vanguard of the world communist movement, and let there be no doubt about it, that vanguard is the Communist Party of the Soviet Union."[60] This was to be the strongest—and the last— of Aidit's pronouncements showing the PKI's decidedly pro-Soviet leanings. But it was a rather blunt admission leaving little doubt that the PKI supported Moscow's handling of the imperialists and expected the Soviet Union to continue to be the major communist power exerting influence on Indonesia.

The preceding analysis of Sino-Indonesian relations between 1959 and 1962 indicates that a bewildering array of contradictions faced Chinese policy makers. Despite a series of major defeats and retreats, at the close of this period the policy of united-front cooperation with Sukarno was theoretically still intact though not really operational. For there was still little evidence that such a policy had any substance or, for that matter, much of a future. As the overseas-Chinese issue and the Indonesian army's largely autonomous power had made apparent, the regime headed by Sukarno was essentially quite reactionary. Even the anti-imperialist justification for an opportunistic rapprochement with Sukarno was extremely weak, since, as the West Irian affair proved, he was quite prepared to move closer to Russia or America, the two powers most anxious to destroy China's influence in Indonesia in order to become dominant themselves. And the PKI had shown pronounced "revisionist" tendencies, both in its

[59] *Ibid.*

[60] *Strengthen National Unity and Communist Unity: Documents of the Third Plenum of the Central Committee of the Communist Party of Indonesia* (Djakarta: Jajasan "Pembaruan," 1962), p. 24.

internal strategy and its inclination to adopt pro-Soviet attitudes; it could not be seriously regarded as a Chinese ally so long as these tendencies were dominant in that party.

What inferences can be drawn from Peking's attempt after the end of the overseas Chinese dispute to revive the prospects for united-front cooperation with Sukarno? Apparently, the Chinese leaders decided that the principal contradiction determining their policy toward Sukarno was international, that is, between imperialism and the Indonesian nation, rather than internal, between the Sukarno-PKI progressive elements and the reactionary anti-communists led by the army and the Moslems. Such an analysis placed the CPR and Indonesia in the same anti-imperialist camp. As long as the international contradiction continued to be the principal one, China would follow a policy of promoting a united front with Sukarno. Other contradictions affecting the relationship between the two powers would, necessarily, have to be regarded as subordinate considerations in the overall determination of Chinese policy.

The important role contradictions theory plays in the Chinese leaders' decisions on global policy is not made less significant by underscoring the evident fact that by 1962 this analytical technique, as applied to Indonesia, had become a convenient means of rationalizing the policies of an aspirant great power. For Peking began to view the contradictions in Indonesia after 1962 as indications that her interests in the overseas Chinese, and even in the fate of the PKI, could be pursued only in accordance with the higher dictates of a realpolitik strategy. How her ranking of priorities was to affect the future evolution of Chinese policy is the theme of the next chapter.

7

Toward Sino-Indonesian Alignment:
The Third-Force Strategy

The decision to conciliate Sukarno at a time when Soviet and American influence in Indonesia clearly seemed to be on the rise soon proved to be highly advantageous for Peking. Between 1963 and 1965, a developing convergence of Chinese and Indonesian foreign-policy aims and interests led to a tacit power alliance that seemed to obscure the conflicts underlying their relationship which had surfaced at the time of the disputes over West Irian and the Chinese residents of Indonesia. During this period Peking acquired pre-eminent influence in Indonesia, not only by forging common interests with Sukarno, but also by finally winning the support of the PKI. These victories in Indonesia were of major significance in Chinese foreign-policy strategy, because they occurred in the larger context of Peking's post-1963 efforts to organize an international anti-American, anti-Soviet coalition. Moreover, since Djakarta was to be one of the key pillars in this coalition, the consolidation of the relationship with Indonesia was essential to the success of Peking's attempt to organize a rival power bloc.

The primary impetus behind the Peking-Djakarta rapprochement was the common threat posed to the two states by the creation of the Federation of Malaysia. To China, this new state was further evidence of the imperialists' intention to establish a chain of anticommunist regimes in Southeast Asia and thus a sufficient reason for Peking to join forces with any power opposed to the federation. The Malaysia issue thus intensified China's determination to pursue a militant anti-imperialist strategy in the region. But the formation of Malaysia had an even more dramatic effect on Indonesia's foreign policy because it led ultimately to the termination of Sukarno's dependence on Moscow and Washington and forced him into an alignment with Peking. This shift necessarily followed from Sukarno's perception of the creation of Malaysia as a scheme designed to block Indonesian hegemony in the Malaya world and possibly also to encourage the dismemberment of Indonesia in the event that any of the outer islands, fearing the growth of communist influence under Sukarno's rule, might attempt to join the new federation.

The PKI also had a strong interest in opposing Malaysia, primarily because the party sorely needed an external crisis in order to regain the momentum it had lost after the West Irian dispute. In the short run at least, only by capitalizing on the danger of a new confrontation could the PKI hope to force its way into the government and, at the same time, keep the army preoccupied with external affairs. When it became clear that the Soviet Union would not, as she had on the West Irian issue, back Sukarno's policy toward Malaysia, the PKI rapidly began to reverse its pro-Moscow stance.

During the 1963 to 1965 period, therefore, the actions of the superpowers in dealing with the Malaysia issue played into the hands of China's diplomatic strategy in Indonesia. The rapidity with which the Sino-Indonesian axis emerged, however, tended to obscure the basic restraints that were still operating against the development of a durable alliance between the two states. (This writer was among those who overestimated the potential of the Peking-Djakarta axis in 1965.) Indonesia's anticommunist elements still controlled all the real levers of power in the system of guided democracy. Although the army rallied in support of the new anti-imperialist struggle, it actually had no intention of allowing the Malaysia question to deflect its attention from the more important internal contest with the PKI. An alliance between Djakarta and Peking, therefore, was possible only insofar as it did not alter the domestic balance of power in Indonesia.

The Aidit group eventually came out in support of China only because Peking's alliance with Sukarno helped the PKI to exploit the Malaysia crisis for its own domestic ends, not because it suddenly converted to Maoism. As events after 1963 soon demonstrated, Aidit's domestic strategy was, in fact, basically in conflict with China's realpolitik foreign policy toward the Sukarno regime. As his earlier flirtations with the great powers imply, Sukarno's attraction to a power alignment with Peking was mainly the product of his increasing international isolation and the worsening of his relations with Moscow and Washington, rather than the outgrowth of a definite convergence of similar long-term interests and goals. As a consequence of these factors, the Peking-Sukarno-PKI alliance was inherently unstable. Only the Malaysia issue held it together. The evidence presented in this chapter points to the conclusion that, despite the obstacles to achieving their goals, the Chinese leaders again seriously misjudged their capacity to control the triangular coalition formed by Peking, Sukarno, and the PKI.

The Malaysia Controversy

When it first surfaced, the formation of the Federation of Malaysia did not immediately appear to present an issue on which Djakarta and Peking would find common ground. On the contrary, the opening phase of the dispute indicated that Sukarno might again turn to Moscow for additional military and economic aid, or, if he decided to accept Malaysia's existence, that Indonesia could expect a grateful outpouring of largess from the United States. For Malaysia resembled West Irian in providing an issue Sukarno could use to force Moscow and the Western powers to compete for Indonesia's favor. Sukarno's handling of the dispute until September 1963 suggested that the lessons learned two years before in the West Irian campaign were still fresh in his mind.

Djakarta did not publicly oppose the British plan to merge her Borneo dependencies with Malaya and Singapore at the time this scheme was first announced in 1961. That Sukarno and his leading generals were, however, hostile to the arrangement rather early seems clear in the light of other developments. Shortly after the British plans became known, it became apparent that the Indonesian army secretly trained, or allowed to be trained, several hundred dissidents from the British Borneo territories on the Indonesian side of the island; they were then sent back to Sarawak, Sabah, and Brunei. Subsequently, on December 8, 1962, a rebellion broke out in Brunei; the rebels pledged to oppose the merger with Malaysia and to establish an independent state. Although Sukarno gave vocal—but lukewarm—support to the Brunei uprising almost immediately, he did not publicly attack the Malaysia federation plan until February 1963. By that time there was little doubt that Sukarno viewed the proposed merger as a neocolonialist scheme directed at Indonesia and at maintaining the economic and military pre-eminence of the Western powers in this area.[1]

The prospect of a new external crisis involving Indonesia was excellent news for the PKI, which had expressed opposition to the Malaysia concept well before Sukarno.[2] Independently, without referring to Sukarno's attitude, on December 15, 1962, Pe-

[1] The most authoritative analysis of the background of the dispute and its impact on Indonesia is George McT. Kahin, "Malaysia and Indonesia," *Pacific Affairs,* 37 (Fall 1964), 253–270. For an analysis of Sukarno's evolving policy during the early phases of the controversy see Frederick P. Bunnell, "The Kennedy Initiatives in Indonesia, 1962–1963," Ph.D. dissertation, Cornell University, 1969, especially chapters i, iii, and v.

[2] In fact, PKI was the first to attack the British plan for a merger. See *Harian Rakjat,* August 31, 1961.

king announced her support of the Borneo rebellion.[3] During the next three months the congruence of interests that was apparently developing among Peking, Sukarno, and the PKI made CPR Chairman Liu Shao-ch'i's visit to Indonesia in April 1963 seem to foreshadow important new diplomatic moves. Liu's visit was part of a larger venture in Southeast Asia which had taken him to Burma and Cambodia, and it marked the preparatory stage of a concerted Chinese effort to forge an anti-Soviet, anti-American coalition in the area. Therefore, if Sukarno and Peking were preparing for joint action on the issue of Malaysia, the timing was perfect. According to the contents of the Liu-Sukarno communiqué of April 26, 1963, however, the possibility of a common position did not seem very good. The two leaders did express "resolute support" for the "righteous struggle of the people of Borneo for self-determination and independence" and warned against "falling into the trap of neo-colonialism in the guise of Malaysia."[4] But this joint expression of support was in a minor paragraph of a document which otherwise supplied no evidence of their having reached an accord on the handling of any specific issues connected with the dispute. It was to become clear two months later that Liu's visit had produced nothing tangible because, in fact, Sukarno had not made up his mind at that time what his policy would be. He was still exploring all diplomatic possibilities.

At a summit meeting of the Malay powers which produced the Manila Accord of June 12, 1963, Sukarno abruptly altered Indonesia's course. He joined the Philippines and Malaya in welcoming the formation of Malaysia, "provided the support of the people of the Borneo territories is ascertained by an independent and impartial authority, the Secretary General of the United Nations or his representative."[5] A second summit meeting of the

---

[3] *Jen-min Jih-pao,* Dec. 15, 1962.

[4] Full text in *Peking Review,* 5 (April 26, 1963), 11–12.

[5] The complete text of the accords appears in the *New York Times,* June 12, 1963.

three states in August produced the concept of Maphilindo—a vague confederation of Malaysia, the Philippines, and Indonesia—and the Manila Declaration, which declared that foreign military bases in the Maphilindo area were regarded as "temporary in nature" and that they should not be used "directly or indirectly to subvert the national independence of any of the three countries." The declaration further pledged the parties to abstain from "the use of arrangements of collective defense to serve the particular interests of the Big Powers" and reserved to themselves "a primary responsibility for the maintenance of the stability and security of the area from subversion in any form or manifestation."[6]

These shifts in Sukarno's policy could only be regarded with suspicion and dissatisfaction in Peking. Read one way, the agreements implied that Sukarno had agreed to accept the inclusion of the Borneo territories in Malaysia, provided the people's will was impartially ascertained; hence Djakarta would be free to oppose the outcome if she did not like it. On the other hand, the Manila Declaration could also mean that Sukarno thought he had succeeded in winning the agreement of the Malay powers to the early elimination of American and British bases in the area, to the adoption by the three states of a neutral policy in the Cold War, and to the establishment of a loose entente among the three under the nominal leadership of Indonesia. Because of the pronounced anticommunist, pro-Western leanings of the Philippine and Malayan governments, Peking could hardly be expected to assume that the latter interpretation, however consistent with Sukarno's desires, was valid.

The absence of any statements by Peking endorsing Sukarno's diplomatic moves of June to August instead indicates that the Chinese leaders drew the same conclusions about his motives as did other interested parties at the time. Most informed observers attached the greatest significance to that portion of the Manila

---

[6] *Ibid.,* Aug. 5, 1963.

Declaration which referred to the three powers' primary responsibility for the region's stability, security, and defense against subversion. These observers, in some instances basing their conclusions on interviews with government officials who had attended the summit meetings, stressed that the declaration really meant that the three powers recognized the common danger to their internal security posed by communist China and, indirectly, by their Chinese communities.[7] Such an assessment was undoubtedly correct, because any regional security arrangements that were not implicitly anti-Chinese and anticommunist would most certainly have been rejected by the Indonesian army. When he signed this document Sukarno must have known very well that Peking and other participants in the Cold War would view his action as another step toward compromise with the anticommunist powers. This reading of Sukarno's motives acquired increasing credibility in the light of his domestic policies between May and August 1963. During this period he adopted an economic stabilization program recommended by the United States; negotiated a settlement with the Western oil companies in Indonesia, whose assets had been threatened a few months before by nationalization plans and PKI harassment; and received tentative assurance that credit would be forthcoming from the United States and the International Monetary Fund. And in moving to the right at this time, Sukarno simply overrode the strong objections raised by the PKI, which had urged the government to seize the foreign oil interests and to denounce Malaysia.

Just as it appeared that Sukarno was on the verge of abandoning radical nationalist policies, however, the whole context of Indonesia's domestic and foreign policies was transformed. The United Nations' "ascertainment" did conclude that the proposed Malaysia federation had the support of the people of the Borneo

[7] Kahin, "Malaysia and Indonesia," pp. 264–267. Also see Mohammad Hatta, "One Indonesian's View of Malaysia," *Asian Survey*, 5 (March 1965), 139–143.

territories. But this finding could hardly be presented to Sukarno
—or any objective audience—as a bona fide implementation of
the Manila Accord, since Malaysia was proclaimed a sovereign
state (September 16, 1963) *before* the ascertainment had even
been officially completed. Sukarno immediately charged, correctly, that the U.N.'s informal plebiscite, conducted with the
close cooperation and guidance of the British colonial admin-
istrators, was improper and, hence, that the findings were invalid.
No doubt he found especially objectionable the fact that, in the
main, only those known to favor the merger were consulted, while
persons who had opposed or might oppose the formation of
Malaysia were largely ignored.[8] Moreover, the existing United
Kingdom–Malaya defense treaty was to be extended to embrace
the newly absorbed territories, and this extension of Western
military power was totally unacceptable to Sukarno. On September 25, 1963, he announced his "confrontation" policy, pledging
that Indonesia would "crush" (*ganjang*) Malaysia, a creature of
imperialism designed to oppose the Indonesian revolution.[9]

The choice of the word meaning "crush" (or "smash") was
no doubt partly a rhetorical device, but it strongly implied
Sukarno's intention to destroy Malaysia. He had been prepared,
in principle, to accept Borneo's merger with Malaysia if the
ascertainment was based on a wide selection of political opinion
in the Borneo territory. But he evidently did not believe findings
derived on this basis would convincingly show popular support
for the merger. Djakarta officially denied any desire to annex the
British dependencies herself.[10] This disclaimer was, however,
hard to square with the statements of some of her leaders, such

[8] For the Indonesian government's objections see Information Division,
Embassy of Indonesia, *A Survey of the Controversial Problem of the
Establishment of the Federation of Malaysia* (Washington, D.C., 1963).

[9] Radio Djakarta domestic service, Sept. 25, 1963.

[10] See *A Survey of the Controversial Problem of the Establishment of
the Federation of Malaysia.*

as Foreign Minister Subandrio, who were saying in effect that it would be only natural if the people of North Borneo someday joined their Indonesian brothers. Since roughly three-fourths of Borneo was already Indonesian territory, any government in Djakarta was likely to feel that a strong interest in security warranted the pursuit of a long-range policy aimed at eventually absorbing the remainder of the island or preventing another power from doing so. How strongly Sukarno was motivated by this consideration is difficult to judge. On the other hand, accepting Malaysia in the form it was presented would mean that the former British territories would be under the control of a Western client state. Such an arrangement would have been totally unacceptable to Sukarno or his generals and would have sparked a desire to break up the federation even if none previously existed.

Although the issues confronting Sukarno in the Malaysian controversy were extremely complex and although not all of his motives can be determined, it is possible to reconstruct the principal objectives of his confrontation policy: (1) He was greatly concerned, as were many other Indonesian leaders—including the generals—because the absorption of the Borneo territories by Malaysia might not prevent political domination of the new state by local Chinese in the future. The perpetuation of Malay political supremacy—if necessary, by artificial and antidemocratic means—had also been a key objective of the British and of Malayan Prime Minister Tengku Abdul Rahman in creating the federation; but Sukarno was not convinced that their scheme would work. (2) A Malaysian state was unacceptable to him because, as a creature of neocolonialism it was an obstacle to Indonesian achievement of leadership in the area. (3) In view of the covert assistance the United States and Malaya had given the 1958 Indonesian rebellion, Sukarno feared the federation was intended not only to block communism and disadvantage Peking and the Chinese living abroad, but also to break up Indonesia. He knew the Western powers were worried about the possibility that the PKI might one day grow beyond its Java base to dominate the outer islands and, hence, that the existence of Malaysia might one day encourage the sessession of Sumatra, Borneo, and Sulawesi. (4) Sukarno also wanted to limit any potential expansion of Chinese communist power and influence in the area. The danger from China, however, he perceived as long-range, whereas the military bases and the economic-political presence of the United States and Britain posed a more immediate threat to Indonesia, not to mention his own regime.

Sukarno might have been prepared to accept a Federation of Malaysia and a Maphilindo entente if these arrangements offered some promise of eliminating British and American dominance, thereby permitting Indonesia to assert a primary role in organizing the area to curb any future internal or external Chinese danger. This aim, of course, could not be pursued when it became clear that Western influence would remain dominant in Malaysia. Since Sukarno was not prepared to accept a humiliating defeat or to abandon his goals, a struggle to decide which powers would determine the geopolitical alignment of the Malay nations was inevitable.

Indonesia's first move to intervene followed a familiar pattern—it sent small armed bands into Malaya and the Borneo territories, as it had in the West Irian campaign. The political objective appeared to be the precipitation of a diplomatic crisis, during which either Washington or Moscow, to advance its own interest in containing the CPR, would be forced to sponsor a settlement that would give Sukarno what he wanted. Sukarno proved to be wrong. Moscow adopted a cool attitude toward his confrontation policy. This time there were no dramatic pledges of major Soviet economic or military assistance to Indonesia. Moscow did not even offer a partial cancellation of the huge Indonesian debt, which was the least it might have done had it wanted to demonstrate Russian support without provoking a possibly hostile response from Washington. The exchange of visits between Subandrio and Mikoyan in July 1964 led to reports that the Soviet Union had agreed to provide Indonesia with an additional small credit of fifty million to a hundred million dollars for arms, but this aid did not materialize.[11] On the other hand, the United States made it clear that she would support Malaysia in a joint communiqué of July 23, 1964, in which Washington announced it would extend military assistance to the federation.[12] Sukarno thereupon accused the United States of "giving Malaysia preference over the Indonesian Republic" and warned of a worsening of Washington-Djakarta relations.[13]

Indonesia's rebuff by the superpowers was followed by a further diplomatic setback, in October 1964, at the conference of nonaligned nations in Cairo. Here Sukarno attempted to win Afro-Asian support for his confrontation policy by lashing out at "the military bases of the big powers built in all strategic positions." But the final conference declaration did not even mention the Malaysia dispute, and it condemned only those foreign bases that were maintained "against the expressed will" of the countries concerned.[14] Because the nonaligned states had implicitly rejected Sukarno's policy, by late 1964 Indonesia found herself diplomatically isolated.

Chinese Attitudes toward Malaysia

Although Sukarno had openly tried to find backing from nearly every quarter except the CPR, the Chinese leaders, by their consistent opposition to Malaysia, left the door open for an eventual Indonesian pact with China. In early 1963, Peking had

[11] That the Soviet Union was considering a new aid grant to Indonesia was reported in the *New York Times,* January 7, 1965.

[12] *New York Times,* July 23, 1964.

[13] Speech of Aug. 17, 1964, commemorating the nineteenth anniversary of the proclamation of Indonesia's independence (Djakarta Radio domestic service, Aug. 17, 1964).

[14] Middle East News Agency, Oct. 6, 1964.

condemned Malaysia virtually without reference to the proposed federation's effect on Indonesian interests. But after Sukarno's September 1963 "crush Malaysia" speech, Chinese editorials and statements increasingly stressed the common danger posed to the CPR and to Indonesia. Malaysia was described as "part of a SEATO move to surround Indonesia" and a "new threat to peace in that region and Asia as a whole."[15] The American agreement to provide Kuala Lumpur with military assistance was attacked as an attempt at "direct armed intervention in North Kalimantan" (Indonesian Borneo), and Peking warned that "should U.S. imperialism dare to launch aggression against Indonesia, the Chinese people will back the Indonesian people with all their might."[16] Peking regarded Malaysia as a serious security threat to both countries. The federation could be "expanded to form a great system of military points for centrally planning the military activities of Britain in the Far East";[17] moreover, opposition to the federation was important because "in the eyes of the U.S. imperialists, to control Malaysia and Indonesia is one of the key factors for carrying out their global strategy."[18]

The expression of these hostile attitudes toward Malaysia involved no immediate conflict of interests for Peking. Over the years a profitable trade had developed for the CPR in this region, especially with Singapore.[19] But this trade had grown despite the absence of diplomatic relations and was likely to continue irrespective of China's attitude toward the merger of territories. Economic considerations aside, furthermore, the CPR had ample political reason to oppose the Malaysia concept. Despite procla-

[15] *Jen-min Jih-pao*, Sept. 29, 1963.

[16] *Ibid.*, Sept. 9, 1963.

[17] Pi Wen, "Ma-lai-hsi-ya lien-pang chi-hua po-shih" (Dissect the Federation of Malaysia Plan), *Shih-chieh chih-shih* (World Knowledge) (Peking), 15 (April 10, 1963), 16.

[18] *Jen-min Jih-pao*, Sept. 9, 1963.

[19] *Far Eastern Economic Review*, 46 (Dec. 1964), 3.

mations of an independent foreign policy, Kuala Lumpur had
already placed herself in the camp of China's enemies by
officially supporting India on the Tibetan boundary question;
and in November 1964, Malaysia reversed her neutral position
on the China-recognition issue (prior to that time Kuala Lumpur
recognized neither the CPR nor Nationalist China) by permitting
Taiwan to open a consulate in Malaysia. This decision Peking
promptly attacked as "an open challenge to the Chinese people"
instigated by the United States.[20] In view of Malaysia's defense
treaty with Britain and the latter's membership in the SEATO-
ANZUS bloc, it seemed to the Chinese communists by late 1964
that the federation had been effectively absorbed into the American security network in Southeast Asia. A policy of open enmity
toward Malaysia, therefore, not only accorded with China's hope
of forging an anti-imperialist united front with Indonesia, but
would, in any event, have followed Kuala Lumpur's alignment
with Peking's enemies.

It was by no means certain, however, that in the long run
Chinese interests and objectives in Malaysia would be compatible
with the policy she was then pursuing in Indonesia. The seemingly expansionist thrust of Indonesian nationalism centered on
the assertion of Djakarta's leadership over the Malay nations.
Peking could support this ambition, in the short run at least,
because any gains Indonesia might make would come at the
expense of China's main and stronger enemies, the Western
powers. But except for the common interest in removing the
Western presence, basic Chinese and Indonesian objectives did
not appear to be harmonious. The Chinese communists undoubtedly believed that the bourgeois nationalist radicals in
Djakarta did not intend to "liberate" the Malaysian people,
particularly not the Chinese population of the federation. From
the Marxist-Leninist perspective the conclusion would have to

[20] *Jen-min Jih-pao*, Dec. 2, 1964.

be that the goal of Sukarno's expansionist nationalism was Indonesian domination over both the Chinese minority and the revolutionary people of the Malay countries; achievement of that goal would help to prop up his own internal regime.

Several factors, nevertheless, suggest that from 1963 to 1965 Peking was prepared to accept temporary Indonesian pre-eminence in the Malay world and that she was quite willing to renounce or sharply scale down any rival Chinese ambitions. There could be no basis for an alliance with Sukarno if he, and especially his generals, believed that China's real objective was a pro-Peking, Chinese-dominated Malaysia. The PKI, if it eventually came to power, would inevitably expect to exert Indonesian communist influence in the Malay countries and would not welcome Peking's interference or competition. Whether Djakarta's government was bourgeois or communist, any attempt by Peking to hold sway in this area by means of ethnic ties to, or revolutionary support for, the predominately Chinese Malayan insurgents was wholly incompatible with China's attempt to promote an Indonesian alliance. No documentary evidence has come to light which indicates that these issues were thrashed out between Peking and Djakarta, or between the CCP and the PKI, during the period of the rapprochement. However, China's efforts to secure an alignment with both Sukarno and Aidit after 1963 strongly suggest that she was not opposed, in principle, to a predominance of Indonesian influence in the Malay area and that her attempts to reach an accord were for the sake of her broader great-power interests. It is difficult to escape this conclusion in view of the rapidity with which the Sino-Indonesian axis developed.

The Emergence of the Peking-Djakarta Axis

At the very time his position on the Malaysian controversy was driving Sukarno into greater diplomatic isolation Peking reached the stage of the open split with Moscow. The signing of the

Nuclear Test Ban Treaty in August 1963 was regarded in Peking as conclusive evidence of Soviet collusion with the United States against China. This treaty inaugurated the most vehement phase of Sino-Soviet polemics. It quickly became apparent that Peking's ideological assault on the Russian leadership formally marked China's departure from the old socialist camp and the establishment of a rival Chinese power center in Asia.

In setting up a third camp the Chinese leaders sought to organize a broad international united front of all those nations, forces, and classes which were opposed to American-Soviet global dominance. Such a front could not, of course, consist exclusively of elements involved in proletarian-led insurrections and liberation struggles but had to include those "national democratic" and capitalist states which were resisting or were otherwise at odds with the two superpowers. Within the communist world, Peking's coalition strategy took the form of attempts to pull various states (notably the Asian ones) from Moscow's orbit and to promote the development of rival pro-Chinese splinter parties in Western Europe and Latin America. In the noncommunist world it involved more extensive economic contacts with industrialized Western nations and Japan, apparently in the hope that the "contradictions" within the capitalist system could be exploited to weaken American influence in these countries. Another group of potential allies to whom the idea of a third camp was directed comprised the radical nationalist regimes, liberation movements, and neutralist states of the Afro-Asian world. Almost the only common characteristic that could link these elements politically to China was their opposition, in varying degrees, to the policies of Washington or Moscow.

The rationale for China's third force was basically an updated version of Mao's 1946 concept of the "intermediate zone." Extending the Leninist idea of the antagonisms between imperialism and the colonies to include relations between imperialism and the lesser capitalist states, early in 1964 Peking began to discuss the possibility of creating a new intermediate zone composed of two elements: (1) the independent states and those oppressed nations still struggling for independence in Asia, Africa, and Latin America; and (2) the second-rank capitalist powers such as France, Germany, Italy, Britain, Australia, Canada, and Japan which, like China, were targets of American-Soviet domination.[21] As is evident from the list of leaders China spent the most time cultivating after the signing of the Test Ban Treaty—Sukarno, Nkrumah, de Gaulle, Ne Win, Nasser, Sihanouk, Ayub Khan, even the Sheik of Yemen—most of the allies she tried to recruit for a united front were staunch nationalists; many had anti-communist records on domestic issues. Anti-Soviet and anti-American they might be; radical revolutionaries they were not.

In effect, this proposed coalition reflected Peking's attempt to project a modified Maoist-type united front (that is, from below and above) onto the international setting of the 1960's. However, it differed from the internal Chinese civil-war model in one crucial respect: except for China, the states that would form this front leaned heavily to the political right. The foreign policy on which it was based stressed the primacy of Peking's desire to establish relations with bourgeois governments and leaders over her desire to influence communist revolutionary movements. The effort to woo the communist states and parties of Asia away from Moscow was an important part of Chinese policy after 1963;[22] however, the great-power strategy she was trying to forge was actually based, not on communists, but on the prospect of alliances with bourgeois-led countries like Indonesia and Pakistan.

Pakistan's long dispute with India over Kashmir presented Peking with an opportunity not only to outflank her enemy New Delhi but also to undermine the American and Soviet positions

[21] See the important article in *Jen-min Jih-pao*, January 21, 1964.

[22] For the history and documents pertaining to this effort see William E. Griffith, *The Sino-Soviet Rift* (Cambridge, Mass.: M.I.T. Press, 1964).

in the subcontinent. On the other hand, Sukarno's conflict with Malaysia might be exploited to counterencircle the SEATO-ANZUS bloc and thus ultimately to weaken the American position in Indochina and the Pacific. In these two areas China had important strategic interests. Compared to these considerations in the period 1963 to 1965, the small, disorganized struggling insurgent groups in Africa, Latin America—and the rest of Asia for that matter—had yet to demonstrate any substantial anti-imperialist or internal revolutionary potential.

The dominance of great-power over revolutionary interests in Chinese policy toward Indonesia became fully apparent during the year following Sukarno's diplomatic defeat at the 1964 conference of nonaligned nations. Shortly after his return from Cairo, Sukarno took his first step toward the Chinese camp. On November 4, 1964, three weeks after the CPR's first nuclear detonation (October 16), he suddenly flew to Shanghai, where he held talks with Chou En-lai. No statements or communiqués were issued from this apparently urgent and unpublicized meeting. However, it evidently produced a decision to carry on subsequent formal negotiations on various types of substantive cooperation between the two states, for Sukarno's visit to China was quickly followed by the arrival of Chen Yi in Djakarta, on November 27, for a week-long series of discussions.

The exceptionally candid Sino-Indonesian joint press release of December 3 revealed an unprecedented degree of agreement between Djakarta and Peking on a wide range of global and regional issues. It openly said that the two powers were working out ways of making their foreign policies mutually re-enforcing. Chen Yi reaffirmed the CPR's full support of Indonesia's struggle "to crush . . . 'Malaysia' which constitute[d] a direct threat to the security and growth of the developing countries of Southeast Asia." The two parties reached "a common understanding and agreed that the struggle against imperialism, colonialism and neo-colonialism [was] a single struggle [whose parts] cannot be separated from one another." They noted that they had exchanged "information and experience on the present stage of the common struggle" and discussed "various world problems now being faced, and others to be faced in the near future," as well as "ways of raising the level of struggle."[23] During the same visit Chen Yi extended Indonesia a fifty-million-dollar credit for economic development and foreign-exchange reserves. As a result of these accords, Peking became the major external force supporting Sukarno's foreign policy and, as the new extension of credit suggested, a source of aid to shore up the deteriorating Indonesian economy.

The full extent of China's desire to remove all obstacles to a rapprochement had become clear earlier, in March 1964, when Peking volunteered to turn over the assets of the Bank of China in Indonesia to Sukarno's government. This institution was regarded by virtually all politically conscious noncommunist Indonesians as the CPR's main source of leverage on the Chinese business community in Indonesia and as the ever ready provider of funds for the PKI.[24] Because the Bank of China was widely believed to be the principal instrument of Peking's suspected subversive activities, when it passed into the hands of the Indonesian government the following November, anticommunist circles in Djakarta were hard-pressed to explain this transaction

[23] NCNA (Djakarta), Dec. 3, 1964.

[24] It was widely believed that the Bank of China lent money to local Chinese businessmen on condition that they contribute to the PKI. The bank was also a source of foreign exchange for Peking since, under a special transfer-of-profits agreement, a percentage of its yearly earnings could be taken out of the country—a practice other foreign enterprises were also permitted by the Indonesian government. This writer was unable to find any reliable data on the sums involved under this arrangement, though several Indonesian Foreign Ministry officials mentioned twenty million to twenty-five million dollars per year. This estimate seems high in view of the economic crisis in Indonesia after 1959 and the government's actions to stem the flow of foreign-exchange reserves.

as another manifestation of "the threat from China." The transfer spoke for itself. Peking had not only given the Sukarno regime new sources of financial power, but she had also liquidated, on her own initiative, the most important base for interfering in Indonesia's internal affairs.

In January 1965, Sukarno announced Indonesia's withdrawal from the United Nations, following the seating of Malaysia as a nonpermanent member of the Security Council. He regarded the recognition accorded to Malaysia by this action as another slap at Djakarta that rendered the United Nations useless as a forum in which Indonesia might expect to advance her national interests. In response, Sukarno soon called for a new international organization, CONEFO (Conference of New Emerging Forces), which would stand in opposition to the United Nations, an institution he charged was dominated by the "old established forces." These were the kinds of sentiments the Chinese leaders had themselves expressed and hoped other nationalists would. They therefore acclaimed Indonesia's withdrawal from the U.N., pledged "resolute" support of Sukarno's decision[25] and condemned the U.N. as a place where genuinely independent and revolutionary nations could no longer "uphold justice" in the face of "manipulations" by the United States.[26] The most significant fact the withdrawal from the U.N. made apparent was that Sukarno's perspective on world affairs had by 1965 essentially become that of Peking. In effect, there was little difference between the concept of a polarization between "new emerging forces" and "old established forces" and China's doctrine of the contradiction between the "imperialists" and the "oppressed nations and peoples."

[25] *Jen-min Jih-pao,* Jan. 6, 1965.

[26] *Jen-min Jih-pao,* Jan. 10, 1965. See also the article "Yin-tu-ni-hsi-ya jen-min te fan ti-kuo ko-ming tou-cheng" (The Indonesian People's Revolutionary Anti-Imperialist Struggle), *Shih-chieh chih-shih,* January 1965, pp. 17–19.

The two countries reached the stage of a *de facto* power axis late in January 1965, when Foreign Minister Subandrio led a forty-two-member delegation of high-level Indonesian civilian and military officials to Peking. This was the largest group of Indonesian leaders ever to visit China, and the inclusion of ranking army, air force, and naval commanders implied an impending new development of considerable political significance. Since the top-echelon Indonesian military leaders had long regarded China as the covert ally of their domestic rival the PKI, and as a potential external threat to their country, it is very unlikely that these feelings had been swept away by Sukarno's recent expressions of friendship for Peking. But the generals also shared Sukarno's nationalistic ambitions, and because the CPR might support the achievement of these goals, they could endorse the alliance with Peking while at the same time carefully scrutinizing it. The Indonesian generals were naturally interested in Chinese economic and, possibly, military assistance; they presumably also had reason to believe that Sukarno had reached an understanding with Peking that was compatible with their own conception of Indonesia's security interests and leadership aspirations in Southeast Asia. For the generals had not abandoned their aims and interests simply because no other major powers were prepared to support Djakarta. As the earlier Soviet arms deal had shown, the Indonesian military was quite prepared to use capitalist or communist aid to further its own ends.

On January 28, 1965, a joint statement was issued which revealed the extent of the Sino-Indonesian accord and its possible future military implications. The statement announced mutual agreement on virtually every major international question. It assailed the United States as the "leader of imperialism, colonialism, . . . carrying on interference, subversion, intimidation, intervention and aggression in Asia, Africa and Latin America." It expressed Sino-Indonesian support of the "peoples of Vietnam, Laos and Cambodia" and stressed that "the anti-imperialist revolutionary movements of all peoples form an integral whole and that they should support and coordinate with each other." Both nations reaffirmed support of Indonesia's "confrontation" policy, and China "solemnly declared that should the British and U.S. imperialists dare to impose a war on the Indonesian people, the Chinese people would absolutely not sit idly by."[27] The last phrase was one Peking would soon use to warn the United States of possible Chinese intervention in Indochina after the bombing of North Vietnam in February 1965.

The Sino-Indonesian declaration of diplomatic and political unity also noted that the two powers had agreed to "strengthen their technical cooperation, expand their trade, develop maritime transportation . . . , and strengthen their friendly contacts in the military field." It was later learned that "friendly contacts in the military field" included a Chinese promise to deliver small arms to Indonesia.[28] But because of the CPR's nuclear test the previous October, the joint statement's references to "technical" cooperation carried the more important implication that the long-range possibilities of an alliance with a China that was a nuclear power was a new factor in Indonesia's calculations. After the Subandrio delegation left Peking, there were persistent statements from Djakarta to the effect that Indonesia intended to become a nuclear power.[29] These assertions seemed incredible, given the primitive state of her industrial capacity; if they were serious, some of Djakarta's military and civilian leaders apparently regarded the alliance with China as a means of obtaining the necessary assistance for making a start in the nuclear direction.

[27] *Peking Review,* 8 (Feb. 5, 1965), 6–8.

[28] *New York Times,* Oct. 19, 1965.

[29] For example, see the statement by General Hartono, Antara, February 2, 1965. The foundations for an Indonesian nuclear-development program were virtually nonexistent. Under an agreement concluded in 1958 the Soviet Union supplied some economic and technical assistance to get a peaceful uses of atomic energy program going, but little progress had been made. However, the construction of a Soviet-built nuclear reactor was supposed to begin in early 1965 (Tass, Jan. 30, 1965).

It seems very unlikely that prospects of nuclear or other aid substantially diminished the Indonesian military's suspicions of China. But the generals were also suspicious of Russian and, to a lesser extent, American intentions.[30] Presumably, Sukarno's generals believed they would benefit from the assistance agreements with Peking—just as they had been the major beneficiaries of all the past aid deals—and there is no persuasive evidence that they seriously tried to block the formation of the axis. The steady exchange of military delegations between the two countries after January 1965 suggests that the Chinese were making a concerted effort to woo the Indonesian officer class, especially its pro-Sukarno elements. Since the viability of the axis ultimately depended on the Indonesian military's support, an attempt had to be made to allay its members' misgivings about China, even though Peking could not offer the quantity, types, or quality of modern military equipment which attracted Sukarno's generals to Moscow and Washington.

The Peking-Djakarta Axis and Indonesian Communism

Numerically and organizationally, by early 1963 the PKI had become the strongest single political force in Indonesia. But the problem of sustaining momentum while the party had no immediate prospect of acquiring or sharing power had become acute. Although the party had tried to achieve a measure of organizational and political independence in the cities and the countryside, in neither type of area had this objective been realized. Under the system of guided democracy only government-approved strikes, seizures, and demonstrations were permitted. The party's large labor, youth, and women's organizations could

[30] During the formation of the Peking-Djakarta axis high-ranking Indonesian military officers frequently condemned the presence of the Western powers in Southeast Asia. On one occasion army chief of staff General Yani—a leading anticommunist—proclaimed Indonesia's role to be that of displacing American and British power in Southeast Asia (Djakarta Radio domestic service, Jan. 27, 1965).

produce splendid rallies for Sukarno to address; such meetings, however, could do little to persuade the rank and file in the cities and towns that the PKI itself was moving closer to power.

In the countryside the situation had become somewhat more favorable as a result of the decision in 1959 to build up strength in rural areas. By 1962 the PKI claimed that the communist-controlled Barisan Tani Indonesia (Indonesian Peasants' Front) had grown to 4,500,000 members.[31] However, much of this expansion was possible because it was more difficult for the army to interfere with or harass the PKI in the villages than in the cities.

In the outer islands social-economic conditions generally did not favor the PKI, and its activities were impeded by the regional military commanders. In Java the communists had better prospects. Middle-income and rich peasants tended to be devout *santri* Moslems, ideologically quite resistant to communism or to agitation for the relief of village grievances. On the other hand, the party's appeals were highly successful among the non-Moslem *abangan* Javanese.[32] Any attempt to play the *abangan* against the *santri* class, however, was almost certain to ignite a communal war which, because of geography and the overall balance of power, the PKI could not possibly win. Moreover, since the army-officer class itself, more strongly *prijaji* (aristocratic-bureaucratic) than Moslem, had a vested social-economic interest in the status quo—there were landed *santri* and *prijaji* relatives to protect—any serious economic threat to the status quo in the villages invited instant repression by the army. This had been demonstrated in the incidents at Kediri, in 1961,[33] when the army had forcefully evicted squatters whom the PKI had encouraged to take over state lands seized from the Dutch by the Indonesian army in 1957.

[31] *Harian Rakjat,* April 30, 1962.

[32] McVey, "Indonesian Communism and the Transition to Guided Democracy," in Barnett, ed., *Communist Strategies in Asia,* p. 158.

[33] *Ibid.,* pp. 178–179.

The PKI knew that pressing a general land-reform campaign, using the dormant 1960 land-reform law as justification, was dangerous. Aidit himself had earlier rejected class warfare in the countryside as unsuited to Indonesian conditions. Therefore careful attempts at developing radicalism in the countryside were about as far as the party could go; Kediri and other showdowns indicated it was dangerous to go even that far.

Because of the obstacles confronting the PKI in the cities and the countryside, only a political breakthrough at the national level was possible for the Indonesian communists. In January 1963, Aidit urged that the PKI be brought into the government in order to achieve national unity in accordance with Sukarno's proclaimed policy of bringing the nationalist, communist and Islamic elements together.[34] By including the PKI's leaders in the cabinet Sukarno hoped not only to unify the country but also to conciliate and domesticate the party. But the Indonesian generals feared the consequences to themselves of this scheme and therefore consistently blocked it.

In the light of the dilemmas facing the Indonesian communists, it is not difficult to see why the onset of the Malaysia dispute appeared to be a development that might break the internal deadlock. The PKI, because of its situation, had a strong interest in a prolonged and militant struggle with Malaysia. This crisis would cause the army to be preoccupied with external dangers and thus give the party a greater opportunity to enlarge its organizations under the banner of anti-imperialist nationalism, as it had with great success during the Irian dispute. Moreover, a protracted crisis might give Sukarno the leverage he needed to bring the communists into the government. Consequently, the last thing the PKI wanted was a settlement of the dispute that would probably result in its facing the handicaps and dilemmas it had confronted under the previous status quo. Its attitude

[34] Antara, Jan. 12, 1963.

toward Russia and China after 1963, therefore, necessarily was determined by the degree to which their policies helped sustain the momentum of the party in Indonesia.

Aidit's shift to the Chinese camp in the dispute with the Soviet Union was a gradual and cumulative process. Moscow's failure to give strong support to Indonesia's confrontation policy was the decisive factor, but the general drift of Soviet policy from 1962 on, especially in Asia, appears to have weakened the Indonesian communists' previous pro-Moscow sentiments even before the onset of the Malaysian issue. The decline of Soviet influence on the Indonesian communists began in October 1962, when the Cuban missile crisis and the border war between China and India forced most communist parties to take a stand in favor of either Moscow or Peking. The Soviets' withdrawal from a confrontation in Cuba that they themselves had precipitated and their siding with bourgeois New Delhi against socialist China evidently had a telling effect on the PKI leaders. If the Soviet Union so prized a détente with the imperialists that it would retreat from Cuba and support India against China, it was doubtful that Moscow would support the interests of the Indonesian communists in the event of a dangerous test. The fact that the PKI took positions on both disputes essentially parallel to those of the CCP[35] indicated that by late 1962 it was about to make a basic reappraisal of its attitudes toward Russia and China.

The turning point came on February 10, 1963, when Aidit delivered a major report to the PKI Central Committee, in which, for the first time, he emphasized that "modern revisionism" (i.e., Soviet policies) was the main danger to the international communist movement. Heretofore, the PKI had condemned both

---

[35] On Cuba, see Aidit's statement of November 7, 1962: "It is a regrettable sacrifice that strategic defensive weapons are being dismounted in Cuba. It is regrettable because a sovereign state, Cuba, was forced to do things against its will" (NCNA [Djakarta], Nov. 7, 1962). On the Sino-Indian conflict, see *Harian Rakjat*, October 30, 1962.

"modern revisionism" and "classic and modern dogmatism" (i.e., Chinese policies).[36] Peking gave this speech the widest possible circulation at home and abroad[37] (previous statements by Aidit had received scant, if any, mention in China). On May 20, 1963, *Hung-ch'i* (Red Flag), the CCP's leading ideological journal, for the first time carried a major article on the Indonesian Communist party. It hailed the PKI as having adopted "the correct political line and policy," not only in opposing "modern revisionism," but also in its domestic united-front strategy. Moreover, the PKI was extravagantly praised for its "theoretical contributions to Marxism-Leninism" and its "influence and prestige" in the communist movement. Peking seemed to be making a bid for an ideological alignment with the Aidit group that would re-enforce her parallel diplomatic policy toward Sukarno.

Aidit did not take his decisive step into the China camp until September 1963, following his unsuccessful attempt to help mediate the Sino-Soviet dispute. In Moscow, the PKI leader was given a brief and cool reception because of his efforts, whereupon he flew to Peking and received a welcome similar to those accorded only to major communist statesmen.[38] Aidit was promptly hailed as "a brilliant Marxist-Leninist theoretician" and a "close friend and comrade in arms of the Chinese people [whose] theoretical generalizations . . . are of vital educational

[36] Hindley, "The Indonesian Communists and the CPSU Twenty-second Congress," *Asian Survey*, 2 (March 1962), 20–27.

[37] D. N. Aidit, *Dare, Dare, and Dare Again!* (Political Report to the First Plenary Session of the Seventh Central Committee of the Communist Party of Indonesia) (Peking: Foreign Languages Press, 1963), p. 66. This statement was broadcast on Radio Peking and published in *Jen-min Jih-pao*, February 14, 1963.

[38] On September 5, 1963, Aidit was made an honorary member of the Chinese Academy of Sciences—clear Chinese recognition of his status as a major theoretician (NCNA [Peking], Sept. 5, 1963). Peking also announced the publication in Chinese of Aidit's selected works (NCNA [Peking], Aug. 30, 1963).

experience to us."[39] Peking also announced its discovery that the PKI's policies and strategy had "ever increasing attraction for the Communists and revolutionary peoples of the capitalist world, particularly of the Asian, African and Latin American countries." Its "great success and rich experience" were considered to be "of great international significance for the international Communist movement."[40]

As Aidit and his Chinese hosts well knew, the "brilliance" and "significance" of the PKI's contributions to Marxism-Leninism consisted solely of an internal united-front program, as a result of which the leadership of the Indonesian revolution had been surrendered to Sukarno, while the party existed by the sufferance of a reactionary, anticommunist army. The PKI was, in fact, a party whose revolutionary rhetoric scarcely concealed its close resemblance to the French and Italian "structural reformist" groups at which Peking was then leveling an unrelenting ideological broadside. The structural reformists' argument that socialism could be achieved by the workers' gradual capture of parliamentary institutions was essentially the same as Aidit's thesis about "peacefully changing the balance of forces" in Indonesia by winning over the "pro-people" elements and isolating the "anti-people" elements.[41] These ideas were a far cry from Maoism any way one looked at them.

The inescapable conclusion to be drawn from the Chinese leader's eulogy of the PKI's "revisionist" strategy is that the ideological and political terms of an alliance between the two

[39] See speeches by Politbureau member P'eng Chen, NCNA (Peking), September 4, 1963; and alternate Politbureau member Kang Sheng, NCNA (Peking), September 2, 1963.

[40] Kang Sheng speech, NCNA (Peking), Sept. 2, 1963.

[41] For an analysis of the PKI's "changing the balance of forces" strategy see Guy J. Pauker, "Indonesia: The PKI's 'Road to Power,'" in Robert F. Scalapino, ed., *The Communist Revolution in Asia* (Englewood Cliffs, N.J.: Prentice-Hall, 1965), pp. 260–265.

parties were being hammered out during the Aidit visit. This was apparent from the contents of the two major speeches Aidit delivered in China.[42] They were not, as might have been expected of a communist party about to align itself with the CCP, scathing attacks on Soviet revisionism or calls for armed struggle. On the contrary, they were lengthy, careful justifications of the PKI's peaceful-road theories, explaining why it was possible to win victory in Indonesia by relying on the masses and the PKI's organizations, even though the party lacked the support of independent military power or rural base areas. (Reliance on such support was the core of Chinese revolutionary doctrine.) Both speeches declared firmly that the PKI had "Indonesianized" Marxism-Leninism and that it would accept no criticism from foreign communist parties.

The bargain that was struck, therefore, apparently involved the CCP's agreement to endorse the PKI's internal "revisionist" line in exchange for the latter's support of Peking on the major issues of global strategy raised in the polemic with Moscow— opposition to the Soviet policies of détente with the United States and abandonment of the anti-imperialist struggles in the Afro-Asian world. When Aidit returned to Indonesia late in September, he spoke for the first time of a "momentous choice" facing all the communist parties, a choice that would reveal "who were the genuine Marxist-Leninists and who were false Marxist-Leninists revisionists."[43] What the PKI meant by "genuine Marxist-Leninists," however, could now include those parties which, like itself, adopted the Soviet-style "peaceful transition" line on the question

[42] D. N. Aidit, "Several Questions on the Revolution in Indonesia and the Indonesian Communist Party," NCNA (Peking), Sept. 4, 1963, and "The Indonesian Revolution Is an Inseparable Part of the World Socialist Revolution," NCNA (Canton), Sept. 25, 1963, also NCNA (Peking), Sept. 25, 1963.

[43] Harian Rakjat, Sept. 30, 1963, as reported in NCNA (Peking), Oct. 3, 1963.

of internal strategy, but joined China's third-force coalition on foreign-policy issues. As their endorsement of the PKI revisionist line indicates, the Chinese leaders accepted an alliance with their Indonesian comrades on these terms.

Sources of Tension in the Sino-Indonesian Axis

What is the main conclusion to be drawn from Peking's gradual embrace of the revisionist PKI and the army-dominated Sukarno regime? It is that Peking's policy in Indonesia had by late 1963 become, essentially, a function of her emerging great-power strategy in the rivalry with America and Russia. According to that strategy, the "principal contradiction" was the international struggle between "imperialism and the oppressed nations and peoples"; the successful resolution of the struggle required that the anti-American, anti-Soviet forces cooperate in forming the broadcast possible united front. The primary "revolutionary" emphasis should be on directing political blows against the United States and the Soviet Union. An important revolutionary corollary, of course, was that in countries like Indonesia (still in the "national democratic" stage) the internal class struggle should be subordinated to the external conflict with imperialism.

Fundamentally, however, Chinese strategy in Indonesia was dependent, not on global events, but on two domestic Indonesian factors: the continuance of Djakarta's assertive, anti-Malaysia foreign policy; and the PKI's avoidance of a showdown with the army, which, if it occurred, would destroy Peking's alliance with Sukarno. Because Peking could not decisively influence either of these factors in Indonesia, in reality the value of the alliance with Sukarno and the PKI to China's global foreign-policy interests depended on its Indonesian partners.

The decisive sequence of events that triggered the fateful confrontation between the PKI and the Indonesian army began well before the October 1, 1965, coup attempt—in fact, with Aidit's December 1963 report to the party's Central Committee.[44] That document raised again the dangerous issue of the government's failure to carry out its land-reform law and announced the PKI's intention of radicalizing the countryside. During most of 1964 the Aidit leadership promoted the "Unilateral Action Movement" (the *Gerakan Aksi Sepihak* campaign), which incited the peasants to seize unoccupied government land or that of absentee landlords and to reduce the amount they paid under crop-sharing agreements. A number of violent clashes between the police and the peasants followed; the most serious were in the towns of Klaten, Indramaju, and Bojolaliis on Java. A number of incidents also occurred on Bali. Sukarno was able to defuse the issue for a time by creating temporary land-reform courts, whose decisions were binding on the rival claimants. But on December 10, 1964, he was forced to bring PKI, government, and army leaders to a conference at the Bogor Palace to warn all concerned that the violence and disturbances must cease. As it had on other issues that had led to a showdown, the PKI did Sukarno's bidding. The party agreed to drop the *Aksi Sepihak* campaign.

Sukarno's timely action thwarted the PKI's latest attempt to gain new momentum in the villages, but the political climate in the countryside had been irreparably disturbed. It was now clear that the communists would, if they could, challenge the rural status quo. On the other hand, it was certain that the anticommunists would take stern countermeasures to protect their vested interests. With the covert assistance and encouragement of the army, after the clashes of 1964 many landowners quietly began to organize Muslim youths into village quasi-military groups that would be ready for the day when it might become necessary to

[44] *Kobarkan Semangat Banteng! Madju Terus, Pantang Mundur* (Awaken the Buffalo Spirit! Forward, Never Retreat) (Political Report to the Second Plenum of the Central Committee of the Communist Party of Indonesia) (Djakarta: Jajasan "Pembaruan," 1964), pp. 21–22.

suppress a tide of peasant demands for land redistribution.[45] (It was these groups, rather than the army directly, which engaged in the most savage phases of the massacre of communists in 1965 and 1966.)

Anxiety among anticommunist circles was further heightened by the growing accumulation of evidence that Sukarno, though he would tolerate no challenge to his own power, had no intention of totally curbing the PKI's militance—indeed, that he regarded it as useful in counterbalancing the army and other conservatives. And Sukarno did, in fact, need the PKI as an instrument to prod and challenge the status quo in order that his own conception of radical nationalism might be realized.

In his annual address on August 17, 1964, Sukarno asserted that "the Indonesian revolution aims at socialism," and he sharply criticized those who opposed his idea of fusing nationalism, Islam, and communism—a fusion he called NASAKOM.[46] A short time before, he had abolished the Committee for Retooling the State Apparatus (PARAN), an organization controlled by the army and intended to indoctrinate government officials with a Sukarnoist ideology. To replace PARAN he created a new body, KOTRAR, in which the PKI was represented, much to the army's dissatisfaction. In December, he banned the Body for the Promotion of Sukarnoism (BPS), another group created by anticommunist political leaders—with army support—to outflank the PKI's increasingly effective efforts to make its own slogans and programs seem the epitome of Sukarno's teachings.[47] When asked by American journalists whether trends in Indonesia portended eventual communist ascendency, Sukarno replied, "I do not care

[45] McVey, "Indonesian Communism and China," in Tang Tsou and Ho P'ing-ti, China in Crisis, II, 377–378.

[46] Djakarta Radio domestic broadcast service, Aug. 17, 1964.

[47] For details of Sukarno's attempt to create a new state ideology see Donald E. Weatherbee, Ideology in Indonesia: Sukarno's Indonesian Revolution (New Haven, Conn.: Yale University Press, 1966).

as long as they [the PKI] do not make trouble for the Indonesian state"[48]—a sentiment hardly reassuring to those elements which were determined to prevent even the party's inclusion in the government.

The PKI took another radical step in January 1965 when Aidit asked Sukarno to agree to the arming of a "Fifth Force" composed of workers and peasants (the Angkatan Kelima). Aidit declared that this militia could provide fifteen million armed citizens to defend the nation from possible attack by the British, who, Djakarta claimed, were preparing for aggression against Indonesia.[49] Shortly thereafter Aidit proposed that a NASAKOM Committee be established in the army, starting at the battalion level, to ensure that it, like all the instruments of the state, received ideological indoctrination in conformity with Sukarno's teachings.[50] During 1965, articles and editorials in PKI organs began to clamor for the resignation of "bureaucratic-capitalists" from government services, plants, and commercial enterprises—a thinly disguised attack on the Indonesian officer corps, which held the managerial positions.

Sukarno did not accede to these proposals, nor did he reject them outright. Opposition to them was very strong in anticommunist circles, and there was never the slightest possibility that the army leadership of the time would have accepted a rival armed militia or what no doubt was intended to be a political-reliability—or commissar—system in its own ranks. Nevertheless, the issues remained very much alive throughout 1965; in his August 17 speech of that year proclaiming the alliance with the CPR, Sukarno said that he was still weighing the matter of the "Fifth Force" and that he would soon make a decision.[51] Shortly

[48] CBS News interview Jan. 31, 1965; as reported in Pauker, "Indonesia: The PKI's 'Road to Power,' " p. 284.

[49] *Antara*, Jan. 14, 1965. See also *Harian Rakjat*, January 19, 1965.

[50] PKI Central Committee statement, May 7, 1965; in *Harian Rakjat*, May 7, 1965.

[51] Djakarta Radio domestic service, Aug. 17, 1965.

before the coup attempt, therefore, an acute state of tension existed between the army and the PKI. However Sukarno decided on the issues, the old balance of power was certain to be disrupted. Either the army's position would be undermined or the PKI's effort to sustain momentum would again be blocked.

In view of the dangers involved, why did the PKI decide to challenge the Indonesian anticommunists directly by radicalizing the countryside and calling for reform of the army? The least likely explanation is that Peking pressured the Aidit group to take this fateful step. Although the historical evidence indicates that the PKI took orders from no external authority, Chinese foreign-policy interests and strategy required, in fact, that the PKI avoid any action that might undermine Peking's relations with Sukarno. Because the preservation of friendship with Sukarno had been uppermost in China's calculations since the late 1950's—during which time relations with the Indonesian communists could scarcely be described as close—it seems very improbable that the quite recent rapprochement with the "revisionist" PKI leadership suddenly led Peking to reappraise the overall situation in Indonesia or the basic policies she was pursuing. It is conceivable that some more extreme leftist elements in the PKI had recently succeeded in forcing Aidit to adopt a more militant line, but there is no solid evidence that the party leadership was beset by important factional disputes.[52] Available evidence points to the conclusion that the sheer size of the PKI and the highly unstable domestic situation it confronted were creating pressures to which the party leadership had to respond. They fatally misjudged what could be done.

---

[52] At one point Aidit did admit that "internal contradictions" existed in the party, but he gave no indication of how serious they were or over what issues they had arisen. See his speech in *Harian Rakjat,* July 6, 1964. It seems unlikely that a severe split existed, since the PKI leadership had experienced no purge since 1951.

By June 1964, the PKI claimed three million party members.[53] The number of women, youth, workers, and peasants associated with, or under the control of, its organizations was estimated as approximately fourteen million. In August 1965, shortly before the coup attempt, the PKI estimated that over twenty-six million people were members of organizations it had created.[54] If allowances are made for exaggeration, it appears that between fifteen and twenty million Indonesians—about one-sixth of the population—were to some degree under the direct political influence of the PKI. In fact, Aidit claimed that the party would poll no less than one-third of the vote if elections were ever held.[55] His claim was probably not exaggerated, in view of the large vote the PKI had received at the polls in 1955 and in 1957 and 1958. Notwithstanding their own historical experience, which inclined them to disregard the worth of electoral support in the absence of independent military power, the Chinese communists themselves published Aidit's boast that "the enemies of communism are unable to openly launch political attacks on the PKI, since many of the Party's political viewpoints have already been incorporated in State documents."[56]

The effect on the PKI of these assessments, combined with the evidence of Sukarno's growing encouragement of its militancy, was obvious. By 1965 the Indonesian communists had concluded that their movement was too large to repress; its very size was a deterrent against a pre-emptive strike by the army, since such an act was likely to ignite a civil war. Moreover, Sukarno's encouragement and protection of the party gave it quasi-governmental

[53] *Harian Rakjat*, June 27, 1964.

[54] *Ibid.*, Aug. 20, 1965.

[55] *Ibid.*, May 6, 1964.

[56] *The Indonesian Revolution and the Immediate Tasks of the Communist Party of Indonesia* (report at the Higher Level Party School of the Central Committee of the Chinese Communist Party), Sept. 2, 1963 (Peking: Foreign Languages Press, 1964), p. 32.

status. Viewing the overall situation, the Aidit group apparently decided that a program of carefully timed but steadily mounting radical demands would meet with Sukarno's favor, help him to achieve his goals during his own lifetime, and thereby eventually clear the path for the PKI to succeed him as the legitimate leader of the revolution.

As a consequence of the PKI's fateful move to a more radical domestic line in 1964 and 1965 the inherent conflict in Peking's policy toward Indonesia finally came to the surface: On the one hand, China's strategy for dealing with the great powers required that the Indonesian communists engage in no adventures which might undermine her alliance with Sukarno. On the other hand, the PKI seemed to be attempting to become, in the Indonesian context, a peasant-based revolutionary movement; such a transformation was bound to alarm and alienate the very elements in Indonesia on which the survival of the Peking-Djakarta axis depended. In failing to resolve—or, possibly, in ignoring—this "contradiction," the Chinese leaders revealed how far they had veered from the original Maoist basis of their foreign policy.

At first glance it appears that the PKI's provocative moves in 1964 and 1965 bore no relation to basic Chinese revolutionary theory and tactics and, moreover, that any genuine Maoists in Peking should have been alarmed by what the PKI was doing. Aidit's decision to press for land reform, the "Fifth Force," and the "Nasakomization" of the army was not, after all, convincing evidence of armed revolution in the countryside, but only a further manifestation of the PKI's attempt to promote militant *legal* struggle within the framework of the unshaken and unchallenged Indonesian bourgeois system. The Indonesian communists still had no independent military force, no peasant population they could rely on or control, and no secure base areas; hence their brand of radicalism merely invited the same kind of suppression that had been suffered by the CCP in 1927 as a result of its pursuit of policies basically similar to those adopted by Aidit after 1964.

In view of their broader foreign-policy interests and the fact that the PKI did not, in any event, possess independent political-military power, the Chinese leaders obviously did not want their Indonesian comrades to take hazardous action. The practical question facing Peking, therefore, was whether, given the situation, the PKI's radicalism was safely below the threshold of adventurism. Since there is some evidence to suggest that Peking approved the land-reform campaign and the Fifth Force idea[57]—which, however, she attributed mainly to Sukarno—presumably Aidit's growing militancy had, at least initially, Peking's tentative support. Moreover, with a little juggling of the finer points of Maoist theory, Peking could view the Indonesian revolution as moving into its "new democratic" stage, under the impetus of the "imperialist" threat posed by Malaysia's formation. The essential requirement of a Maoist-type movement was not that independent military forces be organized immediately, but that the revolutionaries must *eventually* develop them. Although the circumstances confronting the PKI made this requirement exceedingly difficult to fulfill, the radicalizing of the peasants and the striving for a Fifth Force militia indicated that the Aidit leadership might, with Sukarno's assistance, ultimately be able to develop in Indonesia the Chinese equivalent of the Red Army. The PKI's attempt to exploit an Indonesian "national war of resistance" against imperialism—Malaysia—appears to have been regarded in Peking as leading to a revolutionary situation comparable to that in China during the anti-Japanese war period of 1937 to 1945. Indeed, since the famous Lin Piao article of September 3, 1965,[58] explicitly applied the conflict model of the anti-Japanese war to the global situation, asserting that it char-

[57] Peking quoted, without comment, excerpts from statements by Sukarno and also PKI editorials endorsing the need to implement the government's land-reform law (NCNA [Peking], Aug. 17, 18, 24, 1964).

[58] "Long Live the Victory of People's War," *Peking Review*, 8 (Sept. 3, 1965), 9–30.

acterized the contemporary international struggle, it is reasonable to suppose that such a conception governed the Chinese leaders' appraisal of future trends in Indonesia.

The conception of Indonesian adherence to the Chinese model had two fundamental shortcomings. First, unless the imperialists actually attacked or invaded Indonesia, the massive explosion of antiforeign nationalism required to turn control of the revolution over to the PKI was very unlikely to occur. Second, the PKI's time frame was entirely different from China's. As the Lin Piao statement revealed, Peking envisioned a greatly protracted struggle before the imperialists were gradually driven out of Asia, Africa, and Latin America by a China-led alliance between nationalist and communist forces. The PKI, on the other hand, which had no weapons and had only a sixty-four-year-old protector—Sukarno—who would probably not live much longer, could not afford to wait until the unfolding of China's grand design produced the conditions for communist hegemony in Indonesia.

The ambivalence underlying Peking's attitude toward the policies of her Indonesian comrades was revealed at the forty-fifth anniversary of the PKI in May 1965. This occasion provided CCP Politbureau member P'eng Chen, the leader of the Chinese delegation to the ceremonies, with a platform from which to deliver major statements on Peking's global strategy and its implications for the Indonesian communists. He praised the "creativity" and the "correct line and policies" of the PKI leadership, its "resolute struggle" against "the seven devils in the rural areas," and its "call for arming the workers and peasants." "Even more brilliant achievements" lay ahead, P'eng Chen said, for the PKI's struggle against local "feudalism, compradore-capitalism and bureaucratic-capitalism" (i.e., the Indonesian army and its anticommunist allies) and against the external enemies "imperialism" and "modern revisionism."[59]

[59] Speech to PKI Central Committee, May 26, 1965; in NCNA (Peking), May 26, 1965.

That such praise did not, however, constitute full endorsement or encouragement of radical action on the Indonesian domestic front was sharply apparent from P'eng's theses in his second, more significant, address during his visit to Djakarta. The present era, he said, was one in which many "contradictions" faced the communist movement. But "taking the world situation as a whole the contradiction between the oppressed nations of Asia, Africa and Latin America and the imperialists headed by the United States is the most *prominent* and *acute* of all the basic contradictions and is the *principal contradiction* in the contemporary world" (emphasis added). He then cited the "national-democratic revolutionary movements" in Indochina, the Congo, the Dominican Republic, and Indonesia as "the most important force[s] directly hitting imperialism." These "anti-imperialist struggles" were rendering great assistance to the socialist states and those countries in which the proletariat "has not yet won victory."[60]

P'eng went on to argue that "the resolution of the contradiction between the oppressed nations and imperialism" had "a vital bearing," on, and was of "key importance" to, the development of the whole communist movement. "It was," he said, "essential for Marxist-Leninists to *single out* this principal contradiction . . . and *grasp it firmly. Only by so doing can one correctly discern and determine the principal enemy and the principal target of attack . . . , decide which forces to rely on and which to unite with, and formulate the correct strategy and tactics*" (emphasis added). The attitude communist parties adopted on this matter, P'eng said, "constitute[d] the most important criterion for distinguishing between Marxist-Leninists and modern revisionists, between revolutionaries and counter-revolutionaries and between real revolutionaries and sham revolutionaries."

[60] "Speech at the Aliarcham Academy of Social Sciences in Indonesia," May 25, 1965, *Peking Review,* 8 (June 11, 1965), 10–20.

There followed what can only be interpreted as an open Chinese declaration that the present international situation required the PKI to subordinate its internal revolutionary tactics in Indonesia to Peking's global strategy for opposing the imperialists. In the "present stage," P'eng said, the task of the communist parties was "to unite all the revolutionary people [and] forces . . . to combat the imperialists and reactionaries, win world peace, national liberation, peoples' democracy and socialism"; the final objective was to "strive for the *gradual* achievement of complete victory in the proletarian world revolution." (emphasis added) Every communist party's struggle went through "different stages" and had its "own characteristics," P'eng admitted, *"but none can be independent of the general laws governing the development of world history"* (emphasis added). The point he was belaboring was that the contradiction between imperialism and the oppressed nations was "the governing law" of the present era, and no Marxist-Leninist party should conduct its internal revolution in a manner that impaired China's global strategy of uniting as many anti-imperialist oppressed nations as possible. The "future" of the world proletarian revolution, P'eng said, was very "bright," especially in "the next hundred years," during which there would be "still greater revolutionary changes in the world." With this long-range view in mind, P'eng was saying that nongoverning communist parties like the PKI had to give the global anti-imperialist struggle priority over their own immediate revolutionary aspirations.

Sino-Indonesian Relations on the Eve of the Untung Coup

P'eng Chen's lecture to the PKI on the meaning and implications of the present principal contradiction exposed the inherent conflict between the interests of the two parties. From Peking's analysis it followed that the PKI should not take any action which might impair the Chinese alliance with Sukarno. P'eng was also saying that the Indonesian communists should remember that their revolution was still in its anti-imperialist, national-democratic stage. However, the direction in which the PKI was moving clearly threatened to make the principal contradiction in Indonesia an internal one between the bourgeoisie and the proletariat. Such an outcome could only undermine China's global strategy, which required emphasizing the external contradiction between the Indonesian nation and imperialism. The PKI saw its problems and needs differently. It could not carry out a "revolutionary" united-front-from-below strategy. On the other hand, though Sukarno might somehow still bring the party into the government, it had not been able to attain power through his support in nine years; consequently, there was serious doubt whether a prolonged united-front-from-above strategy would help the PKI avoid becoming domesticated.

Although the PKI appeared to be moving in the Maoist direction, the radical action it took after 1964 seemed designed to keep open the options of fronts from both above and below. In essence, the Aidit leadership ended up—willingly or not—with a two-part strategy embodying elements of the conflicting Soviet and Chinese theories on the seizure of power. Its pressures for land reform and the "Fifth Force" were attempts to find, in the Indonesian context, the equivalent of Mao's united front from below. But because it lacked the essential components of such a united front—armed struggle, peasant revolution, and base areas—its Maoism was not genuine. On the other hand, the PKI persistently tried to win converts from the left wing of the Indonesian elite, infiltrate the armed forces and the bureaucracy, and press for a NASAKOM system in the army, and it staunchly aligned itself with Sukarno. It seemed to be forming a united front from above whose aim was an eventual peaceful takeover of the government, which the Soviets had argued was possible. But Khrushchev's theory of "peaceful transition" applied to national-democratic states that were gradually being drawn into the Russian, not the Chinese, orbit—such as Cuba and Egypt, in which the bourgeoisie supposedly was embracing socialism in order to build a modern industrial state. In effect, the PKI attempted to "Indonesianize" the Russian and Chinese models but left out the essential core ideas of both.

The triumph of Chinese diplomacy, marked by Sukarno's August 17, 1965, speech heralding the alliance with Peking, really masked two serious and unresolved problems.

1. Peking finally had achieved the long-sought anti-imperialist alliance with Indonesia and, evidently, had been able to arrive at same preliminary understanding with Djakarta about the two powers' respective roles in Southeast Asia. But Sukarno's record indicated he was an unreliable ally of communism, and, in the final analysis, the stability of the axis depended on his relations with his generals. By wholeheartedly supporting Indonesia's nationalistic foreign-policy objectives, which were shared by the generals, Peking hoped to reduce any danger to the alliance from Sukarno or the generals. Only time would tell whether her efforts would be successful.

2. The PKI had been won over to the Chinese camp because the CCP had endorsed Aidit's revisionist internal strategy. That strategy had been entirely compatible with, indeed essential to, the CPR's primary goal of forging an alliance with Sukarno. In order to maintain her alliance with the PKI after 1964, however, Peking was compelled to endorse Aidit's shift to a more radical line; the endorsement caused her to run the serious risk of undermining her alliance with Sukarno and thus clearly conflicted with China's global strategy.

The pursuit of a great-power policy in Indonesia had ultimately placed the CPR in a position that bore a striking resemblance to that of the Soviets in relation to China forty years before. Peking's struggle with her external enemies necessitated collaboration with Indonesia's anti-imperialist bourgeois nationalist government. This collaboration was expected to help the PKI eventually capture the leadership of the Indonesian revolution in the course of a protracted anti-imperialist struggle. But it also required that Indonesia's internal revolution had to be subordinated to the world revolution; the former would gain momentum as the international balance of forces changed and facilitated the seizure of power by the proletariat in various countries. Theoretically, the PKI was correct in trying to fuse an "above" and a "below" united-front strategy—provided the fusion did not interfere with the dominance of the external over the internal revolution.

The main difference between the situation Moscow faced in the 1920's and that of Peking in 1965 was, of course, that the Chinese communists were not the directors of the PKI. They could urge but could not compel Aidit to follow an internal line that would adjust to Peking's handling of the international situation. The difficulty was that Aidit's views of what was necessary for the advancement of the Indonesian revolution and the preservation of the PKI ultimately did not accord with Peking's foreign policy. Hence, at the zenith of its success in Indonesia Peking's great-power strategy had produced its own "contradiction": it could not solve the fundamental problem inherent in China's attempt to externalize the united-front model. She could not control the behavior of the constituents of the front, Sukarno and the PKI; but what these two actors did or what happened to them would decisively affect the success or failure of her policy.

8

The Collapse of Chinese
Policy in Indonesia

Because many of the crucial facts surrounding the October 1, 1965, Indonesian coup remain unknown, the affair is still largely a puzzling, though highly debated, mystery.[1] An examination of certain aspects of the coup will attempt to discover, first, whether the CPR played a role in the episode; and, second, the immediate and long-range impact of the coup on the Chinese policy of alliance with Indonesia. The main conclusion that emerges from the evidence is that Peking continued to attempt to preserve the alliance with Sukarno after the coup, despite the determination of the anticommunist officers who survived it to provoke a rupture with China. For more than a year after the generals began their campaign to suppress the Chinese minority in Indonesia and to exterminate the PKI, Peking continued to hope that Sukarno might yet bridle the army and prevent the complete destruction of China's diplomatic influence. She clung to this feeble prospect even after the PKI's shift in 1966 to a Maoist program of armed struggle in the countryside, and despite the

[1] Various hypotheses have been advanced concerning the Indonesian coup. See, for example, Arthur J. Dommen, "The Attempted Coup in Indonesia," *China Quarterly,* 8 (Jan.–March 1966), 144–170; Daniel S. Lev, "Indonesia 1965: The Year of the Coup," *Asian Survey,* 6 (Feb. 1966), 103–110; John O. Sutter, "Two Faces of 'Konfrontasi': 'Crush Malaysia' and 'Gestapu,'" *Asian Survey,* 6 (Oct. 1966), 523–546; and Ruth T. McVey, "Indonesian Communism and China," in Tang Tsou and Ho P'ing, eds., *China in Crisis,* II, 357–394.

234

Suharto regime's systematic overthrow of Indonesia's previous anti-imperialist foreign policy. At length China endorsed the "people's war" doctrine in Indonesia—well into 1967, and after the purge of the CCP leadership in the Cultural Revolution had resulted in a more generally militant Chinese foreign policy in Southeast Asia and elsewhere.

The Coup: Its Origins and Actors

Documentary and circumstantial evidence indicates that the October 1 coup was primarily the work of dissident junior officers who were loyal to Sukarno and apparently convinced that the army's anticommunist high command would have to be removed so that the president's conception of the Indonesian revolution might be realized. The main participants in the plot were Colonel Untung (of the Palace Guard), whose forces momentarily seized control of central Djakarta; Vice-Marshal Dhani (commander of the air force); General Supardjo (commander of the Fourth Combat Command, in West Borneo); and Colonels Suherman, Usman, and Marjono (all of the Diponegoro Division, Central Java). Army Colonel Latief and Flight Major Sujono also played prominent roles in the Djakarta coup.

To carry out the coup, which had two centers—Djakarta and Central Java—the plotters had very limited forces. These consisted of units from the Palace Guard, Battalion 454 of the Diponegoro Division, and a small number of young men and women drawn from the PKI-controlled organizations, Gerwani and Pemuda Rakjat. The communist groups had received some military training at Halim Air Force Base outside Djakarta, and, although they played a minor role in the coup, their participation fatally implicated the PKI. Untung's proclamation of a revolutionary council[2] to protect Sukarno and the revolution was apparently timed to coordinate with another coup, within the

[2] Text broadcast by Djakarta Radio domestic service, Oct. 1, 1965, at approximately 7:15 A.M.

army in Central Java, aimed at seizing control of the Diponegoro Division. The fact that at every key location—the palace, air force headquarters, Central Java, and Halim Air Force Base—the success or failure of the whole plot was in the hands of military officers is the most glaring evidence that the coup was mainly the outgrowth of conflict within the Indonesian armed forces.

The political situation in Indonesia immediately prior to the event also suggests that a provocative move within the army was more likely than one by the PKI. As noted earlier, since 1965 tensions between the army and the communists had risen sharply as a result of the latter's increasingly radical demands and Sukarno's apparent receptivity to them. Whether wholly true or not, from the army's standpoint the president had, to a dangerous extent, shifted from his past role of arbitrator between the rivals toward positive encouragement of the communists. Prior to the coup a situation existed which indicated that in the near future either the anticommunist generals would have to stop Sukarno or he would have to remove some of them in order to carry out his policies and programs. It seems very unlikely that the generals ever contemplated more than an attempt at deterring Sukarno from moving too far toward the left, for the Indonesian officer corps was sharply divided in its loyalties, and a move to unseat the president might ignite a crisis in the army and, possibly, civil war. And though it is quite probable that Sukarno wanted—and may have intended—to displace certain generals with officers he could more easily control, if he removed the generals he ran the risk of a showdown which might unite his opponents.

Under these circumstances the least likely prospect was a unilateral move by the PKI to break the deadlock. An attempt to seize power directly would have been suicidal from any standpoint. On the other hand, although the communist leaders greatly feared suppression by the army, Sukarno's gradual progression toward the left advantaged them, especially since he might ultimately be able to dismiss the more reactionary generals and bring the PKI into the government, which only he could do. Hence it is inconceivable that the communists would have involved themselves in any action aimed at removing the main barrier between them and suppression.

It also does not seem likely that the PKI, acting alone, would have risked leading a pre-emptive coup against the generals. For if the party's gradualist and "revisionist" strategy reflected an unpromising but unavoidable meld of the conflicting Soviet and Chinese revolutionary models, a pre-emptive coup against the army might very well have split the party. Those who favored a gradual revolution from "below" would not have wanted to force a direct confrontation they had not prepared for and could not win. Advocacy by any supposed pro-Maoists of a coup would have involved a contradiction in terms, because the core of the Maoist strategy is the precept that coups do not work, that only long, arduous preparation and struggle in the countryside are effective. If the idea of a coup sprang from any group in the PKI that approved the Soviet-style "above" strategy, it could only mean that an ultraradical faction suddenly rejected the Khrushchev peaceful-transition line in favor of a mini-Bolshevik *Putsch,* like Lenin's in 1918. The difficulty here, of course, was that Aidit did not have Lenin's worker-soldier soviets—the famous twenty thousand who seized Petrograd—and in Sukarno and Nasution (Indonesia's Minister of Defense) he faced no bungling Kerensky.

To attempt a coup at all, the PKI would have had to rely on dissident army commanders and units. It requires some stretch of the imagination to believe that even PKI "revisionism" had gone so far as to result in placing the fate of the whole communist movement in the hands of a few bourgeois officers and thus risk a full showdown with no possibility of external help and no reliable strongholds or military forces to fall back on should the operation fail. Finally, it is hard to conceive of a PKI leadership so careful and methodical that it could overcome these handicaps and escape these pitfalls but so stupid that it would endorse the coup in the party's leading journal the day after it had already failed.[3]

The PKI's involvement in the coup seems far more probable if two different assumptions are made: that the coup was initiated and directed by loyalist Sukarno officers; and that its aim was limited to removing the key generals who stood in the way of the president and his allies, so that Sukarno's NASAKOM conception could be realized. The achievement of the goal was contingent on the elimination of all the generals who were the targets of the operation and on the quick gaining of Sukarno's legitimization of the deed. When Generals Suharto and Nasution escaped, Sukarno, whose own motives and role are the crucial missing links in the riddle, temporized, and the coup quickly collapsed.

The fact that members of PKI organizations participated in the murder of the generals and that *Harian Rakjat,* the principal communist newspaper, endorsed the Untung coup implicated the communists in the movement but did not prove that they controlled it. If the party played a leading role, there seems no reason why, at the decisive moment in the early hours—when success still seemed possible—the communists did not mobilize their massive organizations for direct political action in the streets; and why, once the coup had failed, the party's offices and most of its leaders continued to operate openly, even as the army began to arrest party members. Such suicidal behavior does not square with the image of the PKI leaders as infinitely crafty

[3] See *Harian Rakjat,* October 2, 1965. By the late afternoon of October 1 General Suharto was already deploying overwhelmingly stronger forces in the capital. In the absence of a public statement by Sukarno supporting Untung, or direct mass action in the streets by PKI organizations, the ultimate fate of the coup was sealed by this time. Under these circumstances, if the PKI was directing the coup it surely had the strongest reasons and ample time to prevent the publication of this incriminating article supporting Untung.

plotters. At the most, it suggests that if the party played any role, it was that of a supporter rather than a director. For the PKI leaders and organs acted in the immediate postcoup period as if it were clear to everyone that what had occurred was a dispute within the officer corps and that Sukarno would somehow control the situation and protect them.

To explain away the predominant role brother officers played in the coup, the army attempted to assign the guilt exclusively to the PKI. The army's case can neither be proved nor disproved but is nevertheless highly dubious. The army contended that the PKI had duped, misled, persuaded, or otherwise influenced several hundred officers and men to do its bidding, yet not one of them had sense enough to see he was being used in a communist plot to seize power. From the standpoint of the army's postcoup political problems, however, this explanation made very good sense. No other interpretation could justify the subsequent massive extermination of the PKI by the military, and certainly not the army's overthrow of Sukarno, who was the "Supreme Great Leader of the Revolution" and the "Great Teacher"—in fact, the personal embodiment of the state, by law.

How else could the army justify the overthrow of the embodiment of the state on the ground that six generals had been slain by rebellious junior officers working with communist youth and women's groups armed and trained by the air force? Constitutionally, the power to mete out punishment to the assassins was vested wholly in the Sukarno government, not the army. But by charging that the PKI had planned and directed the coup, the army succeeded in displacing Sukarno and made itself the embodiment of the state. The careful and deliberate way in which the army gradually stripped Sukarno of his powers after the coup shows how delicately this abandonment of Indonesian constitutionalism had to be accomplished.

Later events also support the interpretation that the coup was the result of intra-army conflict. Long after the communist party was suppressed, the army continued to carry out a sweeping purge of its own ranks, arresting and imprisoning large numbers of officers and men allegedly involved in the *Gestapu* (September 30 Movement). This purge is hard to reconcile with the army's original contention that only a handful of "dupes" in its own ranks took part in an otherwise PKI-run affair. On the contrary, the purge of officers suggests that the faction in the army which eventually won out as a result of the coup tried to stamp out what was, evidently, a sizable number of officers whose primary loyalty was to Sukarno, not to the anticommunist high command. If Sukarno and the coup planners had this much open and latent support within the army, it seems even less likely that the *Gestapu* was stage-managed by the PKI or, if it had succeeded, that the winners would then have been dependent on the communists.

Although conflicts within the Indonesian military apparently ignited the coup, the PKI surely played a major role in the overall genesis of the crisis. Whatever the internal problems or needs the PKI was responding to, its policies and actions after 1964 were provocative and bound to produce a confrontation eventually unless the army or Sukarno yielded. The PKI's decision to re-open the land-reform issue was a direct challenge to the status quo in the countryside, and the army could not possibly watch the position of the Muslim landholders deteriorate unless it was willing to countenance a drastic political change in the villages that would also, at some point, undermine the balance of power nationally. The whole course of the army's post-1957 rivalry with the communists repeatedly had shown that it would not permit this to happen. For the same reason the army could not tolerate a "Fifth Force" in which PKI-controlled organizations would acquire military training and weapons. The same logic applied to the concept of "Nasakomization" in the armed services, an undisguised plan to break up the officer corps's control over its own units, and hence its base of power.

When the PKI, not satisfied with raising these issues, openly attacked certain segments of the army as "bureaucratic capitalists," it was clear that the party hoped Sukarno would respond by removing the obstreperous generals who blocked radical reforms and communist participation in the government. And since Sukarno seemed almost ready to meet the PKI's demands, one does not have to accept the army's version of the coup to understand that the PKI had given the anticommunist generals ample cause for alarm and a solid reason for suppressing the party after the immediate crisis had passed.

It is equally clear that China's policy toward Indonesia also contributed, indirectly, to the tensions precipitating the coup, though a PKI-army showdown cannot have been Peking's intention or in her interests. China wanted a militant Indonesian ally that was prepared to run substantial risks in the dispute with Malaysia and to alienate herself, as Peking had, from all nations save the members of the CPR's anti-imperialist coalition. Sukarno's commitment to external radicalism was not motivated by Peking's strident calls for action against the imperialists; he was, if complicated and difficult to understand, very much his own man. But Peking's support buttressed Sukarno's disposition to press on with militant nationalism, and his militancy no doubt was opposed by some Indonesian generals who favored more cautious tactics, even though they shared many of his basic foreign-policy aspirations.

The effort China made to cultivate ties with the Indonesian military leaders may have lessened their past suspicions about her motives and may even have inclined some officers to look favorably on Sukarno's alliance with her. But that did not mean the army was prepared to engage in acts which, from the military viewpoint, threatened Indonesia's security or played into the hands of the PKI. After the British military build-up in 1964, the Indonesian army took care to ensure that its actions in the Malaysian campaign would not lead to a direct confrontation.

With or without additional Soviet arms, Indonesia's air and naval forces would have been greatly overmatched in any conflict by those Britain had deployed in Malaysia. If the generals truly feared a British attack, which Djakarta charged was eminent, by encouraging Sukarno's policy of further heightening the anti-imperialist struggle, Peking helped to exacerbate tensions between him and the army. The aid and friendship China was willing to give to advance a militant Indonesian foreign policy, therefore, had the unintended and harmful side effect of strengthening the generals' objections to an alliance with the CPR. Any groups in the Indonesian military who favored the axis with China were quickly silenced after the coup, while the faction that emerged victorious attempted to link Peking to its theory of a PKI plot against the state.

It was not surprising that the Indonesian army failed to produce evidence proving Peking's involvement in the coup and shortly abandoned the effort.[4] China's attempt to forge an alliance with Sukarno, and her theses on how revolutions should be waged, both argued against the likelihood that she favored or would have supported a hazardous move in Indonesia, especially if it was undertaken by the PKI. P'eng Chen's two speeches in Indonesia, the last Chinese statements prior to the coup about the PKI's road to power, smacked of lecturing Aidit not to emphasize the internal class struggle at a time when China and Indonesia should be concentrating their efforts to defeat the external imperialist danger. Moreover, if the Indonesian coup had been

---

[4] Several Indonesian newspapers circulated the story that China had secretly shipped the weapons used in the coup into the country by means of crates ostensibly containing supplies and machinery to be used in building the site for the Conference of "New Emerging Forces" (CONEFO). When it became known that from the moment of their arrival in Indonesia the crates from China were the exclusive possession of the army, the high command, to support its own case that the coup was a PKI-run affair, was obliged to deny the report. See Djakarta Radio broadcast, October 21, 1965.

successful, it could not have been presented as a triumph of the Chinese revolutionary strategy—being just the reverse of it; and what anti-imperialist bourgeois nationalist leadership would thereafter be interested in an alignment with Peking if pro-communist coups like the one in Indonesia were the specters of things to come?

At best, a successful coup would have made army head-quarters in Djakarta more responsive to Sukarno. Would he then have needed the PKI to counterbalance the anticommunists? And if the coup had at length brought the PKI into the government, what would the anticommunist commanders and their Moslem supporters in the outer islands have done? Would they have simply collapsed, or would they have turned to Malaysia and the West (as they had in 1958), with which they had no real quarrel? Would the United States, which was then deploying a massive force in South Vietnam, have stood idly by and per-mitted the still stronger Indonesian anticommunist forces to be gradually defeated when its declared policy was to prevent the expansion of communism and Chinese influence in southeast Asia, by force of arms if necessary? And how would the mercurial Sukarno have veiwed the alliance with Peking if the coup had strengthened his own domestic position? On every occasion in the past when circumstances had permitted, he had invariably turned first to Washington and Moscow, and to Peking only in desperation.

It is reasonable to take at face value Chinese communist ideological pronouncements assailing the prospects of "peaceful transition," and hence to assume that Peking very much doubted that the Aidit policy would succeed in Indonesia. But it does not follow that the Chinese would have urged the PKI to seize power in a manner wholly contrary to their precepts on how power should be seized. In view of their past relations with the inde-pendently minded Aidit group, it is very doubtful that Peking rated the prospect or the value of an alliance with Aidit as high as, or higher than, the possibility or worth of one with Sukarno. To whom would a communist Indonesia—a large Southeast Asian Cuba—turn for military protection and economic aid? To China, groping her way out of the earlier collapse of the Great Leap Forward and on the brink of war with the United States? Or to the Soviet Union, as North Korea and North Vietnam were doing in 1965, mending their fences with Moscow when a real imperialist danger had to be faced? Of all the international parties affected by the Indonesian coup, Peking stood to win the least if it succeeded and to lose the most if it failed.

China's Response to the Coup

The day the coup took place seventeen Indonesian delegations were in Peking, some to attend the celebration of the fifteenth anniversary of the CPR, others to conclude negotiations on technical and economic cooperation as well as trade and payment agreements between the two countries.[5] When Indonesian Trade Minister Saleh left Peking after the issuance of a joint statement on October 4, 1965,[6] there was no indication that China's plans to consolidate the alliance with Sukarno had been at all affected by the turn of events in Djakarta, though by this time the whole world knew that a coup with communist overtones had been put down.

China's first official response to the crisis in Djakarta was a personal message from Liu Shao-ch'i and Chou En-lai to Sukarno on October 3 extending "cordial regards and heartfelt wishes" for his continuing safety and expressing the hope that under his leadership Indonesia would "develop still further the spirit of opposing imperialism and Malaysia."[7] Any hope Peking had that by ignoring the coup she could preserve the previous rela-

[5] *Peking Review*, 8 (Oct. 8), 1965.
[6] Text in NCNA (Peking), Oct. 5, 1965.
[7] Letter in NCNA (Peking), Oct. 4, 1965.

tionship between China and Indonesia was, however, quickly dashed by the Indonesian generals.

Within two weeks of the quashing of the coup, the army's developing campaign to suppress the PKI led to a rash of anti-CPR incidents, including the arrest and detention of suspected Chinese nationals. On October 16 the impending conflict between Peking and the Indonesian generals erupted when the army forcibly entered and searched the offices of the Chinese commercial counselor in Djakarta. The same day the army's newspaper charged that the Indonesian Foreign Ministry had lodged a protest with the CPR about its embassy's refusal to fly its flag at half-mast on October 5 in honor of the generals killed during the attempted coup.[8] This protest announced the official opening of the army's campaign to destroy the alliance with China.

Peking sent a strong protest on October 18 assailing the army's search of her counselor's offices and calling the army's attempts to implicate China in the coup "lies and slander." She warned that "an anti-Chinese wave is starting in Indonesia and if it is not checked the consequences will be serious."[9] The Chinese dismissed as "sheer fabrication" the army's allegation that Djakarta had protested the flag incident; they asserted that no protest note had been sent by Djakarta and that the normal diplomatic custom of the CPR was to lower its flag only after the death of a chief of state.[10] The army, of course, knew that Peking was not going to "honor" the slain anticommunist generals. The Cuban embassy also did not lower its flag, but since the army was interested in provoking a rupture with Peking, not Havana, this slight was overlooked.

For two weeks after the coup was put down China withheld

[8] *Angkatan Bersendjata* (Djakarta), Oct. 16, 1965.
[9] NCNA (Peking), Oct. 18, 1965.
[10] NCNA (Peking), Oct. 20, 1965.

any comment on the overall political situation in Indonesia. On October 19 she released a long and carefully constructed resumé of documents and reports from Indonesian and foreign sources.[11] It stated that the New China News Agency (Hsin Hua) in Djakarta had been prevented by the army from sending any dispatches and that therefore the present report had to rely on information other than that normally supplied by its own correspondent. However, the timing of the October 19 account indicated that China had purposely delayed making a statement until she had appraised the situation. What she saw was most disturbing. The report, as it appeared in *People's Daily* the following day, revealed a great deal about Peking's estimate of the crisis and what her initial response to it would be.

The report began with excerpts from "Documents of the September 30 Movement" showing that Untung's coup was "an internal affair of the Army" designed to forestall a plot to seize power by a CIA-backed "Council of Generals." (The same interpretation was given earlier by the PKI.) Next, it dealt with the attitude of the Indonesian army, plainly indicating that General Suharto, by crushing the Untung group, was in the process of staging a countercoup, was purging the pro-Sukarno air force command and banning the PKI's organizations. Thus far this disguised political editorial said, in effect: "Loyalist officers have attempted to save the Indonesian revolution from a CIA-army plot, but the reactionaries under Suharto are gaining the upper hand." The next items discussed were statements and speeches by Sukarno, which presented a very bleak, though not hopeless, outlook. The discussion noted that on October 1, Sukarno had "temporarily" appointed General Pranoto (a pro-Sukarno officer) to assume "routine charge of Army affairs," had called for "an atmosphere of calm" that would permit the president to make "a political solution," and, on October 2 and 3, had described the

[11] NCNA (Peking), Oct. 19, 1965; reprinted in *People's Daily*, Oct. 20.

coup as "not correct," a "misunderstanding in the Army" which must not be allowed to sow discord beneficial to "imperialism, colonialism and neo-colonialism."

But the report clearly indicated that Peking feared Sukarno's efforts to regain control of the situation were crumbling. The very day he had appointed Pranoto, Suharto declared that he had taken personal command of the army "for the time being." Thereafter Sukarno's power began to deteriorate rapidly. On October 2, Sukarno attempted to divide the army command by reasserting Pranoto's appointment while at the same time giving Suharto the authority to "restore order . . . in compliance with the policy laid down by me." The implication was that Sukarno had been compelled to turn over the real power of the army to the anticommunist officers. According to the October 19 account, Sukarno, leaving a cabinet meeting on October 6, again asked all parties not to "deepen the hatred." But the slain generals (whose funeral he had earlier declined to attend) he now described as "revolutionary heroes." That Sukarno had lost the first round for control over the army was positively established on October 15, when he was forced to replace Pranoto with Suharto, and on the sixteenth, when he was compelled to empower the latter to conduct the "investigation" of the coup, as a result of which, Sukarno said, he would make a judgment.

General Suharto's conception of the investigation evidently produced the raid on the Chinese counselor's offices (October 16) and a decree temporarily outlawing the PKI (October 18). These moves accelerated the army's two-pronged attack on China and the PKI which had been building up since October 5 with the arrest of hundreds of suspects (many of them Chinese nationals), the suppression of party organizations, the closing of left-wing schools, and editorials in the anticommunist press which included such exhortations and indications of things to come as "Hang Aidit" and "Get the Gallows Ready."

Having reviewed the background, the report next discussed

the position of the Indonesian Communist party. It referred to a letter from Aidit of October 2 which called the coup "an internal affair of the Army [in which] the Indonesian Communist Party will not interfere." But also mentioned were Aidit's support of "purification" measures in the state organs, his condemnation of the Council of Generals, and the fatal *Harian Rakjat* statement describing the coup as "patriotic and revolutionary" and urging the people's "vigilance and readiness to face all eventualities." Although the PKI's organizations were already being suppressed, there was no hint in the Chinese news report that Peking thought the time had come for revolutionary struggle. On the contrary, if China was giving any advice, it seemed to be "Stand your ground; don't panic."

The account evidenced an attitude similar to the one Chinese statements and editorials were to adhere to until mid-1966. China would verbally respond to the gauntlet thrown down by the Indonesian army and expose the generals' anti-Chinese, anticommunist actions. By doing so she probably hoped to strengthen Sukarno's position, the collapse of which would mean the end of the alliance. Despite growing provocation from the right wing of the Indonesian army, Peking did not early consign Djakarta to reactionary status or call for an Indonesian "people's war," as might have been expected given the precarious position of the PKI and the militant-sounding revolutionary line China had been identified with since the early 1960's, especially following the 1965 Lin Piao statement. Instead, Peking responded to the immediate post-October 1965 crisis in Indonesia as if the threat it posed to her was similar to that she faced during the overseas Chinese dispute of 1959 and 1960 and could be checked, ultimately, when Sukarno managed to regain the upper hand. A similar attitude was adopted by the PKI; after the coup had failed and the army suppression had begun, it refrained from resisting, in the mistaken hope that Sukarno would sooner or later save the situation.

Beginning in mid-October 1965, the Indonesian army engaged in numerous—almost weekly—provocative acts against the CPR, including the mistreatment of Chinese residents and a series of demonstrations against its diplomatic mission. Predictably, these incidents were followed by official Chinese protests condemning the anticommunist generals.[12] The main theme running through these documents, however, was that the army's behavior was contrary to President Sukarno's policies of friendship with China and Indonesia's adherence to the anti-imperialist struggle. In turn, the Indonesian anticommunist press tried to present Peking's verbal opposition to army brutality against the Chinese in Indonesia and suspected communists as evidence of China's complicity in the coup or as another form of foreign intervention in Indonesian affairs. To some extent, as in 1959 and 1960, China's open defense of her friends and allies actually played into the army's hands.

The Destruction of the Peking-Djakarta Axis

By February 19, 1966, friction with China had been so exacerbated that the generals were able to demand the recall of Ambassador Djawoto from Peking, ostensibly to face charges of involvement in the Gestapu. While Peking's vitriolic attacks on the army made a diplomatic break more likely than ever, presumably they also helped to force the ultimate showdown between Sukarno and his generals. On February 21, Sukarno removed General Nasution from his post as defense minister—an attempt to regain the authority he had lost over the army since the coup. This political comeback, however, proved to be very short-lived. On March 11, 1966, Sukarno was forced to make General Suharto acting president and to give him sweeping powers. Suharto promptly installed a new cabinet which was devoid of the old Sukarno supporters and dominated by the army. This

[12] See CPR Foreign Ministry protest notes in NCNA (Peking), November 3 and 5, 1965.

Chinese Policy toward Indonesia

event marked the *de facto* fall of the Sukarno regime and fore-shadowed the end of the alliance with Peking.

Once the army had emerged victorious from the showdown with Sukarno, the formal dismantling of the Peking-Djakarta axis proceeded rapidly. In early April, Peking charged that a "rightist military clique," in collusion with the United States and the Soviet Union, had "coerced" Sukarno and "seized state power by staging a coup d'etat."[13] Apparently convinced that there was no longer much possibility of ensuring the protection of the most ill-treated of the Chinese residents of Indonesia, on May 18, 1966, Peking announced that ships would be sent to repatriate those CPR nationals wishing to leave Indonesia.[14] Although the abuse to which the Chinese in Indonesia were subjected was far more extreme in 1966 and 1967 than in 1959 and 1960, this time Peking Radio broadcast no appeals for a massive exodus. Fragmentary reports indicate that apparently no more than ten thousand availed themselves of the option to leave Indonesia.[15]

The impossibility of providing protection for the Chinese in Indonesia after Sukarno fell led to a series of diplomatic and political decisions. The first of these was the announcement on March 26, 1966, that Peking had closed "temporarily" her consulates in Medan, Bandjarmasin, and Makassar.[16] In April the CPR granted Ambassador Djawoto political asylum—thus openly siding with former friends of Sukarno and sympathizers with the PKI—and in May she dramatized the break with Suharto's new regime by recalling Yao Chung-ming, the ambassador to

[13] NCNA (Peking), April 4, 6, 1966.

[14] CPR Foreign Ministry note, NCNA (Peking), May 18, 1966.

[15] In the province of Atjeh (north Sumatra) alone several hundred Chinese were killed. Elsewhere the Chinese endured widespread destruction of property, looting, and innumerable acts of vandalism in what was tantamount to a pogrom.

[16] CPR Foreign Ministry statement, NCNA (Peking), March 26, 1966.

Indonesia. These acts were followed by the suspension of all Chinese economic aid and technical assistance, the abrogation of the 1965 agreement to establish a Sino-Indonesian shipping line, and the closing of the New China News Agency in Djakarta.

General Suharto quickly proceeded to destroy the axis from the other end. In July 1966 the Indonesian consulate and the Antara News Agency in Peking were closed. A short time later airline flights to Canton were suspended and all trade with China was cut off. However, Djakarta's most dramatic attempts to break up the alliance were reflected in her relations with China's enemies. After the army took over the government, Indonesia terminated the confrontation with Malaysia (June 1, 1966); secured assurances of forthcoming economic aid from the United States (September 19, 1966); reclaimed her U.N. seat (September 27, 1966); and obtained a rescheduling of the extensive payments owed to Western powers (September 29, 1966) and the Soviet Union (November 24, 1966). In taking these steps, Suharto's government clearly was not only committed to destroying domestic communist influence and the alliance with China, but also intended to revive in Indonesia's foreign policy a brand of nonalignment which, in practice, served the interests of the United States.

The PKI's "Self-Criticism" and Sukarno's Fall

According to every ideological test—the massacre of the PKI, suppression of the resident Chinese, destruction of the alliance with China, and restoration of close ties to Malaysia and Washington—the Suharto regime should have been immediately singled out as the target for a Chinese declaration calling for revolutionary war in Indonesia. Peking made no such call, though she began making inflammatory statements as early as April 1966, when she labeled the Indonesian military forces "loyal agents of U.S. imperialism and diehard reactionaries" who were "opposing China and wrecking the Afro-Asian cause of solidarity against imperialism [and had] shamelessly trampled underfoot the Bandung principles and soiled the glorious name of Bandung."[17] The attacks on Suharto, however, stopped short of advocating a revolutionary line toward Indonesia; the restraint suggested that Peking still had not completely abandoned hope that a Sukarnoist restoration was possible.

The perfect opportunity—which afforded a seemingly compelling reason—to call for revolution in Indonesia was presented to the Chinese leaders between May and September 1966, but they chose to ignore it. During this period the remanent leadership of the Indonesian Communist party met somewhere in Central Java to conduct a "self-criticism" of the party's past mistakes and to map out a new strategy. As a result of these deliberations, the PKI underground Politbureau published three documents[18] which repudiated the "petty-bourgeois" and "revisionist" line of its slain leader D. N. Aidit and announced a new Maoist path of armed revolutionary struggle in the countryside.

Among the many revelations contained in the PKI self-criticism documents, three warrant mention at this point because they shed useful light on the relationship between the Aidit leadership and the CCP prior to the 1965 coup. First, it is clear that PKI

[17] The basic condemnation of the Suharto regime was spelled out in a "Commentator" editorial in *Jen-min Jih-pao*, April 27, 1966. For other attacks on Suharto see NCNA (Peking), May 27, 1966, and June 12, 1966; and the CPR Foreign Ministry protest note of June 9, 1966, in *Peking Review*, 9 (June 17, 1966), 31–35.

[18] See "Uphold the Honour and the Reputation of Communists," Political Bureau statement of May 23, 1966, and "Take the Road of Revolution to Realize the Tasks That Should Have Been Accomplished by the August Revolution of 1945," Political Bureau statement of August 17, 1966, *Indonesian Tribune* (Tirana, Albania), 1 (Nov. 1966), 6–20; and "Build the PKI along the Marxist-Leninist Line to Lead the People's Democratic Revolution in Indonesia," Political Bureau statement of September 1966, *ibid.*, 1 (Jan. 1967), 6–29.

strategy, to the extent that it was influenced by external advice at all, was more in accord with Khrushchev's than with Mao's views. The documents charge that after 1951, and especially after the CPSU Twentieth Party Congress in 1956, the Aidit line "merged with the influence of modern revisionism in the international Communist movement" and that until the coup Moscow's influence on the party "was by no means eradicated." The PKI leadership committed errors because it allegedly wanted to be on good terms with the CPSU in order to preserve the united front with the Indonesian national bourgeoisie.[19] Second, the self-criticism openly admits that the PKI had a hand in the coup, though it is not clear what the hand actually did. Apparently the charge that the PKI's leader had engaged in "adventurism" and that by "violating organizational rules they had easily involved themselves in the September 30th Movement"[20] was an elliptical means of confessing that Aidit had conspired with the Sukarnoist army officers in their plot without the approval or knowledge of the party Central Committee, and perhaps not even the full Politbureau. Third, the documents explicitly deny that the PKI suffered disaster because "it had adhered to the so-called Peking line" but, "on the contrary," that its defeat was "precisely the result of its Right opportunist and revisionist mistakes, of its failure to consistently put into practice Comrade Mao Tse-tung's teaching on Party buildings, on armed struggle and on revolutionary united front."[21]

Two of the revelations point to the conclusion that the Indonesian communists had never been seriously committed to, or under the influence of, a Maoist-type revolutionary strategy. They also support the interpretation presented in Chapter 6, above, that P'eng Chen's visit in May 1965 exposed the existence of important differences, rather than similarities, between the

[19] "Build the PKI . . . ," pp. 8–9.
[20] *Ibid.*, p. 6.
[21] Editor's note, *Indonesian Tribune*, 1 (Jan. 1967), 5.

CCP's and the PKI's ideas about strategy. The third revelation implies that if Aidit "violated organizational rules" and "easily involved" the leadership in the junior officers' plot by not telling the Politbureau about it, it is very unlikely that he conferred with, or was influenced by, anyone in Peking. Moreover, Aidit's failure to rally the party organization to resist after the coup and his decision to wait for a Sukarno comeback are hardly proof of his slavish enthusiasm for the Chinese revolutionary line, especially since that stern code regards coups from the top and reliance on the bourgeoisie as cardinal sins.

On the contrary, the self-criticism documents seem to charge the Aidit group, fairly, with "adventurism" for allowing the party to be trapped in a situation in which the leadership participated in a reckless act, isolating itself from the party organizations and the masses; and with "capitulationism," in making the fate of the movement depend on Sukarno after counterrevolutionary suppression had left the party with no alternative but to go underground and engage in resistance. The commission and admission of these errors by the PKI constitute yet another link in the chain of evidence which indicates that, except for their common interest in a Peking-Djakarta anti-imperialist alliance, the CCP and the PKI were far apart on the question of the correct strategy to be followed in the Indonesian revolution, long before the coup and after it.

China's failure to endorse immediately the PKI's shift to Maoism did not necessarily mean that she had reservations about the PKI's shift. If the CCP intended to back the PKI's armed-struggle line, presumably Peking preferred to wait for an occasion when she could announce this backing with appropriate fanfare and drama. Such an occasion presented itself during the first week of November 1966, when the Albanian communists held their Fifth Party Congress. Indeed, that gathering of Peking's staunchest ideological allies could hardly have been improved on as a suitable occasion to hail the triumph, at long last, of Maoism in Indonesia. Since, in May 1966, the Albanians themselves had foreshadowed the PKI's shift by issuing a major statement arguing that the Indonesian communists now had to wage an "armed struggle of workers and peasants,"[22] the stage seemed to be well prepared for a Chinese ideological finale calling for revolutionary war against the Suharto government.

The leader of the PKI delegation to the congress, Politbureau member Adjitorop (who had been given asylum in Peking since the coup) spelled out the essence of his Party's previous errors and reiterated the self-criticism documents' call for a new three-point program: reconstruction of the PKI "on Marxist-Leninist lines"; preparation "to lead a long, armed struggle fused with the agrarian revolution of the peasantry in the countryside"; and formation of a united front of "all forces opposed to the right-wing generals" and based on "the alliance of the working class with the peasantry, under the leadership of the proletariat." Adjitorop declared that the PKI, thus armed with "Marxism-Leninism and the thought of Mao Tse-tung," would "vanquish" the Suharto-Nasution regime and establish "the people's power."[23] The Chinese communist spokesman at the congress, far from taking this declaration as the cue to welcome the repentant Indonesian communists into the fold, made no mention of the PKI's recent complete about-face.[24] Moreover, Peking's subsequent report, intended for international audiences, on Adjitorop's speech was limited to brief excerpts which did not include the passages admitting past PKI errors or Adjitorop's main point that hence-

[22] For the Albanian communist position on the PKI's past mistakes and what it should do to correct them see "The Fascist Coup d'Etat in Indonesia and Its Lessons for Communists," *Zeri I Popullit* (Tirana), May 11, 1966.

[23] See the greeting to the Fifth Congress of the Albanian Workers' Party from the Central Committee of the Indonesian Communist Party, Radio Tirana, Nov. 4, 1966.

[24] See the speeches by CCP Politbureau member Kang Sheng, in *Peking Review*, 9 (Nov. 11, 1966, 13–18; Nov. 18, 1966, 31–33).

forth the Indonesian communists would follow a Maoist armed struggle line.[25] Clearly, the PKI's shift to a Maoist strategy had not, in itself, been sufficient to cause the CCP to escalate further the dispute with Djakarta at this time.

Insofar as events in Indonesia influenced Peking's decision to withhold a declaration of revolutionary war against the Suharto regime, the only factor that concerned her after the Albanian party congress was whether a Sukarno comeback was even remotely possible. The fact that the Indonesian army had not felt strong enough to depose him completely and officially in March 1966 must have sustained Peking's hope that the counterrevolutionaries would not be able to consolidate their power. Western reporters who observed the Indonesian scene in mid-1966 saw evidence that Sukarno still had considerable political support in Java.[26] East and Central Java were also the main strongholds of the PKI; hence the party's move to an armed-struggle policy in the period between May and September 1966 may have been viewed in Peking, not as a shift to a strictly revolutionary, class-war line, but as a means of triggering a broadly based uprising of nationalist and communist groups that might bring down the generals and restore Sukarno. An endorsement of the PKI's position that was indicated in the 1966 self-criticism obviously would have conflicted with China's hope for a Sukarno comeback, since the Indonesian comrades had prematurely repudiated their former policy of collaboration with him. It therefore appears that the different objectives and interests of the two communist parties were still operative, even after the PKI had shed its revisionist ideas and programs.

If the Indonesian situation of 1966 had resulted in a civil war advantageous to the Sukarnoist elements, no doubt more information would be available about the extent of the discord between

[25] *Peking Review,* 9 (Nov. 25, 1966), 20.

[26] For example, Donald Kirk, "Sukarno's Holdouts in Central Java," *The Reporter,* 36 (Sept. 8, 1966).

Peking and the PKI. But the resistance of Sukarno's disorganized supporters was not spirited, and the PKI's shift to armed-struggle tactics did not ignite a national resistance movement. On the contrary, the army was able to continue the communist-suppression campaign without unleashing a civil war.

By April 1967 the Suharto regime felt strong enough to complete the last phase of Sukarno's overthrow and thereupon formally divested him of the presidency. Confined thereafter to the palace at Bogor, he no longer constituted a serious threat to the generals' consolidation of power. At this point Peking's last hope for a political miracle vanished, and with it her interest in maintaining even the semblance of normal diplomatic ties. On April 24, 1967, Indonesia expelled the CPR's chargé d'affaires and her consul general from Djakarta. The following day China responded by expelling the Indonesian chargé d'affaires from Peking. Diplomatic relations between the two states were suspended in October 1967[27] and have not been restored.

The Revival of a Revolutionary Policy

Peking's long-delayed endorsement of the PKI's Maoist revolutionary line came in July 1967,[28] three months after Sukarno was stripped of the presidential title. Ironically, the firm establishment, for the foreseeable future at least, of anticommunist rule in Indonesia doubtless made possible a closer identification between Peking's and the PKI's views and interests than at any previous time. That the Chinese leaders waited three months after Sukarno's final fall to endorse the new line of their Indonesian comrades suggests that the implications of adopting an

[27] CPR Foreign Ministry note Oct. 27, 1967; in *Peking Review*, 10 (Nov. 3, 1967), 5–6.

[28] "People of Indonesia, Unite and Fight to Overthrow the Fascist Regime," *Hung-ch'i*, No. 11 (July 7, 1967), 14–17. The appearance of this article in the CCP's leading theoretical journal indicated that it was a major statement of policy on Indonesia.

unequivocally revolutionary attitude toward Djakarta had been carefully weighed. The timing of the decision also had been influenced by profound changes in China's foreign and domestic situation.

Soon after the Indonesian coup and the overthrow of Sukarno, China was in the throes of an unprecedented internal upheaval—the Great Proletarian Cultural Revolution. The disruption of national policies during this crisis was so extensive that virtually no governmental activity or agency escaped intact. The Ministry of Foreign Affairs was subjected to considerable harassment by the Red Guards, and many of its top policy-making officials were purged. Relations with a number of countries were inevitably impaired when the ideological momentum built up by the Cultural Revolution spread from China to the external world. The hostile attitude Peking adopted toward many countries with which she had previously been on good terms did not subside until late in 1968, by which time normal relations with most of these states had had begun to be re-established

Although Chinese policy toward Indonesia was undoubtedly affected by the generally militant fervor of the Cultural Revolution, the substance of that policy was not the product of irrational emotion. Peking did not take a "hard line" toward the Suharto regime until a year after the May 1966 launching of the Cultural Revolution, and it was not abandoned after the Chinese domestic situation had calmed down after late 1968. The more sensational episodes of that two-year period obscured the fact that in the course of the Cultural Revolution a major shift was quietly occurring in Chinese policy. The defeat in Indonesia and an analysis of its lessons were among the main factors causing this shift.

A general reappraisal of CPR foreign policy began in the latter half of 1966, as indicated by the fact that Peking called home her ambassadorial corps. The review itself appears to have been an outgrowth of the political realignment taking place in

Peking at that time and a series of disastrous external setbacks suffered by China in 1965.[29] But it soon became caught up in the power struggle between the supporters of Mao Tse-tung and Liu Shao-ch'i, whose conflicting approaches to both foreign and domestic policy came to a head in the Cultural Revolution. After Liu was purged from the leadership in 1968, the Maoists charged that he had generally favored "revisionist" and "capitulationist" policies toward the United States, Russia, and foreign "reactionaries," and that he had long opposed Mao's concept of armed revolutionary struggle.

Liu's alleged role in the formation of the policies in the 1960's adopted toward Indonesia and Burma in particular were brought up in the indictment against him. During his 1963 visit to Indonesia, the Maoists charged, he had supported the Krushchev line on "capitulating to imperialism, revisionism and reaction and stamping out the flames of revolution," and "desperately advocated the 'parliamentary road.'" Liu was further charged with acclaiming the bourgeois leader Sukarno and supporting Indonesia's membership in the "imperialist-sponsored" Maphilindo bloc, though such membership "completely departed from Chairman Mao's teaching." Finally, the Maoists alleged that Liu urged the PKI to take the "peaceful transition road" and advanced the theory of "structural reform"; he used reform as a "trick" to "hold

[29] These setbacks were: (1) the collapse of the Second Asian-African Conference in Algiers, which deprived Peking of a forum to attack Russia, the United States, and India in the hope of rallying the Afro-Asian states to support an anti-imperialist stance; (2) the beginning of the massive American ground intervention in Vietnam, which changed the nature of the war and constituted a direct threat to China; (3) the Indonesian coup which destroyed the Peking-Djakarta Axis; (4) Pakistan's poor military performance in the September 1965 war with India, which obliged Ayub Khan to accept Soviet diplomatic cooperation to restore peace; (5) the defection of the Korean, Vietnamese, and Japanese communist parties from the Chinese ideological camp after the American escalation in Vietnam.

back the Indonesian proletariat from smashing the old state apparatus by violent revolution and setting up a dictatorship of the proletariat." Liu "wanted the Indonesian revolution to take the reformist path, which ultimately leads to failure."[30]

Whether or not these charges are true, the Maoists' attempt to blame Liu for the defeat in Indonesia (and Burma) in effect constituted self-criticism of China's past policies toward the bourgeois nationalist regimes in Southeast Asia. It is also clear that the decision to declare ideological war on both countries simultaneously in July 1967[31] was a major step in Peking's return to a more revolution-oriented foreign policy. In essence, Chinese foreign policy during the Cultural Revolution called for a united front from below with the genuinely revolutionary forces in all countries and especially those groups led by antirevisionist communist parties. Except for Cambodia and Pakistan, which remained on good terms with China, her return to revolutionary policies between 1967 and 1969 made virtually impossible cooperative relationships with bourgeois-nationalist regimes—the very nations Peking had assiduously cultivated during the previous decade.

China's endorsement of a revolutionary line in Indonesia had been long delayed, but when it came, the approval was complete. In assessing the PKI's 1966 self-criticism as "correct," the Chinese stressed that the Indonesians had indeed committed "Right opportunist errors," had allowed themselves to be injured by "Khrushchev's counter-revolutionary line," and had "deviated" from Marxism-Leninism by stressing the possibilities of the "peaceful

---

[30] "Renegade to Socialism; Lackey of Imperialism, Revisionism and Reaction," Peking Review, 12 (Jan. 17, 1969), 25–28.

[31] Peking published and broadcast a major attack on the Ne Win government by the Burma Communist party (White Flag) Central Committee's vice-chairman, Thakin Ba Thein, on July 5. See NCNA (Peking) July 5, 1967, and Peking Review, 10 (July 14, 1967), 10–15.

road."[32] However, once the PKI had accepted "Mao Tse-tung's Thought," the future, though arduous, would be much brighter, provided this party established a "broad anti-imperialist and anti-feudal united front led by the working class and based on the worker-peasant alliance." *Hung-ch'i's* observation that it was "particularly important" for the PKI to "grasp that form of armed struggle in which it integrates with the peasants and wins their support" was a pointed reminder that the Indonesian comrades henceforth must abandon their past tradition of concentrating on the cities. "This change [would] not be easy" but "the objective realities of the revolutionary struggle [would] compel people to make the change and compel them to learn armed struggle."[33]

Furthermore, China stood "unflinchingly on the side of the Indonesian Communist Party . . . , the Indonesian revolutionary people" and would "firmly support" them in their struggle to overthrow the "Suharto-Nasution fascist regime."[34] This declaration was made in 1967 and marked the nadir in relations between the two countries. Since then diplomatic ties have not been restored and there has been no strong impetus on either side to explore the possibilities of a new beginning.

The defeat China suffered in Indonesia may have been beneficial, because the main dilemma which had confronted her since the late 1950's has been eliminated, at least for the foreseeable future. Peking's subsequent hostility toward the Suharto government no longer creates a conflict between her revolutionary and great-power interests, because, as a result of the overthrow of Sukarno and the suppression of the PKI, Indonesia has become, according to the Chinese perception, an appendage of American, Japanese, and European capitalism. Accordingly, Peking's support of the underground PKI is in harmony, not only with her commitment to anti-imperialist revolutionary movements in the

---

[32] "People of Indonesia, Unite."
[33] *Ibid.*
[34] *Ibid.*

Third World, but also with her security interest in siding with any forces which resist American and Soviet global domination.

Does this mean that the basic contradictions which previously undermined Chinese policy in Indonesia have been resolved? Probably not. Like the CCP after its suppression in 1927, the PKI has now fled to the countryside in the course of another Long March which it apparently believes will one day spark the flames of peasant revolution. Here the parallel must end, for the road to an Indonesian Yenan seemingly requires an Indonesian Mao Tse-tung. Such a leader would inevitably be forced to adapt theories of peasant revolution to Indonesian conditions, as Mao had to revise Leninism in China. In considering what such a development might mean for the future relations between the Chinese and Indonesian communist movements, it is worth remembering that the roots of Sino-Soviet conflict go back to Mao's Sinicization of Leninism. Any successful latter-day Maoist revolutionary leader in Indonesia would be very unlikely to ape the Chinese model slavishly. On the contrary, like Mao, he probably would eventually create another highly independent and nationalistic movement. Insofar as history provides clues about future trends, it seems that such movements will continue to be among the most important factors in the gradual but steady disintegration of the international communist movement and its pretensions to centralism or secular orthodoxy.

Although the Chinese cannot expect the Indonesian communists to become their disciples, neither can they afford to rule out the possibility of establishing amicable relations with Djakarta's noncommunist rulers. The same ideology that envisions future peasant revolutions also insists that the contradictions between Indonesia and imperialism will intensify. And according to that ideology, Peking's foreign policy should exploit these contradictions, not only for China's sake, but also to make possible the ultimate independence of Indonesia from foreign control. From the Chinese point of view, the rise of the Suharto government is merely another stage in Indonesia's struggle to attain genuine independence. This struggle is marked by the dual nature of the Indonesian bourgeoisie, which alternately opposes and submits to foreign domination. Because, however, its own desire to establish native capitalism is insatiable, this class must eventually come into irreconcilable conflict with the imperialists, which will lead to another liberation struggle. That is to say, the more American, European, and Japanese capitalism penetrates and controls Indonesia, the sooner the fundamental contradictions between these powers and Djakarta will become politically operative.

Hence, while Peking has condemned the Suharto government's policy of inviting the wholesale return of foreign capitalism, she also expects that this policy will eventually spawn serious conflicts within the Indonesian elite and between it and the capitalist powers. And should the contradictions come to the surface again, the same diplomatic and strategic interests that led China to pursue a policy of friendship and support for Indonesian nationalism in the past may very well cause China to revive that policy in the future.

Conclusion

The preceding analysis has tried to show how the Chinese leadership attempted to externalize a united-front strategy which would serve to further the achievement of its goals in Indonesia and throughout the world. Two general conclusions about the evolution of Chinese policy seem warranted by the evidence: (1) During the period 1949 to 1967 the policy in Indonesia gradually became a function of her needs and aspirations as a great power. (2) Although considerations of global strategy predominantly influenced the design and execution of that policy, the decisive factor affecting the outcome of the Sino-Indonesian relationship consistently proved to be the domestic political process in Indonesia, over which Peking had little or no control. In the end, the growing tension between China's realpolitik interests, which required an alliance with the Sukarno regime, and her revolutionary ethos, which seemingly called for an endorsement of the PKI's bid for power, could not be resolved.

With the advantage of hindsight it is easier to see the causes of the Chinese defeat than it was during the apparently triumphant days of the Peking-Djakarta axis. Foremost, of course, was the fact that China was never able to influence decisively the behavior of the principal actors and forces contending for political power in Indonesia. Yet the outcome of this rivalry had, at every point from 1949 to 1967, determined the extent to which Chinese purposes could be achieved, irrespective of what those purposes were. The 1965 coup and its disastrous consequences

264

were only the most dramatic examples in a historical pattern which had repeatedly demonstrated Peking's feeble leverage on Indonesia and the unreliability of her communist and noncommunist allies in that country.

The PKI's self-criticism of 1966 indicates that the Aidit group had never considered the essential features of the Maoist path applicable to Indonesia. On the other hand, Sukarno, who might have saved the PKI and the alliance with China if he had thrown his great prestige behind the coup group on October 1, when the issue was still in the balance, did not—at the crucial moment—act like the ally of communism or the loyal client of Peking. Instead, he tried to regain his authority by various maneuvers short of a call for civil war, and when these failed he passively bowed to the right-wing counterrevolution. Until the end Sukarno carried on his lifelong struggle to achieve his country's independence, refusing to legitimize the generals' decision to pull Indonesia back into the Western capitalist system. But he was not prepared to lead the Left in a civil war on behalf of a social revolution, much less to serve or follow China.

Peking was consistently unable to manipulate events in Indonesia or to take the initiative herself. Actually China scored her major diplomatic victories by adroitly taking advantage of fortuitous opportunities, such as Sukarno's confrontation .with Malaysia or the periodic ups and downs of American and Soviet influence in Djakarta. Limited to an essentially defensive policy, the evolution of Sino-Indonesian relations during the period examined in this study was characterized by the steady accommodation of China to the desires of Sukarno and the PKI, rather than the other way around. But it cannot be shown that the accommodation to either one actually brought Peking much closer to any fundamental objectives or gave her any significant advantages. The compromises and accommodations did cause China to become ever more deeply involved in the fate of the Sukarno regime and the Indonesian communists, unreliable allies whom she could neither bend to her own purposes nor bail out of difficulties.

There are good reasons for assuming that the Sino-Indonesian relationship would have remained unstable, or perhaps have become more so, even if the 1965 coup attempt had succeeded. The elimination of the army's anticommunist hierarchy would have strengthened, first and foremost, Sukarno and the conservative elite classes he represented. It is of course possible that he would have continued the policy of alliance with China. But if his domestic power was increased Sukarno would have had a new opportunity, and no doubt strong incentives, to explore what Moscow and Washington might be prepared to offer him in exchange for abandoning his Chinese friends. Sukarno had an impressive record of avoiding excessive dependence on external powers, capitalist or communist. And at every juncture, when circumstances had permitted, he had invariably turned first to Washington and Moscow, and only to Peking as a last resort. Faced with the choice of seeing the Indonesian revolution come under the control of the anticommunists, who really wanted to re-enter the American orbit, or the radicals led by the PKI, by 1965 Sukarno was apparently reconciled to helping the communists. But a successful removal of the pro-Western generals would have revived the NASAKOM idea, the political solution he had always favored. For Sukarno really wanted a fusion of the various political groups which could harness the energy of the Indonesian communists while at the same time containing their strength. To the extent that he was able to achieve this goal Sukarno's hand would have been greatly strengthened at home and in dealing with the great powers, especially China, which had never been dominant in the relationship with his country, even when Indonesia was weak and disunited.

As for the PKI, a successful coup, far from making it more subject to Chinese influence, would have immediately vindicated Aidit's "revisionist" line (and Moscow's as well), thereby strengthening the PKI's prestige and independence, not to mention its capacity to undercut the CCP, in the international communist movement. Whether a successful coup also would have ensured the PKI's domestic position is highly questionable. Although a Sukarnoist regime purged of West-leaning officers presumably would have been less inclined to suppress the PKI, the Aidit group would not have been politically secure, and it certainly would still have been a long way from taking power. An army more malleable by Sukarno would still have held all the guns and, though its threshold of tolerance toward the communists might have been higher with the pro-American generals gone, it was, after all, the instrument of conservatism and the status quo in Indonesia, and undoubtedly it would have happily crushed any reform-minded radicals whenever Sukarno gave the word.

Under certain conditions the Aidit leadership might, in the long run, have been able to avoid becoming domesticated or being suppressed. If the Sukarno regime had ultimately crumbled through some combination of its own corruption and external Western pressures, it is conceivable but not probable that the PKI would have been able to acquire the independent military power necessary to capture a radicalizing nationalist revolution. Presumably, if Indonesia eventually acquired a communist government, the divergence between the policies and interests of Peking and the PKI, which had clearly developed by the time of the abortive coup, would lessen. But there are better reasons to assume, especially on the basis of the earlier record, that a successful coup would have pulled the CCP and PKI further apart after 1965. The history of independent communist parties—like that of sovereign states—shows that the strong ones have invariably developed nationalistic sentiments incompatible with foreign control.

When we look at the more subjective factors which impelled Peking to court, and later to gamble on an alliance with, Indonesia, the primary cause of the Chinese defeat becomes clear. Fundamentally, the false appraisals of Indonesia which led to the earlier and the final defeats were rooted in the assumptions and expectations underlying Chinese foreign-policy theory and strategy. Acting in accordance with their conception of the truly dynamic factors in international politics and of the best means of using Chinese communist doctrine creatively to advance Chinese and worldwide revolutionary interests, Peking's leaders repeatedly entertained unwarranted optimism about what their policy could achieve in Indonesia and about that country's potential role in regional and global affairs. Why they so over-rated weak, vacillating, unreliable countries like Indonesia is the central riddle that must be solved before the diplomatic strategies and moves of Chinese policy fall into place.

The major concepts that comprise the Chinese communist political-military philosophy were developed during the period of the war with Japan, an enemy whose ferocity mortally damaged a weak and narrowly based Kuomintang government, and whose cruelty enabled the CCP to mobilize and lead the aroused forces of antiforeign nationalism. The core ideas about guerrilla warfare, building a party-army apparatus, and the role and tactics of the united front—whether attributed solely to Mao or to other CCP leaders—were formulated and tested during this crucial struggle. The Chinese leaders conceived the notion of applying these ideas to the understanding and solution of the problems of foreign policy as a consequence of the lessons of the war against Japanese imperialism. Their Marxist-Leninist world outlook also made them apply the doctrine from which it originated to other nations, since that doctrine recognized no inherent distinction between the applicability of successful revolutionary strategy and tactics to internal as opposed to external spheres of politics. Therefore, what the Chinese communists had learned and successfully used in solving the political-military problems of seizing power within the nation could be transferred to the arena of international grand strategy. In their glorification of the exportability of the national myth, America and China have had much in common.

The expectations and assumptions underlying Chinese communist foreign policy after World War II thus seemed to adhere to a specific historical model derived from the essential class alignments and national-international "contradictions" of the anti-Japanese war period. As early as 1946, after the defeat of Japan but well before the Chinese leaders had won victory on the mainland, they proclaimed that the United States had replaced Japan as the "main enemy" of China and the people of all countries. Subsequently Peking's foreign policy was largely predicated on the assumptions that the role of American imperialism in the post-1949 international situation was analogous to that of Japan in the Chinese civil war, and that American intervention in China and other Third World countries could be combated successfully by using the strategies the Chinese had employed in the earlier conflict.

In other words, the kind of political chain reactions to which Chinese united-front strategies can most adeptly respond—whether for revolutionary or realpolitik purposes—require a truly virulent imperialist enemy. The crucial expectations responsible for her tactics in dealing with the intervention-minded United States was that she would behave like Japan, and that the more aggressive America became, the greater would be the prospect of rallying an international coalition of nations and peoples against her—as the CCP had done against the Japanese in China. Eventually the Chinese also expected the revolutionary forces to gain the upper hand in certain Afro-Asian nations as the struggle against the imperialists reached its later stages.

The international behavior of the United States seemed to fit Peking's model admirably, especially since the imperialists were indeed intervening in the affairs of many countries; according to Chinese assumptions, vigorous antiforeign movements would emerge. Except for the intervention in Vietnam, however, where the local and international reactions to American policy ultimately vindicated Chinese assumptions, the imperialism of the United States takes forms quite different from the Japanese invasion of China and produces altogether different social and political consequences. American global influence is maintained primarily by means of an elaborate and sophisticated network of economic, political, and military relationships which are designed to aid, undermine, or otherwise manipulate foreign governments and societies. Even when it engages in direct interventions, the United States prefers to rely on covert instrumentalities and to work through its allies in the native elite. If possible, the United States employs it own military forces only as a last resort—when diplomacy, rewards, sanctions, coups, or threats have failed. In most countries like Indonesia, this form of neocolonialist intervention has not, to date, precipitated massive antiforeign nationalist movements and has, consequently, deprived the Chinese of the heavy-handed imperialist adversary their foreign-policy strategy requires in order to oppose successfully the further penetration and consolidation of the imperialist powers in the Third World.

Since straightforward imperialist aggression is not the American style of intervention, Third World nationalist governments are rarely driven into the arms of communist powers. More often, the neocolonialist methods Washington employs actually help to sustain and lubricate the bourgeois systems of Afro-Asian countries. Consequently, the important native classes, far from becoming radicalized or disposed to throwing the imperialists out, become increasingly wedded to the existing order and desirous of maintaining their countries' dependence on Western capitalism. Afro-Asian nationalist leaders often loudly condemn imperialism, sometimes restrict or confiscate foreign capitalist assets, and welcome aid from the socialist states. But invariably they do so in order to shore up the existing social-economic order in their country and ordinarily in a cautious manner, so that the native elite will not be entirely cut off from future economic and military assistance from these same imperialist powers. And if a more radical bourgeois government is bold enough to engage in more than pin-prick anti-imperialism, one of two things usually happens: the native elite splits and its rightist faction, frequently with covert help from the United States or other Western governments, overthrows the anti-imperialist wing (as happened in postcoup Indonesia, Ghana, Iran, Guatemala, Cambodia, and Chile); or the radical nationalists successfully use the anti-imperialist issue themselves to consolidate power vis-à-vis other contending left- or right-wing groups (as happened in Egypt, Burma, Iraq, and precoup Indonesia, Cambodia, and Ghana). In both types of cases the nationalist elites have compiled an impressive record of manipulating Peking and Moscow to further their own ends. It would be difficult to prove that any of these elites have become the captive allies of communism, certainly not of Peking.

Similarly, since there has been no outright aggression by the imperialist powers, except in Vietnam, the long-range revolutionary expectations underlying Chinese foreign policy seem not to have been realized. For the revolutionary element of the Chinese model to become operational requires that the imperialist intervention take such an extreme form that it ignites a local upheaval resembling a national war of resistance. In the course of this struggle, the Chinese theory asserts, a communist party—provided it is not afflicted with the disease of revisionism—will gradually come to dominate a multiclass coalition which will be formed to oppose the foreign invader, and the insurgent leaders will learn how to develop their own military forces and tactics. Consequently, the local communist party will eventually displace its temporary antiforeign, bourgeois-nationalist allies.

Since the bourgeoisie has no clear program for attracting, much less mobilizing, mass support, this class loses control of the revolution because it does not know what to do with it.

But this scenario has actually unfolded only in China and, to a lesser extent, in Vietnam. In the vast majority of cases, two very different patterns have emerged: the aggression of the imperialists is short-lived or half-hearted and eventually leads to a political accommodation with the native bourgeoisie before the necessary radicalization of the revolutionary process can occur (nearly all the former colonial countries have followed this pattern); or, where the anti-imperialist struggle has been severe or prolonged, the bourgeoisie early gains the dominant position in the revolution and simply suppresses, or proves to be more vigorous than, the local communists (as occurred in Algeria and Indonesia). Both patterns again indicate that when communist states assist anti-imperialist revolutions the hand of the native bourgeoisie has usually been strengthened. Thus the efforts of China or other communist powers to weaken the position of Western capitalist states in the former colonial areas usually are at the expense of the radical elements in these countries, especially the communists.

It therefore is clear that the classic model of China's political-military strategy when applied to developing a foreign policy in the Third World is beset by a fundamental ambivalence. One of its declared revolutionary purposes is to assist in driving the imperialists out of these countries—an objective which has been very often best advanced by supporting primarily the noncommunists, rather than the communists, in the antiforeign elite. On the other hand, the Chinese strategy argues that revolution abroad is more likely to go forward rapidly if the imperialists struggle violently to remain in the Third World, since capitalist exploitation allegedly will result in a deepening social conflict and, at some point, national liberation movements which, under certain conditions, will be led by communists. The Indonesian experience demonstrates that the problem the Chinese faced in trying to orchestrate their ideas on political-military strategy so that they might serve both types of revolutionary objectives was never successfully solved.

The effectiveness of united-front strategies in furthering China's great-power aims is also questionable. The historical record shows that until 1967 Peking's policies were most successful in relations with united-front partners which were dissatisfied (like the CPR) with the status quo imposed by Soviet-American power but whose internal revolutionary potential was weak. These two conditions permitted an essentially straightforward united-front-from-above policy that disregarded issues related to social revolution. Again, however, the cementing of the alignments depended on the severity and duration of the actions of the common imperialist enemy which drove the Chinese and their allies together. For the pattern of China's diplomacy with Indonesia and a number of other nations indicates that Chinese united-front relationships proved to be quite vulnerable to shifts in Soviet and American policy toward her allies. On the other hand, in her relations with countries allied to, or dominated by, the United States—or, since the rift, those nations considered to be under Soviet control—China seemed to serve her great-power and strategic interests by encouraging insurgent causes, whether the local revolutionaries were weak or strong. The rationale apparently was that, by giving moral and material help to anti-American or anti-Soviet revolutionaries, Peking was helping to tie down, weaken, and disperse the power of the imperialist enemies, thereby rendering them less capable of concentrating their strength against China.

Again the assumptions behind Chinese united-front strategy do not adequately take into account the possibility of sudden changes of fortune. Governments at one time branded as "lackeys of U.S. imperialism" or "Soviet social-imperialism" may, even from the point of view of Chinese "contradictions" theory, be regarded in a quite different light if their relations with the superpowers sour in the future. Past Chinese condemnation of these regimes has not, of course, helped lay the basis for cooperation with them in the future if the Chinese leaders believe this desirable.

An analysis and explanation of the Sino-Indonesian relationship are important for an understanding of Chinese foreign policy in the period before the Cultural Revolution. For the attempted but unsuccessful merger of great-power and revolutionary aspirations in the policy toward Indonesia was, in a larger sense, a test of the fundamental assumptions and methods of Chinese policy throughout the Third World. In the emphasis Peking has attached, since 1968, to renouncing superpower ambitions, while quietly but steadily retrenching her commitments in the still volatile Afro-Asian nations, there is an unspoken acknowledgment that her previous policy was deficient. The defeat in Indonesia was only one symptom, not a cause, of this weakness; but the Chinese leaders undoubtedly pondered—and learned from—this experience as they began to chart the new policies which have emerged in the 1970's.

The failure in Indonesia and other external setbacks indicate that China's leaders overestimated the strength and the intensity of Third World anti-imperialist movements during the 1950's and 1960's. That misappraisal was largely responsible for a series of decisions which tied Chinese foreign policy more closely to the fate of some movements than their actual potential and performance justified. On balance, however, it is easier to fault the Chinese for misjudging the size of the revolutionary floodtide during those two decades than it is to charge them with failing to comprehend the nature of the forces at work in the Third World over the long term. While an international anti-imperialist front did not come about as quickly as the Chinese apparently expected, certainly the basic trends in the Third World have moved and continue to move in a direction that confirms China's leaders' expectation of a progressive weakening of the power and influence of the imperialist nations.

It is therefore entirely possible that those elements of Chinese foreign policy which have reflected the anti-Japanese-war syndrome may be entirely abandoned or sharply modified. It does not necessarily follow, however, that as a result of this, Chinese policies in the 1970's and beyond would more closely resemble those of America and Russia, which have sought the extension and consolidation of superpower influence in the Third World. Indeed, Peking's continuing opposition to Soviet-American global hegemony is likely to reinforce the past emphasis China's foreign policy has placed on the strategic importance of the Afro-Asian countries, since her own independence will be affected by whether or not they too escape domination by the superpowers.

Selected Bibliography

OFFICIAL PUBLICATIONS
China

Government Departments and Documents

Chinese People's Political Consultative Conference. *The Common Program and Other Documents of the First Plenary Session of the Chinese People's Political Consultative Conference.* Peking: Foreign Languages Press, 1950.

——. *The Electoral Law of the People's Republic of China.* Peking: Foreign Languages Press, 1953.

——. *New China Forges Ahead: The Achievements of the Chinese People in 1950–1951.* Peking: Foreign Languages Press, 1952. Important documents of the Third Session of the First National Committee of the Chinese People's Political Consultative Conference.

Embassy of the People's Republic of China in Indonesia. *Chung-hua jen-min kung-ho-kuo ta-shih-kuan shou-yin-jen te sheng-ming* (Statement by the Spokesman of the Embassy of the People's Republic of China), May 13, 1960, Djakarta.

——. *Keterangan Dari Pihak Ambassade Republik Rakjat-Tionghwa Mengenai Soal Pembukaan Konsulat-Konsulat* (Statement by the Embassy of the People's Republic of China on the Question of Opening Consulates), Nov. 18, 1950. Djakarta, 1950.

——. *News Bulletin,* No. 43/1960. Djakarta: Cultural and Information Office of the Embassy of the People's Republic of China in Indonesia, July 4, 1960.

——. *News Bulletin,* Special Issue. Djakarta: Cultural and Information Office of the Embassy of the People's Republic of China in Indonesia, April 20, 1961.

Foreign Ministry

Asian Solidarity against Imperialism. Peking: Foreign Languages Press, 1964.

China and the Asian-African Conference. Peking: Foreign Languages Press, 1955. Documents.

"China-Indonesia Joint Statement," Jan. 28, 1965, *Peking Review,* 8 (Feb. 5, 1965), 6–8.

Chung-hua jen-min kung-ho-kuo tui wai kuan-hsi wen-chien chi (Selected Documents on the Foreign Relations of the People's Republic of China). 5 vols. Peking: Shih-chieh chih-shih ch'u-pan-she (World Knowledge Publishers), 1949–1958.

Drive U.S. Imperialism out of Asia! Peking: Foreign Languages Press, 1960.

The First Year of Victory. Peking: Foreign Languages Press, 1950.

Imperialism and All Reactionaries Are Paper Tigers. Peking: Foreign Languages Press, 1958.

"New Page in Sino-Indonesian Comradeship-in-Arms," *Peking Review,* 6 (Sept. 14, 1963), 36.

"Resolutely Support the Indonesian People's Just Struggle against 'Malaysia,' " *Peking Review,* 7 (Sept. 11, 1964), 8.

"The Significance of Chairman Liu Shao-ch'i's Fruitful Visits," *Peking Review,* 6 (April 26, 1963), 11–12.

"Sino-Indonesian Joint Statement," April 20, 1963, *Peking Review,* 6 (April 26, 1963), 3.

"Sino-Indonesian Joint Statement," Oct. 4, 1965, *Peking Review,* 8 (Oct. 15, 1965), 3.

"Statement on the SEATO Council Session," March 10, 1958, *Peking Review,* 1 (March 18, 1958), 22–23.

"Statement on United States Intervention in Indonesia," May 15, 1958, *Peking Review,* 1 (May 20, 1958), 19–20.

Su-chia-no tsung-t'ung tsai chung-kuo (President Sukarno in China). Hong Kong: Chung-hua shu chu yin-hsing (China Book Printers), 1957.

Tung-nan-ya t'iao-yueh tsu-chih (The Southeast Asia Treaty Organization). Peking: Shih-chieh chih-shih ch'u-pan-she (World Knowledge Publishers), 1958.

Ya-chou t'ai-p'ing-yang chu-yu ho-p'ing hui-i chung-yao pao-kao chi chueh-i (Important Reports and Resolutions of the Peace Conference of the Asian-Pacific Region). Peking: n.p., 1952.

Yin-tu-ni-hsi-ya ti-i-tze min-tsu ch'i-i (Indonesia's First Nationalist Uprising). Peking: Shih-chieh chih-shih ch'u-pan-she (World Knowledge Publishers), 1963.

National People's Congress. *Chung-hua jen-min kung-ho-kuo hsien-fa* (The Constitution of the People's Republic of China). Peking: Jen-min ch'u-pan-she (People's Publishers), 1954.

——. *Documents of the First Session of the First National People's Congress of the People's Republic of China*. Peking: Foreign Languages Press, 1955.

——. *Main Documents of the First Session of the Third National People's Congress of the People's Republic of China*. Peking: Foreign Languages Press, 1965.

Overseas Chinese Affairs Commission. *Ch'iao-shih cheng-ts'e wen-chi* (Collected Documents on Overseas Chinese Policies). Peking: Jen-min ch'u-pan-she (People's Publishers), 1957.

Government Spokesmen

Chen Yi. *Vice Premier Chen Yi Answers Questions Put by Correspondents*. Peking: Foreign Languages Press, 1966.

Chou En-lai. *Mu-ch'ien kuo-chi ch'ing-hsing ho wo kuo wai-chiao cheng-ts'e* (The Current International Situation and Our Country's Foreign Policy). Peking: Shih-chieh chih-shih ch'u-pan-she (World Knowledge Publishers), 1958.

——. *Note to Prime Minister Ali Sastroamidjojo on the Implementation of the Dual Nationality Treaty, June 3, 1955.* Djakarta: Cultural and Information Office of the Embassy of the People's Republic of China in Indonesia, 1955.

——. "On the Current International Situation and China's Foreign Relations," *Peking Review*, 3 (April 12, 1960), 7–9.

——. *Political Report of the Second Session of the Second National Political Consultative Conference, Jan. 30, 1956.* Peking: Foreign Languages Press, 1956.

——. "The Present International Situation and China's Foreign Policy," *People's China*, 6 (Aug. 16, 1955), 3–8.

——. *Report on the Work of the Government at the First Session of the First National People's Congress of the People's Republic of China, September 23, 1954.* Peking: Foreign Languages Press, 1954.

Fan Hsiu-chu. *A Struggle between Two Lines over the Question of How to Deal with U.S. Imperialism.* Peking: Foreign Languages Press, 1965.

Ho Cheng. "The Great Asian-African Conference," *People's China,* 6 (May 16, 1955), 3–6.

Hsieh Pien. "A Visit for Friendship, Unity and Peace," *Peking Review,* 6 (April 19, 1963), 7.

Hung Lan. "SEATO—Instrument of U.S. Aggression," *Peking Review,* 5 (March 2, 1962) 7–8.

Pi Wen. "Ma-lai-hsi-ya lien-pang chi-hua po-shih" (Dissect the Federation of Malaysia Plan), *Shih-chieh chih-shih* (World Knowledge) (Peking), 15 (April 10, 1963), 16.

Sha Ping. "Lessons from Indonesia," *China Digest,* 5 (April 5, 1949), 5–6.

Soong Ching-ling. "The Difference between Soviet and American Foreign Policies." In *700 Millions for Peace and Democracy.* Peking: Foreign Languages Press, 1950, 23–36.

———. "On Peaceful Coexistence," *People's China,* 2 (June 1, 1951), 1–6.

Tsung Shan. "Indonesia's Anti-Imperialist Record," *Peking Review,* 8 (Jan. 22, 1965), 11–12.

Yao Teng-shan. "The Blood Debts Owed by the Reactionary Indonesian Government to the Chinese People Must Be Settled," *Peking Review,* 10 (May 19, 1967), 22–24.

Yeh Chi-chuang. "China's Economic Relations with Asian and African Countries: Progress and Prospects," *People's China,* 7 (March 16, 1956), 12–15.

Wang En-yuan. "President Sukarno in Peking," *People's China,* 7 (Nov. 1, 1956), 8–12.

Chinese Communist Party
    Central Committee of the Chinese Communist Party

Documents of the National Conference of the Communist Party of China. Peking: Foreign Languages Press, 1955.

"The Indonesian People's Revolutionary Armed Struggle: A Great Beginning," *Peking Review,* 11 (Jan. 26, 1968), 21.

"Outstanding Contributions of the Communist Party of Indonesia," *Peking Review,* 6 (Sept. 13, 1963), 36.

"People of Indonesia, Unite and Fight to Overthrow the Fascist Regime," *Peking Review,* 10 (July 14, 1967), 15.

The Polemic on the General Line of the International Communist Movement. Peking: Foreign Languages Press, 1965.

The Political Report of the Central Committee of the Communist Party of China to the Eighth National Congress of the Party, Sept. 15, 1956. Peking: Foreign Languages Press, 1956.

The Seventh All-China Congress of Trade Unions. Peking: Foreign Languages Press, 1953.

"Some Questions Concerning the Indonesian Revolution and the Communist Party of Indonesia," *Peking Review,* 6 (Sept. 13, 1963), 37.

Yin-tu-ni-hsi-ya kung-ch'an-tang ti ssu-shih nien (Forty Years of the Indonesian Communist Party). Peking: Jen-min ch'u-pan-she (People's Publishing House), 1963.

Yin-tu-ni-hsi-ya kung-ch'an-tang yin-tu kung-ch'an-tang ho jih-pen kung-ch'an-tang ti tiao-chien (Documents on the Communist Parties of Indonesia, India, and Japan). Peking: Shih-chieh chih-shih ch'u-pan-she (World Knowledge Publishers), 1957.

Spokesmen for the Chinese Communist Party

Fu Hsiung. "The Indonesian People's Revolutionary Struggle and the Indonesian Communist Party," *Peking Review,* 6 (June 7, 1963), 7.

Hu Chiao-mu. *Thirty Years of the Communist Party of China.* 4th ed. Peking: Foreign Languages Press, 1959.

Hu Sheng. *Imperialism and Chinese Politics.* Peking: Foreign Languages Press, 1955.

Li Wei-han. "The Struggle for Proletarian Leadership in the Period of the New Democratic Revolution in China," *Peking Review,* 5 (March 2, 1962) 12.

Lin Piao. "Long Live the Victory of People's War," *Peking Review,* 8 (Sept. 3, 1965), 9–30.

Liu Shao-ch'i. *Lun kuo-chi chu-i yu min-tsu chu-i* (On Internationalism and Nationalism). Peking: Hsin Hua (New China), 1949.

——. "Speech at the Asian-Australasian Trade Union Conference," Nov. 16, 1949. New China News Agency (Peking), Nov. 23, 1949.

——. *The Victory of Marxism-Leninism in China.* Peking: Foreign Languages Press, 1959.

Lo Jui-ch'ing. *Commemorate the Victory over German Fascism! Carry the Struggle against U.S. Imperialism through to the End!* Peking: Foreign Languages Press, 1965.

——. *The People Defeated Japanese Fascism and They Can Certainly Defeat U.S. Imperialism, Too.* Peking: Foreign Languages Press, 1965.

Mao Tse-tung. *Selected Work.* 4 vols. Peking: Foreign Languages Press, 1965.

——. *Selected Works.* 5 vols. London: Lawrence and Wishart, 1954.

——. *Selected Works.* 5 vols. New York: International Publishers, 1954.

P'eng Chen. "Speech at the Aliarcham Academy of Social Sciences in Indonesia," *Peking Review,* 8 (June 11, 1965), 10–20.

Shao Tieh-chen. *Revolutionary Dialectics and How to Appraise Imperialism.* Peking: Foreign Languages Press, 1963.

Shih Tung-hsiang. "The Distinction and Link-up between the Two Stages of the Chinese Revolution," *Peking Review,* 4 (Jan. 20, 1961), 9–18.

Teng Hsiao-p'ing. *The Great Unity of the Chinese People and the Great Unity of the Peoples of the World.* Peking: Foreign Languages Press, 1959.

Yü Chao-li. "Imperialism—Source of War in Modern Times—and the Path of the People's Struggle for Peace," *Hung-ch'i* (Red Flag), 3 (April 1, 1960), 1–12.

Indonesia
Government Departments and Documents

Army. *Keputusan Penguasa Perang Daerah Swatara I Djawa Barat* (West Java War Administrator's Decree), No. KPTS. 70/8/PPD/1959, Aug. 28, 1959.

——. *Pengumuman Penguasa Perang Pusat,* No. Prt/Peperpu/039/1959, May 12, 1959 (Central War Administrator's Announcement No. 039). Djakarta, 1959.

Embassy of the Republic of Indonesia in the United States. *A Survey on the Controversial Problem of the Establishment of the Federation of Malaysia.* Washington, D.C., 1963.

Ministry of Foreign Affairs. *The Era of Confrontation.* Djakarta, 1964.

——. *Joint Communique of Foreign Minister Subandrio of the Republic of Indonesia and Foreign Minister Chen Yi of the People's Republic of China,* October 11, 1959. Special Release on Current Indonesian Affairs, No. 8. Djakarta, 1959.

——. *Keumuman Kementerian Luar Negri* (Announcement of the Ministry of Foreign Affairs), March 16, 1951. Djakarta, 1951.

——. Press Release No. P/27/60, Djakarta, May 19, 1960.

——. Press Release No. P/52/59, Djakarta, Dec. 13, 1959.

——. *The Question of West Irian.* Djakarta, 1955.

Ministry of Information. *A Chronology of Indonesian History.* Djakarta, 1960.

——. *A History of the Armed Forces of the Republic of Indonesia.* Djakarta, 1960.

——. *The Indonesian Revolution: Basic Documents and the Idea of Guided Democracy.* Djakarta, 1960.

——. *Keterangan dan Djawaban Pemerintah atas Program Kabinet Ali Sastroamidjojo* (Government Statement and Replies on the Program of the Ali Sastroamidjojo Cabinet). Djakarta, 1953.

——. *The Malaysia Issue: Background and Documents.* 2d ed. Djakarta, 1965.

——. *Neo-Colonialism, a Threat to World Peace.* Djakarta, 1964.

——. *Peraturan Pemerintah* (Government Regulation) No. 10, 1959. Djakarta, 1959.

——. *Political Manifesto, Republic of Indonesia, of 17th August 1959.* Djakarta, 1960.

——. *The Resounding Voice of the Indonesian Revolution.* Djakarta, 1963.

——. *Sukarno: President, Supreme Commander, Prime Minister of the Republic of Indonesia.* Djakarta, 1960.

Ministry of Trade. *SK Menteri Perdagangan Tanggal 14 Mei, 1959,* No. 2933/M (Ministry of Trade Decree, May 14, 1959). Djakarta, 1959.

Government Spokesmen

Sukarno. *The Birth of Pantja Sila.* Djakarta: Ministry of Information, 1952.

——. *Dibawah Bendera Revolusi* (Under the Banner of the Revolution). 2 vols. Djakarta: Panitya Penerbit Dibawah Bendera Revolusi, 1963.

——. *Go Ahead, PKI.* Djakarta: Jajasan "Pembaruan," 1965.

——. *Indonesian Students Meet the Challenge of the Times.* Djakarta: Ministry of Information, 1958.

——. *Like an Angel That Strikes from the Skies: The March of Our Revolution.* Djakarta: Ministry of Information, 1960.

——. *Marhaen and Proletarian.* Trans. Claire Holt. Ithaca: Cornell Modern Indonesia Project, 1960.

——. *Reach to the Stars!: A Year of Self-Reliance.* Djakarta: Ministry of Information, 1965.

——. "Speech at the Joint Session of the Standing Committee of the National People's Congress and the National Committee of the Chinese People's Political Consultative Conference," Oct. 4, 1956. New China News Agency (Peking), Oct. 5, 1956.

——. *Tahun "Vivere Pericoloso"* (The Year of "Live Dangerously"). Djakarta: Jajasan "Pembaruan," 1964.

——. *To Build the World Anew*. Djakarta: Ministry of Foreign Affairs, 1960.

——. *Toward Freedom and the Dignity of Man*. Djakarta: Ministry of Foreign Affairs, 1961.

Tirtoprodjo, Susanto. *Hasil-Kerdja Panitya-Bersama* (Work Report of the Joint Committee). Djakarta: Djambatan, 1961.

Yamin, Muhammad. *Nasah Persiapan Undang-Undang Dasar, 1945* (The Drafting of the 1945 Constitution). Vol. I. Djakarta: Jajasan Prapantja, 1959.

Indonesian Communist Party
Central Committee of the Indonesian Communist Party

"Build the PKI along the Marxist-Leninist Line to Lead the People's Democratic Revolution in Indonesia," Sept. 1966, *Indonesian Tribune*, 3 (Jan. 1967), 6–29.

Documents of the Sixth Plenum of the Central Committee of the Communist Party of Indonesia. Djakarta: Jajasan "Pembaruan," 1958.

40 Tahun PKI (Forty Years of the Communist Party of Indonesia). Djakarta, 1960.

"Hold Aloft the Banner of Marxism-Leninism, Mao Tse-tung Thought! March Forward along the Road of Revolution," *Indonesian Tribune* (Tirana, Albania), 1 (Aug.–Sept. 1967), 4–8.

Materials of the Sixth National Conference of the Communist Party of Indonesia. Djakarta: Agitation and Propaganda Department of the Central Committee of the Communist Party of Indonesia, 1958.

"Self-Criticism by the Political Bureau of the Central Committee of the Indonesian Communist Party" (excerpts), Sept. 1966, *Peking Review*, 10 (July 21, 1967), 13.

"Statement by the Political Bureau of the Central Committee of the Indonesian Communist Party" (excerpts), Aug. 17, 1966, *Peking Review*, 10 (July 14, 1967), 18.

Strengthen National Unity and Communist Unity: Documents of the Third Plenum of the Central Committee of the Communist Party of Indonesia. Djakarta: Jajasan "Pembaruan," 1962.

"Take the Road of Revolution to Realize the Tasks That Should Have Been Accomplished by the August Revolution of 1945," Aug. 17, 1966, *Indonesian Tribune*, 1 (Nov., 1966), 6–20.

"Uphold the Honor and Reputation of Communists," May 23, 1966, *Indonesian Tribune*, 1 (Nov. 1966), 6–29.

Spokesmen for the Indonesian Communist Party

Aidit, Dipta Nusantara. *The Birth and Growth of the Communist Party of Indonesia*. Djakarta: Jajasan "Pembaruan," 1958.

———. *Dare, Dare, and Dare Again!* Political Report to the First Plenary Session of the Seventh Central Committee of the Communist Party of Indonesia. Peking: Foreign Languages Press, 1963.

———. *The Indonesian Revolution and the Immediate Tasks of the Communist Party of Indonesia*. Report at the Higher Level Party School of the Central Committee of the Chinese Communist Party. Peking: Foreign Languages Press, 1964.

———. "The Indonesian Revolution Is an Inseparable Part of the World Socialist Revolution," New China News Agency (Canton), Sept. 25, 1963.

———. *Indonesian Society and the Indonesian Revolution*. Djakarta: Jajasan "Pembaruan," 1958.

———. *Kobarkan Semangat Banteng! Madju Terus, Pantang Mundur* (Awaken the Buffalo Spirit! Forward, Never Retreat). Political Report to the Second Plenum of the Central Committee of the Communist Party of Indonesia. Djakarta: Jajasan "Pembaruan," 1964.

———. *The Road to People's Democracy for Indonesia*. Djakarta: Jajasan "Pembaruan," 1955.

———. "Several Questions on the Revolution in Indonesia and the Indonesian Communist Party," New China News Agency (Peking), Sept. 4, 1963.

Musso. *Djalan Baru untuk Republik Indonesia* (The New Road for the Republic of Indonesia). Djakarta: Jajasan "Pembaruan," 1953.

Setiati Surasto. "The Peaceful Road Is the Suicidal Road," *Indonesian Tribune*, 1 (April–May 1967), 16–18.

Malaysia

Department of Information. *Background to Indonesia's Policy towards Malaysia*. Kuala Lumpur, 1964.

———. *Indonesian Involvement in Eastern Malaysia*. Kuala Lumpur, 1964.

Muhammad Ghazali bin Shafie, Dato. *Confrontation: A Manifestation of the Indonesian Problem*. Kuala Lumpur: Department of Information, 1964.

Rahman, Tengku Abdul. *Malaya's Stand on Communist China's Aggression against India*. Kuala Lumpur: Department of Information, 1962.

SECONDARY SOURCES
Books

Ambekar, G. V., and V. C. Divekar, eds. *Documents on China's Relations with South and Southeast Asia (1949–1962)*. Bombay: Allied Publishers Private, 1964.

Anderson, Benedict R. O'G., and Ruth T. McVey. *A Preliminary Analysis of the October 1, 1965, Coup in Indonesia*. Ithaca: Cornell Modern Indonesia Project, 1971.

Baperki. *Segala Sesuatu Tentang Kewarganegararaan Republik Indonesia* (Concerning the Problem of Indonesian Nationality). Djakarta: Pengurus Pusat Harian Baperki, n.d.

Bardjo, Imam. *Masaalah Kewargaan Negara Republik Indonesia* (The Problem of Republic of Indonesia Citizenship). Semarang: Baperki, 1958.

Barnett, A. Doak. *Communist China and Asia: Challenge to American Policy*. New York: Harper, 1960.

——, ed. *Communist Strategies in Asia: A Comparative Analysis of Governments and Parties*. New York: Praeger, 1963.

Benda, Harry J. *The Crescent and the Rising Sun: Indonesian Islam under the Japanese Occupation, 1942–1945*. The Hague: W. van Hoeve, 1958.

Benda, Harry J., and Ruth T. McVey, eds. *The Communist Uprisings of 1926–1927 in Indonesia: Key Documents*. Ithaca: Cornell Modern Indonesia Project, 1960.

Black, Cyril E., and Thomas P. Thornton, eds. *Communism and Revolution: The Strategic Uses of Political Violence*. Princeton, N.J.: Princeton University Press, 1964.

Blum, Robert. *The United States and China in World Affairs*. New York: McGraw-Hill, 1966.

Boeke, J. H. *The Evolution of the Netherlands Indies Economy*. New York: Institute of Pacific Relations, 1946.

Bone, Robert C., Jr. *The Dynamics of the Western New Guinea (Irian Barat) Problem*. Ithaca: Cornell Modern Indonesia Project, 1958.

——. *The Role of the Chinese in Indonesia*. Washington, D.C.: Foreign Service Institute, Monograph Series, 1951.

Boyd, R. G. *Communist China's Foreign Policy*. New York: Praeger, 1962.

Brackman, Arnold C. *The Communist Collapse in Indonesia*. New York: Norton, 1969.

——. *Indonesia: The Gestapu Affair*. New York: American-Asian Educational Exchange, 1969.

——. *Indonesian Communism: A History*. New York: Praeger, 1963.

——. *Southeast Asia's Second Front: The Power Struggle in the Malay Archipelago*. New York: Praeger, 1966.

Brimmel, J. H. *Communism in Southeast Asia: A Political Analysis*. London: Oxford University Press, 1959.

Bunnell, Fredrick P. *American Reactions to Indonesia's Role in the Belgrade Conference*. Ithaca: Cornell Modern Indonesia Project, 1964.

Cator, William J. *The Economic Position of the Chinese in the Netherlands Indies*. Chicago: University of Chicago Press, 1936.

Chang Chao-ch'iang. *Chan-hou yin-tu-ni-hsi-ya ti cheng-chih ho ching-chi* (Politics and Economics of Postwar Indonesia). Peking: Shih-chieh chih-shih (World Knowledge), 1956.

Chatham House Study Group. *Collective Defence in Southeast Asia: The Manila Treaty and Its Implications*. London: Oxford University Press, 1956.

Ch'en I-ling. *Yin-ni hsien-chuang yü hua-ch'iao* (The Present Situation in Indonesia and the Overseas Chinese). Taipei: Chung-yang wen-wu kung-ying she, 1954.

Chen Po-ta. *Mao Tse-tung on the Chinese Revolution*. Peking: Foreign Languages Press, 1953.

Chiang Kai-shek. *China's Destiny*. New York: Macmillan, 1947.

Ch'iu Shou-yü. *Tung yin-tu yü hua-ch'iao ching-chi fa-chan shih* (The East Indies and the Historical Development of the Overseas Chinese Economy). Shanghai: Cheng-chung shu chü, 1947.

Clark, Marilyn W. *Overseas Chinese Education in Indonesia: Minority Group Schooling in an Asian Context*. Washington, D.C.: U.S. Department of Health, Education and Welfare, 1965.

Dahm, Bernard. *Sukarno and the Struggle for Indonesian Independence*. Trans. Mary F. Somers Heidhues. Ithaca: Cornell University Press, 1969.

Degras, Jane, ed. *The Communist International, 1919–1943*. 3 vols. London: Oxford University Press, 1956–1965.

Dutt, Vidya Prakash. *China and the World: An Analysis of Communist China's Foreign Policy*. Rev. ed. New York: Praeger, 1966.

Elegant, Robert S. *The Dragon's Seed: Peking and the Overseas Chinese*. New York: St. Martin's Press, 1959.

Elsbree, Willard H. *Japan's Role in Southeast Asian Nationalist Movements, 1940–1945*. Cambridge, Mass.: Harvard University Press, 1953.

Fairbank, John King, ed. *The Chinese World Order: Traditional China's Foreign Relations.* Cambridge, Mass.: Harvard University Press, 1968.

Federation of Chinese Associations. *Memorandum Outlining Acts of Violence and Inhumanity Perpetrated by Indonesian Bands on Innocent Chinese before and after the Dutch Police Action Was Enforced on July 21, 1947.* Batavia, 1947.

Feith, Herbert. *The Decline of Constitutional Democracy in Indonesia* Ithaca: Cornell University Press, 1962.

——. *The Indonesian Elections of 1955.* Ithaca: Cornell Modern Indonesia Project, 1957.

——. *The Wilopo Cabinet, 1952–1953: A Turning Point in Post-Revolutionary Indonesia.* Ithaca: Cornell Modern Indonesia Project, 1958.

Fifield, Russell H. *The Diplomacy of Southeast Asia: 1945–1958.* New York: Harper, 1958.

Fischer, Louis. *The Story of Indonesia.* New York: Harper, 1959.

Fitzgerald, C. P. *The Chinese View of Their Place in the World.* London: Oxford University Press, 1964.

——. *The Third China: The Chinese Communities in Southeast Asia.* Vancouver: University of British Columbia Press, 1965.

Fried, Morton H., ed. *Colloquium on the Overseas Chinese.* New York: Institute of Pacific Relations, 1958.

Gittings, John. *A Survey of the Sino-Soviet Dispute, 1963–1967.* New York: Oxford University Press, 1968.

Gnoeneveldt, W. P. *Historical Notes on Indonesia and Malaya.* Djakarta: Bhratara, 1960.

Griffith, Samuel B. *Peking and People's Wars: An Analysis of Statements by Official Spokesmen of the Chinese Communist Party on the Subject of Revolutionary Strategy.* London: Pall Mall Press, 1966.

Griffith, William E. *Sino-Soviet Relations, 1964–1965.* Cambridge, Mass.: M.I.T. Press, 1967.

——. *The Sino-Soviet Rift.* Cambridge, Mass.: M.I.T. Press, 1964.

Hall, D. G. E., ed. *A History of Southeast Asia.* London: Macmillan, 1955.

Halpern, A. M. *Policies toward China: Views From Six Continents.* New York: McGraw-Hill, 1965.

Hanna, Willard A. *Bung Karno's Indonesia.* New York: American University Field Staff, 1959.

Hindley, Donald. *The Communist Party of Indonesia.* Berkeley: University of California Press, 1964.

Hinton, Harold C. *China's Relations with Burma and Vietnam: A Brief Survey.* New York: Institute of Pacific Relations, 1958.

———. *Communist China in World Politics.* Boston: Houghton Mifflin, 1966.

Hsieh, Alice L. *Communist China's Strategy in the Nuclear Era.* Englewood Cliffs, N.J.: Prentice-Hall, 1962.

Hsien-tai ti yin-tu-ni-hsi-ya (Contemporary Indonesia). Shanghai: Hsin chih-shih ch'u-pan-she (New Knowledge Press), 1956.

Hudson, G. F., Richard Lowenthal, and Roderick MacFarquhar. *The Sino-Soviet Dispute.* New York: Praeger, 1963.

Hughes, John. *The End of Sukarno: A Coup That Misfired: A Purge That Ran Wild.* London: Angus and Robertson, 1968.

———. *Indonesian Upheaval.* New York: McKay, 1967.

Jaspan, M. A. *Social Stratification and Social Mobility in Indonesia.* Djakarta: Gunung Agung, 1959.

Kahin, George McT. *The Asian-African Conference, Bandung, Indonesia, April 1955.* Ithaca: Cornell University Press, 1956.

———. *Nationalism and Revolution in Indonesia.* Ithaca: Cornell University Press, 1952.

Kautsky, John H. *Moscow and the Communist Party of India: A Study in the Post-War Evolution of International Communist Strategy.* Cambridge, Mass.: M.I.T. Press, 1956.

Kennedy, Captain Malcolm D. *A History of Communism in East Asia.* New York: Praeger, 1957.

Kroef, Justus van der. *The Communist Party of Indonesia: Its History, Program and Tactics.* Vancouver: University of British Columbia Publications Centre, 1965.

Legge, J. D. *Central Authority and Regional Autonomy in Indonesia: A Study in Local Administration.* Ithaca: Cornell University Press, 1961.

———. *Indonesia.* Englewood Cliffs, N.J.: Prentice-Hall, 1964.

Lev, Daniel S. *The Transition to Guided Democracy: Indonesian Politics, 1957–1959.* Ithaca: Cornell Modern Indonesia Project, 1966.

Levi, Werner. *Modern China's Foreign Policy.* Minneapolis: University of Minnesota Press, 1953.

Lewis, John Wilson. *Leadership in Communist China.* Ithaca: Cornell University Press, 1963.

Lowenthal, Richard. *World Communism: The Disintegration of a Secular Faith.* New York: Oxford University Press, 1966.

Lu Yu-san. *Programs of Communist China for Overseas Chinese.* Communist China Problem Research Series, No. 12. Hong Kong: Union Research Institute, 1956.

MacNair, Harley F. *The Chinese Abroad*. Shanghai: Commercial Press, 1924.

McLane, Charles B. *Soviet Strategies in Southeast Asia: An Exploration of Eastern Policies under Lenin and Stalin*. Princeton, N.J.: Princeton University Press, 1966.

McVey, Ruth T. *The Calcutta Conference and the Southeast Asian Uprisings*. Ithaca: Cornell Modern Indonesia Project, 1958.

——. *The Development of the Indonesian Communist Party and Its Relations with the Soviet Union and the Chinese People's Republic*. Cambridge, Mass.: Center for International Studies, 1954.

——, ed. *Indonesia*. New Haven, Conn.: Human Relations Area Files Press, 1963.

——. *The Rise of Indonesian Communism*. Ithaca: Cornell University Press, 1965.

——. *The Soviet View of the Indonesian Revolution*. Ithaca: Cornell Modern Indonesia Project, 1957.

Mintz, Jeanne S. *Mohammed, Marx, and Marhaen: The Roots of Indonesian Socialism*. New York: Praeger, 1965.

Morse, Hosea Ballou. *The International Relations of the Chinese Empire*. 3 vols. London: Longmans, Green, 1910–1918.

Mossman, James. *Rebels in Paradise: Indonesia's Civil War*. London: Jonathan Cape, 1961.

Mozingo, David P. *Sino-Indonesian Relations: An Overview, 1955–1965*. RM-4641-PR. Santa Monica, Calif.: RAND Corp., 1965.

Muaja, A. J. *The Chinese Problem in Indonesia*. Djakarta: New Nusantara, 1958.

Müller, Kurt. *The Foreign Aid Programs of the Soviet Bloc and Communist China*. Trans. Richard H. Weber and Michael Roloff. New York: Walker, 1967.

Neuhauser, Charles. *Third World Politics: China and the Afro-Asian People's Solidarity Organization, 1957–1967*. Cambridge, Mass.: Harvard University Press, 1968.

North, Robert C. *The Foreign Relations of China*. New York: Dickenson, 1969.

Nugroho, Notosusanto, and Ismail Saleh. *The Coup Attempt of the "September 30 Movement" in Indonesia*. Djakarta: Pembimbing Masa, 1968.

Palmer, Leslie H. *Indonesia and the Dutch*. London: Oxford University Press, 1962.

Pauker, Guy J. *Communist Prospects in Indonesia*. RM-4135-PR. Santa Monica, Calif.: RAND Corp., 1964.

Purcell, Victor W. W. S. *The Chinese in Southeast Asia*. London: Oxford University Press, 1951.

Schram, Stuart R. *The Political Thought of Mao Tse-tung*. New York: Praeger, 1963.

Schurmann, Franz. *Ideology and Organization in Communist China*. Berkeley: University of California Press, 1966.

Schwartz, Benjamin I. *Chinese Communism and the Rise of Mao*. Cambridge, Mass.: Harvard University Press, 1951.

Simon, Sheldon W. *The Broken Triangle: Peking, Djakarta and the PKI*. Baltimore: John Hopkins Press, 1969.

Siong, Gouw Giok. *Warga Negara dan Orang Asing [Citizens and Foreigners]*. Djakarta: Keng Po, 1960.

Skinner, G. William. *Report on the Chinese in Southeast Asia*. Ithaca: Cornell Southeast Asia Program, 1950.

Steiner, H. Arthur. *Communist China in the World Community*. New York: Carnegie Endowment for International Peace, 1961.

———. *The International Position of Communist China: Political and Ideological Directions of Foreign Policy*. New York: American Institute of Pacific Relations, 1958.

Taylor, Alastair M. *Indonesian Independence and the United Nations*. Ithaca: Cornell University Press, 1960.

Trager, Frank N., ed. *Marxism in Southeast Asia*. Stanford, Calif.: Stanford University Press, 1959.

Vandenbosch, Amry. *The Dutch East Indies: Its Government, Problems, and Politics*. Berkeley: University of California Press, 1942.

Van Leur, J. C. *Indonesian Trade and Society: Essays in Asian Social and Economic History*. The Hague and Bandung: W. van Hoeve, 1955.

Van Ness, Peter. *Revolution and Chinese Foreign Policy*. Berkeley: University of California Press, 1970.

Van Slyke, Lyman P. *Enemies and Friends: The United Front in Chinese Communist History*. Stanford, Calif.: Stanford University Press, 1967.

Vlekke, Bernard H. M. *Indonesia in 1956: Political and Economic Aspects*. New York: Institute of Pacific Relations, 1957.

——, ed. *Indonesia's Struggle, 1957–1958.* The Hague: Netherlands Institute of International Affairs, 1959.

——. *Nusantara: A History of the East Indian Archipelago.* 2d rev. ed. The Hague: W. van Hoeve, 1960.

Wang, Gung-wu. *A Short History of the Nan Ying Chinese.* Singapore: Eastern Universities Press, 1959.

Wehl, David. *The Birth of Indonesia.* London: Allen and Unwin, 1948.

Wertheim, W. F. *Indonesian Society in Transition: A Study of Social Change.* 2d rev. ed. The Hague and Bandung: W. van Hoeve, 1959.

Williams, Lea E. *Overseas Chinese Nationalism: The Genesis of the Pan-Chinese Movement in Indonesia, 1900–1916.* Glencoe, Ill.: Free Press, 1960.

Willmott, Donald E. *The National Status of the Chinese in Indonesia, 1900–1958.* Ithaca: Cornell Modern Indonesia Project, 1961.

Wu, Chun-hsi. *Dollars, Dependents, and Dogma: Overseas Chinese Remittances to Communist China.* Intro. by C. F. Remer. Stanford, Calif.: Hoover Institution on War, Revolution and Peace, 1967.

Ying, Hsin. *The Foreign Trade of Communist China.* Communist China Problem Research Series. Hong Kong: Union Research Institute, March 1954.

Zagoria, Donald S. *The Sino-Soviet Conflict, 1956–1961.* Princeton, N.J.: Princeton University Press, 1962.

Articles

Anderson, Benedict R. O'G. "Indonesia: United against Progress," *Current History,* 48 (Feb. 1965), 75–81.

Baldwin, Hanson W. "China as a Military Power," *Foreign Affairs,* 30 (Oct. 1951), 51–62.

Barnett, A. Doak. "A Choice of Nationality: Overseas Chinese in Indonesia." American Universities Field Staff Report, ADB-7-55. Djakarta, May 28, 1955.

——. "Echoes of Mao Tse-tung in Djakarta." American Universities Field Staff Report, ADB-6-55. Djakarta, May 21, 1955.

Benda, Harry J. "Communism in Southeast Asia," *Yale Review,* 45 (March 1956), 417–429.

Boorman, Howard L. "Sources of Chinese Communist Conduct," *Virginia Quarterly Review,* 42 (Autumn 1966), 512–526.

Boorman, Howard L., and Scott A. Boorman. "Strategy and National

Psychology in China," *Annals of the American Academy of Political and Social Science,* 370 (March 1967), 143–155.

Bunnell, Fredrick P. "Guided Democracy Foreign Policy: 1960–1965," *Indonesia,* No. 2 (Oct. 1966), 37–76.

Butwell, Richard. "Communist Liaison in Southeast Asia," *United Asia* (Bombay), 6 (June 1954), 146–151.

Castles, Lance. "Notes on the Islamic School at Gontor," *Indonesia,* No. 1 (April 1966), 30–45.

Ch'en, Jerome. "China's Conception of Her Place in the World," *Political Quarterly,* 35 (July–Sept. 1964), 260–269.

Derkach, Nadia. "The Soviet Policy towards Indonesia in the West Irian and the Malaysian Disputes," *Asian Survey,* 5 (Nov. 1965), 566–571.

Dommen, Arthur J. "The Attempted Coup in Indonesia," *China Quarterly,* No. 25 (Jan.–March 1966), 144–170.

Donnithorne, Audrey G. "Western Business in Indonesia," *Pacific Affairs,* 27 (March 1954), 27–40.

Fairbank, John King. "China's Foreign Policy in Historical Perspective," *Foreign Affairs,* 47 (April 1969), 449–463.

——. "China's World Order: The Tradition of Chinese Foreign Relations," *Encounter* (London), 27 (Dec. 1966), 14–20.

——. "The People's Middle Kingdom," *Foreign Affairs,* 44 (July 1966), 574–586.

Fairbank, John King, and Ssu-yu Teng. "On the Ch'ing Tributary System," *Harvard Journal of Asiatic Studies,* 6 (June 1941), 135–246.

Feith, Herbert. "Dynamics of Guided Democracy," In Ruth T. McVey, ed., *Indonesia.* New Haven, Conn.: Human Relations Area Files Press, 1963. Pp. 309–547.

——. "Indonesia." In George McT. Kahin, ed., *Governments and Politics of Southeast Asia.* 2d ed. Ithaca: Cornell University Press, 1964. Pp. 183–278.

——. "Indonesia's Political Symbols and Their Wielders," *World Politics,* 16 (Oct. 1963), 79–97.

——. "President Soekarno, the Army and the Communists: The Triangle Changes Shape," *Asian Survey,* 4 (Aug. 1964), 969–980.

——. "Toward Elections in Indonesia," *Pacific Affairs,* 27 (Sept. 1954), 236–254.

Feith, Herbert, and Daniel S. Lev. "The End of the Indonesian Rebellion," *Pacific Affairs,* 36 (Spring 1963), 32–46.

Fitzgerald, Stephen. "Overseas Chinese Affairs and the Cultural Revolution," *China Quarterly,* No. 40 (Oct.–Dec. 1969), 103–126.

Halpern, Abraham Meyer. "Communist China and Peaceful Coexistence." *China Quarterly*, No. 43 (July–Sept. 1970), 16–31.

——. "The Foreign Policy Uses of the Chinese Revolutionary Model," *China Quarterly*, No. 7 (July–Sept. 1961), 1–16.

Hanna, Willard A. "Moscow Comes to Bung Karno—and So Does Peking." *Newsletter of the American University Field Staff*, 5 Nov. 30, 1956.

Hanssens, V. "The Campaign against the Nationalist Chinese in Indonesia." In B. H. M. Vlekke, ed., *Indonesia's Struggle, 1957–1958*. The Hague: Netherlands Institute of International Affairs, 1959.

Harcourt, Wilfred. "Indonesia's Chinese under Threat," *Dissent* (Melbourne), No. 20 (Winter 1967), 42–43.

Hatta, Mohammad. "Indonesia's Foreign Policy," *Foreign Affairs*, 31 (April 1953), 441–452.

——. "One Indonesian's View of Malaysia," *Asian Survey*, 5 (March 1965), 139–143.

Hawkins, Everett D. "Labor in Transition." In Ruth T. McVey, ed., *Indonesia*. New Haven, Conn.: Human Relations Area Files Press, 1963. Pp. 257–269.

Heidhues, Mary F. Somers. "Peking and the Overseas Chinese: The Malaysian Dispute," *Asian Survey*, 6 (May 1966), 1–12.

Hindley, Donald. "Communist Party Strategy in Indonesia, 1948–1959," *Australian Outlook*, 13 (Dec. 1959), 253–271.

——. "The Indonesian Communist Party and the Conflict in the International Communist Movement," *China Quarterly*, No. 19 (July–Sept. 1964), 99–119.

——. "The Indonesian Communists and the CPSU Twenty-second Congress," *Asian Survey*, 2 (March 1962), 20–27.

——. "Political Power and the October 1965 Coup in Indonesia," *Journal of Asian Studies*, 26 (Feb. 1967), 237–249.

——. "President Sukarno and the Communists: The Politics of Domestication," *American Political Science Review*, 56 (Dec. 1962), 915–926.

Hinton, Harold. "The Overseas Chinese and Peking," *Far Eastern Economic Review*, 19 (Oct. 6, 1955), 417–424.

Houn, Franklin W. "The Principles and Operational Code of Communist China's International Conduct," *Journal of Asian Studies*, 27 (Nov. 1967), 21–40.

Kahin, George McT. "The Chinese in Indonesia," *Far Eastern Survey*, 5 (Oct. 23, 1946), 326–329.

——. "Communist Leadership in Indonesia," *Far Eastern Survey,* 18 (Aug. 10, 1949), 188–189.

——. "The Communist Revolt in Java: The Crisis and Its Aftermath," *Far Eastern Survey,* 17 (Nov. 17, 1948), 261–264.

——. "Indonesia." In George McT. Kahin, ed., *Major Governments of Asia.* 2d ed. Ithaca: Cornell University Press, 1963. Pp. 535–700.

——. "Malaysia and Indonesia," *Pacific Affairs,* 37 (Fall 1964), 253–270.

Klein, Donald W. "Peking's Evolving Ministry of Foreign Affairs," *China Quarterly,* No. 4 (Oct.–Dec. 1960), 28–39.

Lasker, Bruno. "The Role of the Chinese in the Netherlands Indies," *Far Eastern Quarterly,* 8 (Feb. 1949), 162–171.

Leng Shao-chuan. "Communist China's Economic Relations with Southeast Asia," *Far Eastern Survey,* 28 (Jan. 1959), 1–11.

Lenin, V. I. "Imperialism, the Highest Stage of Capitalism." In *Selected Works.* Moscow: Foreign Languages Publishing House, 1952. I, 433–568.

Lev, Daniel S. "Indonesia 1965: The Year of the Coup," *Asian Survey,* 6 (Feb. 1966), 103–110.

——. "The Political Role of the Army in Indonesia," *Pacific Affairs,* 36 (Winter 1963–1964), 349–364.

Lowenthal, Richard. "Communist China's Foreign Policy." In Tang Tsou, ed., *China in Crisis.* Chicago: University of Chicago Press, 1968. II, 1–18.

——. "Soviet and Chinese Worldviews." In Donald W. Treadgold, ed., *Soviet and Chinese Communism: Similarities and Differences.* Seattle: University of Washington Press, 1967. Pp. 374–404.

Mancall, Mark. "The Persistence of Tradition in Chinese Foreign Policy," *Annals of the American Academy of Political and Social Science,* 349 (Sept. 1963), 14–27.

McVey, Ruth T. "Indonesian Communism and China." In Tang Tsou and Ho P'ing-ti, eds., *China in Crisis,* Chicago: University of Chicago Press, 1968. II, 357–394.

——. "Indonesian Communism and the Transition to Guided Democracy." In A. Doak Barnett, ed., *Communist Strategies in Asia: A Comparative Analysis of Governments and Parties.* New York: Praeger, 1963. Pp. 148–195.

——. "The Southeast Asian Insurrectionary Movement." In C. E. Black and T. P. Thornton, eds., *Communism and Revolution: The Strategic*

Uses of Political Violence. Princeton, N.J.: Princeton University Press, 1964. Pp. 145–184.

——. "The Strategic Triangle: (2) Indonesia," *Survey,* No. 54 (Jan. 1965), 113–122.

Mintz, Jeanne S. "Marxism in Indonesia." In Frank N. Trager, ed., *Marxism in Southeast Asia.* Stanford, Calif.: Stanford University Press, 1959. Pp. 171–239.

Modelski, George. "Indonesia and Her Neighbors." In Alastair Buchan, ed., *China and the Peace of Asia.* London: Chatto and Windus, 1965. Pp. 160–174.

Mortimer, Rex. "Class, Social Cleavage and Indonesian Communism," *Indonesia,* No. 8 (Oct. 1969), 1–20.

Mosely, Philip E. "Soviet Policy and the Revolutions in Asia," *Annals of the American Academy of Political and Social Science,* 276 (July 1951), 91–98.

Mozingo, David. "China and Indonesia." In Tang Tsou, ed., *China in Crisis.* Chicago: University of Chicago Press, 1968. II, 333–356.

——. "New Development in China's Relations with Indonesia," *Current Scene,* 1 (Feb. 5, 1962), 1–7.

——. "The Sino-Indonesian Dual Nationality Treaty," *Asian Survey,* 1 (Dec. 1961), 25–31.

North, Robert C. "Two Revolutionary Models: Russian and Chinese." In A. Doak Barnett, ed., *Communist Strategies in Asia: A Comparative Analysis of Governments and Parties.* New York: Praeger, 1963. Pp. 34–60.

Pauker, Guy J. "Current Communist Tactics in Indonesia," *Asian Survey,* 1 (May 1961), 28–35.

——. "General Nasution's Mission to Moscow," *Asian Survey,* 1 (March 1961), 13–22.

——. "Indonesia: The PKI's Road to Power." In Robert A. Scalapino, ed., *The Communist Revolution in Asia.* Englewood Cliffs, N.J.: Prentice-Hall, 1965. Pp. 256–289.

——. "Indonesia in 1964: Towards a 'People's Democracy?' " *Asian Survey,* 5 (Feb. 1965), 88–97.

——. "The Role of the Military in Indonesia." In J. J. Johnson, ed., *The Role of the Military in Underdeveloped Countries.* Princeton, N.J.: Princeton University Press, 1962. Pp. 185–230.

——. "The Soviet Challenge in Indonesia." *Foreign Affairs,* 15 (July 1962), 612–626.

Pelzer, Karl J. "The Agricultural Foundation." In Ruth McVey, ed.,

Indonesia. New Haven, Conn.: Human Relations Area Files, Press 1963. Pp. 118–154.

Purcell, Victor H. "The Overseas Chinese and the People's Republic," *Far Eastern Survey,* 19 (Oct. 25, 1950), 194–196.

Ra'anan, Uri. "The Coup That Failed," *Problems of Communism,* 15 (March–April 1966), 37–43.

Rey, Lucien. "Dossier of the Indonesian Drama," *New Left Review,* No. 36 (March–April 1966), 26–40.

Scalapino, Robert A. "Moscow, Peking and the Communist Parties of Asia," *Foreign Affairs,* 41 (Jan. 1963), 323–343.

Schwartz, Benjamin I. "The Maoist Image of World Order," *Journal of International Affairs,* 21 (1967), 92–102.

Steiner, H. Arthur. "Ideology versus National Interests in Chinese Foreign Policy." In E. F. Szczepanik, ed., *Symposium on Economic and Social Problems of the Far East.* Hong Kong: Hong Kong University Press, 1962. Pp. 246–258.

Sutter, John O. "Two Faces of 'Konfrontasi': 'Crush Malaysia' and 'Gestapu,' " *Asian Survey,* 6 (Oct. 1966), 523-546.

Tirtawidjaja, D. "Jus Sanguinis and Dual Nationality," *Indonesian Review,* 2 (Feb. 1954), 26–29.

Townsend, James R. "Communist China: The New Protracted War," *Asian Survey,* 5 (Jan. 1965), 1–11.

Tretiak, Daniel. "Changes in Chinese Attention to Southeast Asia, 1967–1969: Their Relevance for the Future of Asia," *Current Scene,* 7 (Nov. 1, 1969), 1–17.

Tsou Tang. "Mao Tse-tung and Peaceful Coexistence," *Orbis,* 8 (Spring 1964), 36–51.

Tsou Tang and Morton H. Halperin. "Mao Tse-tung's Revolutionary Strategy and Peking's International Behavior," *American Political Science Review,* 59 (March 1965), 80–99.

Van der Kroef, Justus M. "Agrarian Reform and the Indonesian Communist Party," *Far Eastern Survey* (Jan. 1960), 5–13.

——. " 'Gestapu' in Indonesia," *Orbis,* 10 (Summer 1966), 458–487.

——. "How Dead Is the Indonesian Communist Party?" *Communist Affairs,* 5 (Jan.–Feb. 1967), 3–10.

——. "Indonesia, Malaysia and the North Borneo Crisis," *Asian Survey,* 3 (April 1963), 173–181.

——. "Indonesian Communism under Aidit," *Problems of Communism,* 7 (Nov.–Dec. 1958), 15–23.

———. "Lenin, Mao and Aidit," *China Quarterly*, No. 10 (April–June 1962), 23–44.

———. "The Sino-Indonesian Partnership," *Orbis*, 8 (Summer 1964), 332–356.

———. "The Sino-Indonesian Rupture," *China Quarterly*, No. 33 (Jan.–March 1968), 17–46.

———. "The Vocabulary of Indonesian Communism," *Problems of Communism*, 14 (May–June 1965), 1–9.

Wertheim, W. F. "Indonesia before and after the Untung Coup," *Pacific Affairs*, 39 (Spring and Summer 1966), 115–127.

Wilson, David A. "China, Thailand and the Spirit of Bandung," *China Quarterly*, No. 30 (April–June 1967), 149–169; No. 31 (July–Sept. 1967), 96–127.

Yahuda, Michael B. "Chinese Foreign Policy after 1963: The Maoist Phases," *China Quarterly*, No. 36 (Oct.–Dec. 1968), 93–114.

Zhdanov, A. "The International Situation," *For a Lasting Peace for a People's Democracy* (Bucharest), 1 (Nov. 10, 1947), 2–4.

Unpublished Doctoral Dissertations

Bunnell, Fredrick P. "The Kennedy Initiatives in Indonesia, 1962–1963." Cornell University, 1969.

Idle, Dunning, IV. "Indonesia's Independent and Active Foreign Policy." Yale University, 1955–1956.

Somers, Mary Frances Ann Heidhues. "Peranakan Chinese Politics in Indonesia." Cornell University, 1965.

Index

Chinese Policy toward Indonesia

Designed by R. E. Rosenbaum.
Composed by Joe Mann Associates,
in 11 point linotype Fairfield, 2 points leaded,
with display lines in monotype Deepdene.
Printed offset by LithoCrafters, Inc.,
on Warren's Number 66 text, 50 pound basis.
Bound by LithoCrafters
in Columbia book cloth
and stamped in All Purpose foil.